Praise for *Whispers of Cruel Wrongs*

"Through brief biographies, family trees, and extensive endnotes, Maillard takes her reader through the letters. The story they tell is not necessarily the one that readers expect." *Pennsylvania Magazine of History and Biography*

"Maillard provides extensive but unobtrusive editorial apparatus to aid the reader in understanding the complex web of relationships represented in the letters and the historical context in which the authors and their associates lived."
Resources for American Literary Study

"A rich and fascinating portrait of Philadelphia's and Washington, D.C.'s black elite after the Civil War. Even as the letters depict the increasingly troubled political status and economic fortunes of the correspondents, they offer rare glimpses into private homes and inner emotions."

Carla L. Peterson,
author of *Black Gotham:*
A Family History of African Americans
in Nineteenth-Century New York City

Wisconsin Studies in Autobiography

WILLIAM L. ANDREWS
Series Editor

Whispers
of Cruel Wrongs

*The Correspondence of Louisa Jacobs
and Her Circle, 1879–1911*

Edited by
Mary Maillard

The University of Wisconsin Press

The University of Wisconsin Press
728 State Street, Suite 443
Madison, Wisconsin 53706
uwpress.wisc.edu

Gray's Inn House, 127 Clerkenwell Road
London EC1R 5DB, United Kingdom
eurospanbookstore.com

Printed in the United States of America

This book may be available in a digital edition.

Library of Congress Cataloging-in-Publication Data
Names: Maillard, Mary (Manuscript editor), editor.
Title: Whispers of cruel wrongs: the correspondence of Louisa Jacobs and her circle,
1879–1911 / edited by Mary Maillard.
Other titles: Wisconsin studies in autobiography.
Description: Madison, Wisconsin: The University of Wisconsin Press, [2017]
| Series: Wisconsin studies in autobiography |
| Includes bibliographical references and index.
Identifiers: LCCN 2016041576 | ISBN 9780299311803 (cloth: alk. paper)
Subjects: LCSH: Jacobs, Louisa Matilda, 1833–1917—Correspondence.
| Purvis, Annie (Harriet Ann), 1848–1917—Correspondence.
| Webb, Eugenie, 1856–1919—Correspondence.
| African American women—Correspondence.
Classification: LCC E185.96 .W475 2017 | DDC 305.48/896073—dc23
LC record available at https://lccn.loc.gov/2016041576

ISBN 9780299311841 (pbk.: alk. paper)

For

Del and Carole

Mizpah

You know a woman can whisper her cruel wrongs in the ear of a dear friend much easier than she can record them for the world to read.

Harriet Jacobs to Amy Post,
1859

I know the cruel wrongs that crush
The young and ardent heart;
But falter not; keep bravely on,
And nobly bear thy part.

Charlotte Forten,
"The Angel's Visit,"
1858

One by one the sands are flowing,
One by one the moments fall;
Some are coming, some are going;
Do not strive to grasp them all.

One by one thy duties wait thee,
Let thy whole strength go to each,
Let no future dreams elate thee,
Learn thou first what these can teach.

One by one (bright gifts from Heaven)
Joys are sent thee here below;
Take them readily when given,
Ready too to let them go.

One by one thy griefs shall meet thee,
Do not fear an armed band;
One will fade as others greet thee;
Shadows passing through the land.

Do not look at life's long sorrow;
See how small each moment's pain;
God will help thee for to-morrow,
So each day begin again.

Every hour that fleets so slowly
Has its task to do or bear;
Luminous the crown, and holy,
When each gem is set with care.

Do not linger with regretting,
Or for passing hours despond;
Nor, the daily toil forgetting,
Look too eagerly beyond.

Hours are golden links, God's token,
Reaching Heaven; but one by one
Take them, lest the chain be broken
Ere the pilgrimage be done.

Adelaide Anne Proctor,

"One by One"

Contents

Illustrations

Charts

Photographs

Preface

I was in rural Pennsylvania, holding a box of letters from "Lulu," written from Washington, DC, and addressed to Genie Webb in Camden, New Jersey. No one in the family who owned the letters knew who Lulu was; they didn't even know her last name, but her middle initial was "M." *Please let it be Matilda*, I thought. If I hadn't been saturated in the history of Edenton, North Carolina, if I hadn't recently devoured the two-volume edition of the *Harriet Jacobs Family Papers*, if I hadn't known that Genie Webb's grandfather was a cousin of Louisa Jacobs's father, I would not have immediately hoped that the author would be the only Lulu I had ever heard of—Louisa Matilda Jacobs. We frantically searched the letters and found the lines, "You want to know what the M in my name stands for, not Minerva the wise, oh no, only plain Matilda. Turn it as you will there is no poetry in it."

I had been brought to Louisa Jacobs's letters by a series of nagging questions, obscure footnotes, odd intuitions, unbridled curiosity, and the freedom, as an independent scholar, to follow my nose. I hadn't been looking for Louisa Jacobs; I had been looking for Annie Wood Webb. My documentary editing work on the slaveholding Skinner family of Edenton had led me to an interest in the town's free and enslaved African Americans, especially those who had made their way north to antebellum Philadelphia, Boston, New Haven, and New Bedford. One particularly intriguing émigré was Geoffrey Iredell, the brother of a former Skinner slave, who had moved to Philadelphia and shared a home with Annie Wood Webb, another North Carolina native. Who was Annie and what was her connection to Iredell?

After many twists and turns, I speculated that Annie Wood Webb might be the mixed-race daughter of wealthy Edenton bachelor James Cathcart Johnston—and that she might also be connected to African American novelist Frank J. Webb and activist writer Charlotte Forten. As I moved forward in my

Annie Wood (Webb), ca. 1847, was Genie Webb's mother. (AWWP)

search in a distressingly nonlinear manner, signs that at first had seemed to be insignificant began to point the way: historian Julie Winch's footnote about the sisters Annie and Mary Virginia Wood, coming originally from Hertford, Perquimans County, North Carolina; John Zehmer's highlighting of Annie Wood Webb's claim to be Johnston's daughter; the appearance of Edenton's Geoffrey Iredell in all the right times and places in Philadelphia, his marriage to Elizabeth Susan Webb, and the death of his son, Frank Webb Iredell; Charlotte Forten's diary entries about her aunt Annie, "Mrs. J." and "Lu"; William Cooper Nell's observations about Miss Wood in Salem, Massachusetts; a typescript history of the Wood family of Hertford, Perquimans County, noting slave Edy Wood and her daughter Mary. An accumulation of minutia began to add up to something.

I had tried to ignore Annie Wood Webb, but she would not go away. She was an alluring mystery, the linchpin of a fascinating story of antebellum anti-slavery activism and a crucial missing piece to the story of the famous 1867 Johnston estate trial. One day I found a photograph of someone named Annie Wood Webb buried among old family pictures on an artist's personal website. She had the right birth year—1831. She appeared to be white. I stared at her picture in amazement and could not get over the fact that she was the spitting image of James Cathcart Johnston of Edenton. Could I approach the owner of the website on the basis of a photographic resemblance? Did he know that his great grandmother was African American? Did he really have boxes of old family papers? The answer to all of those questions was yes.

My deepest thanks go to Del Thomas, the owner of the Annie Wood Webb Papers, who welcomed me into his home in November 2012 and invited me to his family's Thanksgiving table. My first American Thanksgiving showed me the simplicity and grace of Quaker tradition and the open-hearted abundance of Jewish hospitality. I sat in the proverbial empty chair reserved for the un-expected stranger. Del wanted his great-grandmother's story told—in her own words. Raised an only child by his Victorian aunt and mother, Del had grown up in Philadelphia immersed in the spirited presence and haunting absence of Annie Wood Webb.

It was Del's wife, Carole, who first discovered the "Lulu" letters eighteen years ago. She felt a pull toward and a fascination with this mysterious woman and always intended to come back to the letters and discover her identity. When I arrived at their home, Carole suggested I look at these letters, but in the midst of all the excitement, I was too busy jumping for joy at the discovery of letters from James Cathcart Johnston and Frank J. Webb Jr. Carole approached me on another day with a handful of letters she had transcribed, and this time she got my attention. If it were not for Carole's careful, accurate transcriptions and her kindness and encouragement over the past three years, this project might not have proceeded.

I am writing in the first person with my own thoughts and memories, but I must emphasize that this project has always been a "we" endeavor. My greatest supporters from the very beginning were Ray and Liz Hayes of Silver Spring, Maryland. If it were not for Ray's family Bible records, we would not have had enough information about Geoffrey Iredell to figure out his movements and connection to Annie Wood Webb and to Louisa and Harriet Jacobs. If it were not for Liz's untiring genealogical work and her knack for leaving no stone unturned, we would not have had numerous clues and slivers of evidence that pointed to not only Frank J. Webb but also to his grandfather Vice President Aaron Burr. Liz and Ray were always there for me. If it were not for their support, my first trip to Philadelphia would have been delayed by a crucial half year, and I would not have had the opportunity to meet Del, who tragically died in May 2013.

I am grateful to the Library Company of Philadelphia and the Historical Society of Pennsylvania for my one-month Albert M. Greenfield Fellowship in African American History in 2013 and for fellowship privileges in 2012, including my opportunity to stay at Cassatt House. Krystal Appiah, curator of African American history, provided me with hidden gems from the collections and offered quiet, steady support through a number of unexpected crises. Cornelia King, Linda August, Sarah Weatherwax, Erika Piola, and Nicole Janiec all helped me to navigate my way through the collections. Alison McMenamin very ably took care of guest lunch details with practically no advance notice. John Van Horne and his wife, Christine, kindly entertained me at their home, along with Jean and Ed Yellin, and I had the chance to meet Richard S. Newman while he taught summer National Endowment for the Humanities students. Special thanks go to Beverly Brown Ruggia and Cordelia Hinkson Brown, who, at ninety-three, provided invaluable assistance in identifying photographs in the Library Company's Stevens-Cogdell-Sanders-Venning-Chew collections. Chief librarian Jim Green, always available for advice and guidance, took a genuine interest in all aspects of my research.

I arrived at the Library Company during a time of transition and had the very good fortune to meet Phil Lapsansky, the recently retired curator of African American history after forty-one years. My research had taken me into the heart of northern antebellum racism and the savagery of Philadelphia's race riots in the 1830s and 1840s; it was Phil who helped me through my shock as I came to realize that this 180-year-old story was not widely known or taught. In Philadelphia I heard analogies drawn between late-nineteenth-century lynching and the travesty of justice known as the Trayvon Martin murder trial. After Trayvon, came Mike Brown, Tamir Rice, Eric Garner, Walter Scott, the 2015 Charleston church massacre, Sandra Bland, Freddie Gray, Philando Castille, and far too many other names. Just as we must say their names now, I learned from Phil that we must also recover African American names and biographies from our past.

When I needed to ask specialists for advice, I turned to my bookshelves, to the historians who first brought old Philadelphia and Edenton to life for me. I still can't believe the incredible generosity and openness of the scholars I approached. Julie Winch, thank you for your groundbreaking scholarship and your willingness to help me step into the field. Carla Peterson, how could I have managed without your encouragement? Beverly Wilson Palmer, my mentor from the Association for Documentary Editing, you met me in Philadelphia, read sample letters, and gave good, practical tips. Jean Fagan Yellin, without your scholarship these letters would never have come to light; you were wonderfully supportive in Philadelphia and proved to be every bit as passionate and courageous in person as you are in your work. Quintard Taylor, you took a chance on an unknown writer and taught me the basics of the biographical entry. Connie Schulz, you actually looked at the Louisa Jacobs poster at the 2014 ADE conference and could see the southern kinship patterns in these women's lives. Susan Goodier, your enthusiasm for the project kept me motivated. Sheila Jones, at Eden Cemetery in Collingsdale, Pennsylvania, you provided invaluable documentation for the Forten, Purvis, and Cassey families. Thank you. Everyone needs a trustworthy friend in the profession who will always be direct and honest, encouraging and sympathetic. That true friend for me is the wonderful historian and documentary editor Giselle Roberts, coeditor of the Women's Letters and Diaries of the South series. My other true friends—women's historian Marjory Lang, her husband, David Johnstone, and Lynne Quarmby—have supported me in so many ways I will never be able to say thank you enough.

I have several good-hearted cousins in North Carolina who helped me immensely during my 2013 research trip. In Chapel Hill, I stayed with Rebecca Warren, who provided me with stimulating company and introduced me to historians Jane Pease, Jean Bradley Anderson, and Anne Firor Scott. Susan Inglis offered her home and car, not to mention her precious parking spot near UNC's Wilson Library. My cousin Elizabeth Matheson of Hillsborough cheered me on. Frances Inglis hosted me at the Homestead in Edenton, where, sitting on her porch overlooking the bay, I could close my eyes, drenched in details of Harriet Jacobs's life, and imagine a once-vibrant African American community.

At the University of Wisconsin Press, I wish to thank Raphael Kadushin, senior acquisitions editor; Amber Rose, acquisitions assistant; Adam Mehring, managing editor; Sheila Leary, communications director; Meg Wallace, copy editor; and Carla Marolt, associate production manager. The manuscript could not have received more thought and care. Special thanks go to William L. Andrews, series editor.

In Vancouver, I must thank Sonia Zagwyn and Andrea Bennett for saving me from complete meltdown with their methodical ordering of hundreds of digital photographs and scans, and for transcribing numerous old news articles and miscellaneous letters. Finally, my husband, Keith, took it all in good humor when I would vanish for weeks at a time. He, more than anyone, understands the long project, and he deserves the greatest thanks of all.

Editorial Principles

All of the seventy-eight documents reproduced in this volume are held in a single private collection, the Annie Wood Webb Papers. Because of the rarity of these documents as examples of nineteenth-century African American personal correspondence, there has been no selection process: all documents written by Louisa Jacobs (fifty-eight) and Annie Purvis (thirteen) to Eugenie Webb are included. In addition, the collection includes three letters from Frank J. Webb Jr. and one each from Sarah L. Forten (Purvis), Charlotte Forten (Grimké), Francis J. Grimké, and Edith Willis (Grinnell). There are no extant reciprocal letters from Eugenie Webb. Enclosures in Louisa Jacobs's letters have not been counted as separate documents. One undated note has been placed early in the exchange (1881) according to context. Other documents from the Annie Wood Webb Papers are cited in the notes.

The location and date are placed at the top right of each letter. Envelope addresses and postmarks are considered to be relevant information and are placed at the beginning of each document. Strikethroughs indicating change of address and forwarded mail are included. Salutations are rendered as they appear in the original. Closings are right justified. Editorial comments indicating enclosures, marginal writing, pencilings, and other descriptors are contained in square brackets. Annotations—identifying people, places, and events—are included in the notes. Identifications are usually provided at the point where the person, place, or event first appears in the text.

The letters were transcribed as faithfully possible. Original spelling, punctuation, and capitalization have been preserved except for Louisa's initial misspellings of "Genie" as "Jenie" and the name Grimké, which has been standardized to include the accent. Louisa Jacobs's inscription errors—for instance, "think" for "thing," "hear" for "heard," "pay" for "play"—have been retained without the use of [*sic*]. Conjectural readings of illegible words and characters are enclosed in square brackets. Underlined words in the original text appear as underlined words in the transcription. A missing letter at the end of a word is supplied by the editor in square brackets. Interlinear insertions have been incorporated into the text, and superscripts have been lowered. Occasionally, a paragraph break was inserted when a sentence started on a new line and there was a clear change in subject. In some cases, a new paragraph was introduced when a separate line of thought coincided with a slightly larger space between the end of a sentence and the start of a new one.

The overriding editorial principle of this volume is one of clarity and simplicity, reflecting the relative clarity of the original letters. Editorial comments and marks have been kept to a minimum to ensure a flowing, readable text.

Notes on Photograph Identifications

With the exception of William Claflin, everyone who appears in photographs in this volume is African American. Many of the photographs found in Genie Webb's album and among the Annie Wood Webb papers are unidentified. Of the four Webb sisters pictured in their youth, only Ada and Cordelia are positively identified. I identified Miriam Webb by comparing images of her as an older woman. Eugenie "Genie" Webb is identified by the date and place of the photograph in Corry, Pennsylvania, where the Webbs lived in the late 1860s and early 1870s, and by comparison to a daguerreotype taken of Genie and her sister Edith in 1858.

I made positive and tentative identifications by first determining the date of the photograph, using photography studio names and places, and women's hair and dress fashions. Next, after establishing a photograph date, I attempted to determine the age of the sitter. I then consulted family trees to see who in the family circle was that age at that time in that place. In some instances I was able to make an identification by linking an unidentified younger person with an identified portrait of her as an older person. The danger, however, in linking photographs by resemblance is that these are family albums and different family members sometimes look alike. Confirmation bias is always possible when one is making a tentative identification.

My final identification method resulted from the process of elimination. After identifying as many family members as possible, I searched the family tree for those who should be in the album and were not yet identified. Fortunately for this project, only one of the five Webb sisters had children, and thus most of the family documents remained together in the Annie Wood Webb Papers in the possession of Miriam Webb's oldest and youngest daughters.

Identification of historical photographs in the Annie Wood Webb Papers is an ongoing process, and I look forward to any new information that might clarify my tentative identifications.

Whispers of Cruel Wrongs

Introduction

After reading Harriet Jacobs's fugitive slave narrative, *Incidents in the Life of a Slave Girl*, who has not wondered what happened to her daughter, Louisa? Who can forget the poignant scene when six-year-old "Lulu," sworn to secrecy by her great-grandmother, is allowed to spend a single night wrapped in the arms of the slave mother she had never known before being taken away to the north by her white father? Louisa never forgot that night and never betrayed her mother. Long after they were reunited in New York—and throughout the rest of her life—she remained silent on their shared history. She was so intensely private that she did not divulge the details of her life even to her closest, oldest friend until 1905, when she was over seventy years old.[1] Who did she become, this mixed-race, mixed-place child of the South and grown woman of the North? What did she think, how did she feel, what were her beliefs, who were her friends? If only we could hear her speak, see her smile, understand a bit of her heart.

Now we can.

New voices call out from the silence of nineteenth-century African American women's writing. Unidentified for nearly one hundred years, seventy-one rare, personal letters from Louisa Jacobs and Annie Purvis to their friend Genie Webb shed new light on the lives of women of color who created a warm and sympathetic private world in spite of the racist strife that marked their times. By the twentieth century their story of enduring friendship was forgotten. Scholars did not go looking for it because these women were not supposed to exist in a world where letter writing was considered to be the province of educated white women, where scholarship on black women concentrated on slavery, oppression, identity politics, racial uplift, civil rights, and resistance. Through neglect and forgetting, these women's quiet stories were erased.[2]

Genie Webb is the recipient of all of the letters in this collection, and Louisa Jacobs the main correspondent. What unites Louisa and Genie and Annie Purvis—aside from kinship—is their membership in Philadelphia's elite black society of the 1850s and 1860s. The city's "colored aristocracy" fell roughly into three subgroups: freeborn native citizens, descendants of West Indian immigrants, and mixed-race children of the South.[3] Louisa, Genie, and Annie belonged to the last group, but Genie and Annie also claimed descent from some of Philadelphia's earliest free black families dating back to the eighteenth century. Their parents, grandparents, aunts, and uncles were closely connected with William Lloyd Garrison in the 1830s and lived at the hub of early abolitionism; they were founding members of the American Anti-Slavery Society, the Philadelphia Female Anti-Slavery Society, the Pennsylvania Anti-Slavery Society, the Library Company for Colored People, the Colored Conventions, and the Vigilance Committee, which was dedicated to aiding fugitive slaves.

Louisa, Genie, and Annie grew up in reenergized activism after the passage of the Fugitive Slave Act in 1850 and the *Dred Scott* case of 1857. They were educated by tutors and in private schools, and they studied French, the classics and mathematics, drawing and painting, botany and physiology. They sang in choirs and played musical instruments; practiced elocution; enjoyed fine music, opera, and oratory; visited museums and science exhibits; and appreciated country walks and visits to the seaside. The men in this society were barbers, caterers, carpenters, tailors, printers, and businessmen. The women were dressmakers, teachers, housekeepers, nurses, and milliners. They were reformers, their families deeply involved in the temperance movement and Underground Railroad work, and, during the war, with the organization of soldiers' and freedmen's aid societies. Wealth was not a prerequisite for membership in Philadelphia's black elite society, and neither Genie, Annie, nor Louisa had much in the way of money or property. What mattered most was education and propriety—and, in Genie's and Annie's case, an impeccable pedigree.

Genie Webb is closely connected to the owners of the only known African American friendship albums: those of her aunt, Mary Virginia Wood Forten; her mother's adoptive mother, Amy Matilda Cassey; and Martina and Mary Ann Dickerson, whose mother, Delia Dickerson, had been a close friend of Genie's paternal grandmother.[4] Annie Purvis's mother and her Forten aunts and uncles were frequent contributors to the Wood and Cassey albums. Members of the early network of prominent African American antislavery activists—including Frederick Douglass, William Whipper, Bishop Daniel Alexander Payne, Sarah Mapps Douglass, and Patrick H. Reason—contributed an assortment of poems, sketches, essays, abolitionist sentiments, and gorgeous floral watercolors. Many of the contributors allude to specific events in the owners' lives: a birthday (Mary Virginia Wood), leaving school (Mary Ann Dickerson), love and courtship (Mary Virginia Wood), marriage (Amy Matilda Cassey), motherhood (Amy Matilda Cassey), and death (Joseph Cassey's in 1848). James Forten Jr.'s poem "On Time," written in 1840 to Genie's aunt, Mary Virginia Wood Forten, stands out for its serious tone. Unlike other album contributions, his somber verse offers no congratulations, good wishes, or jesting remarks; instead, it diminishes earthly human accomplishments in the context of "all powerful Time" and then, in its last line, turns the entire conceit on the idea of immortal life. "The final trump proclaims that time shall be no more!" He could not have written better-intentioned words than these to his young sister-in-law, who lay dying of consumption.[5]

By the 1870s the three friends had scattered in search of work and a better life. Genie Webb settled in Camden, New Jersey, to teach. Her 1880s autograph album echoes the names of the previous generation of elites: William Adger, Lydia A. Bustill, journalist Florence A. Lewis, inventor William B. Purvis, antislavery poet Sarah Forten Purvis, physicians Alexander T. Augusta and Frank J. Webb Jr., educators Lottie Bassett, Henry Boyer, Joseph E. Hill, Ada H. Hinton, Anna L. Jones, and Emily D. Bass, and the prominent Bishop family of Annapolis.[6] Reflecting the contributors' education and literary sensibility, these autographs quote such authors as James Russell Lowell, Elizabeth Barrett Browning, Fanny Kemble, Tennyson, Robert Southwell, and Charles Kingsley. Louisa Jacobs and Annie Purvis followed their friends and family to Washington to search for government jobs. There they connected with poet and diarist Charlotte Forten Grimké—a cousin to all three women—and other Philadelphia family members who had already established themselves in the District as teachers, students, government clerks, doctors, and lawyers.

Louisa's social spheres radiated well beyond Philadelphia and Washington. She also maintained contact with family friends in New York, New England, and Edenton, North Carolina. She identified as a woman of color but was equally comfortable in white social circles, such as those of the abolitionist Brocketts in central New York state, biographer James Parton's literary friends in New York City, and Grinnell Willis's "houseful of young people" in Jamestown, Rhode Island, where "not one of them suspected her race—all treated her with the greatest deference and respect." A white family friend, Robert Apthorp Boit, observed that "Louisa was white and passed for white everywhere," but not deliberately. He noted that "when she stayed with Edith or the Willis family she lived as one of them as their guest and was never then known as anything but white." He emphasized that "she never sought whites—rather avoided them," and added that although she "never obtruded it—nor alluded to it— . . . when it was necessary to explain did not hesitate to say she was a negro."[7]

Most of the letters in this collection were sent from Washington during the early post-Reconstruction years. Only four of Louisa's letters written after 1900 are extant. We are literary eavesdroppers in a world that has otherwise been closed to us—that of gentlewomen of color who, despite their education and social standing, were forced to struggle to survive in a world dominated by sexism, racism, bigotry, and Jim Crow laws. A generation older than the "smart set" of powerful black elites in late-nineteenth-century Washington[8]—and themselves the product of Philadelphia's mid-century "colored aristocracy"—these ladies maintained their dignity, always guided by Christian ideals of hope and love.

The story the letters tell is simple, timeless, and universal; they chronicle a compassionate friendship between single, resourceful women who must provide for their families through hard times. The larger story is one of loss: the deaths, aging, and sickness that deplete these women's lives. The other side of that story is the faith that sustains them. A motherless young teacher and a childless middle-aged lady begin the long journey that will transform their mutual grief into a lasting familial bond. When Louisa addresses Genie Webb as "Childie," we can almost hear her own mother's voice and feel the warmth of her embrace. As she delivers news about Genie's Washington cousins—Charlotte Forten and Annie Purvis—Louisa evokes their shared North Carolina heritage, and we, the readers, begin to feel the full significance of southern kinship ties.

Until now, only seven of Louisa Jacobs's personal letters were known to exist.[9] The new letters confirm her unique voice, what Robert Boit noted as her "great intelligence, a rare fancy & imagination, and a way of expressing herself that was quaintly and delightfully her own." He described Louisa as "quiet, cheerful, sweet, refined, intelligent," and wrote that her "letters were always interesting in the graceful and quite unusual turns of thought and of expression." She "passes simply on without a murmur at the injustice of man."[10] Yet late in life—after attempting unsuccessfully to resolve a nearly fifty-year-long dispute over North Carolina property bequeathed to her mother—Louisa did break through her long-held guard of discretion and equanimity. "The South," she wrote, "never did anything for me and to know that white Southern men have the benefit of my great grandmother's labor is too unjust to bear quietly."[11] Louisa's fifty-eight letters in this collection are probably the closest we will ever come to knowing the mature heart and mind of the grave little girl who long kept her promise to her great-grandmother: *Do not tell.*

What might have been a personal survival tactic for Louisa seems to have served as a general rule for an entire class of elite black women who had been taught not to tell. Pulitzer Prize–winning critic Margo Jefferson remembers learning in mid-twentieth-century Chicago that "you don't tell your secrets to strangers—certainly not secrets that expose error, weakness, failure." Elite black women, she writes, were denied the white privilege of "freely yielding to depression." Full self-expression was not an option. Their legacy of "duty, obligation and discipline" compelled them to be strong, to persevere, to set an example, and to succeed.[12] Louisa Jacobs was no exception, as her entry in a young friend's autograph album indicates: "Precept is good but example is better."[13]

Readers of Jacobs's private letters, then, should not expect confessional writing but rather reflection marked by pragmatism, tempered with faith. Louisa reveals her self-restraint but hints at a secret persona when she advises Genie: "Beneath the quiet exterior that you know runs another stream that leaps out on occasions and no doubt is too emphatic in expression."[14] Critical of a black newspaper editor for scandal mongering, Louisa censors herself outright in one letter. "Burn this up," she scrawls at the top, after eloquently advocating racial uplift. "I know we are poor and have not the wherewith to compete with the other race. . . . For that very reason a colored man who undertakes to edit a paper should make its tone high and elevating, imbue it with a spirit of self respect that will make his readers reach out and struggle for something better than the old life."[15] Silences in Louisa's correspondence could well be construed as evidence of the stress, anxiety, fatigue, and despair she chose not to disclose while she herself struggled for that better life. As she reminded Genie early in the correspondence, "'Unsaid' is a pretty picture of real life."[16]

In her letters to Genie, Louisa noted that she often visited the cozy home of Reverend Francis J. Grimké and his wife, Charlotte Forten, at 1608 R Street in Washington. Annie Purvis, who forwarded a list of their wedding gifts to Genie, still lived in her grandfather James Forten's grand residence on Lombard Street in Philadelphia, and Genie, a frequent visitor at the Forten home, would also have been familiar with such elegance. For anyone with a historical imagination it is not hard to imagine that the Grimké parlor, with all its trappings of culture and discreet comfort, represented a microcosm of the sheltered society of light-skinned African American elites in Washington and a reflection of the gracious, cultivated interior life of an educated woman of color.

From Annie's list of the Grimkés' wedding presents[17] we can form a good sense of the interior of their home in all its Victorian richness, and we can guess

"Thy love shall chant itself its own beatitudes / After its own life wakings. A child's kiss / Set on thy sighing lips, shall make thee glad, / A poor man served by thee shall make thee rich, / A sick man helped by thee shall make thee strong. / Thou shalt be served thyself by every sense / Of service which thou renderest." Charlotte Forten (Grimké)'s autograph poem to Genie Webb, September 1, 1884. (AWWP)

at the atmosphere of those intimate literary soirees where Reverend Grimké ceremoniously poured amber-colored tea for his guests. Its parlors—as Annie Purvis described them—were tastefully furnished with easy chairs, books, and paintings, and were heated by a Latrobe stove in the front parlor and a grate fire in the back parlor, where Doctor Grimké had his study. When the middle doors were opened, the two parlors made an inviting space with "a pleasant spirit over all."[18]

The front parlor was furnished with a "handsome ingrain" carpet, given by the Fifteenth Street Presbyterian Church, and four parlor chairs, both "ornamental and useful." The walls were hung with thirteen or fourteen pictures, including landscapes and flowers; a large, magnificent engraving titled "Christ as the Good Shepherd" from William E. Matthews of Baltimore; two "exquisite ones, 'Mignon,' from Cordelia Ray, and a transparency, 'Hamlet & Ophelia,' from Florence Ray";[19] and, in wax, the motto "God is Love." Carefully arranged were two pairs of vases, a glass vase on a bronze stand, a pair of elegant bronzes, four Japanese card trays, two clocks, and a hanging basket. Two student lamps lit Reverend Grimké's study. His desk was equipped with three inkstands and one pen wiper shaped like a dog. Among the many books were "one cookery book, an elegant copy of Shakespeare & Mr. Still's Underground book (from himself, of course)."[20] Civil rights activist Katie Jennings and Mrs. Elizabeth Keckley (Mary Todd Lincoln's former dressmaker) had presented the Grimkés

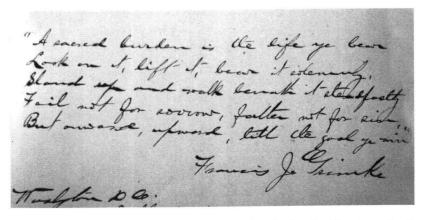

"A sacred burden is the life ye bear / Look on it, lift it, bear it solemnly, / Stand up and walk beneath it steadfastly / Fail not for sorrow, falter not for sin / But onward, upward, till the goal ye win." Francis J. Grimké's autograph poem to Genie Webb, September 1, 1884. (AWWP)

with an elegant china chamber set, and Annie Purvis's uncle, equal rights leader Robert Purvis, had given them a cluster of autumn leaves and frames.

For elegant dining, Francis Grimké's mother, who lived upstairs, had given the newlyweds a full set of French China for ten. The Grimkés had also received an abundance of silver: a fruit basket, napkin rings, knives, forks, spoons, and a gold-lined silver salt cellar from Cherry Vogelsang. There were five linen tablecloths—four white and one gray and red, for breakfasts—and three table covers, one elegantly embroidered. Dozens of table napkins of all kinds and sizes and four sets of fancy mats were laid away in drawers. The kitchen was well furnished with a teakettle, table mats, thermometer, wall baskets with two silk pin cushions, a table, crockery, aprons, and a kitchen stone. For the bedroom the Grimkés had received a handsome carpet, a "tidy walnut bedstead & mattress," a large number of towels, four or five white bedspreads, two "splendid" pairs of blankets—one pair from Annie Purvis's cousin, Dr. Charles B. Purvis's wife, Ann Hathaway—and two pairs of pillow shams. Finally, there were the personal gifts: the knit shawl, three pairs of finest woolen stockings, a winter cloak, a knit fascinator for the head, and a mother-of-pearl pin from Spain, given by Ednah Dow Cheney.

The oasis of the Grimkés' charming home stood in contrast to Louisa's and her mother's unsettled and often uncomfortable life. They moved often, at least twice a year, as they followed the opening and closing of Washington's seasons. Their pattern for many years was to rent a house in the District for the winter, then pack up, put their things in storage, and stay with friends in New England during the summer. Sometimes they rented a small apartment that they furnished themselves; at other times they leased a more spacious, furnished residence, where they could sublet rooms and employ servants to assist them. The need for servants and the ability to pay their wages depended entirely on the number of boarders the Jacobses attracted, often through their Boston connections. In 1883, Louisa's main concern was finding the right kind of help. Although she kept three servants and sent the washing out, she complained that the "trouble is in getting competent help, and the want of it leaves so much care and responsibility on me."[21]

The following year, although she eventually hired another person to help with her canning business, Louisa juggled several jobs, working days at Howard University, early evenings helping her mother board the Bailey Willis family, and nights at the vacant residence of her former employer, where she made her jams and jellies. On one occasion she and her mother, without proper kitchen facilities of their own, used the kitchen of their friend Julia Wilbur to make twelve quarts of chicken salad for a party given by wealthy socialite Josephine Willson Bruce.[22] Louisa had always wished for her own quiet little home, but she foretold her own future when she wrote, "I am afraid I shall never have enough of this world's goods to buy the most modest shanty."[23]

The letters in this collection allude to a number of public topics. Jacobs writes of the rhythms of life in 1880s Washington: incoming and outgoing presidential administrations (including President Garfield's assassination),[24] politics, employment, church affairs, housing, summer travel to New York and Boston, and her work at Howard University. We do not know how and to what extent increased segregation, political corruption, post-Reconstruction government retrenchment, and news of southern lynchings and disfranchisement negatively affected Louisa during her Washington years because she does not dwell on many of these subjects. Given her acuity, education, and equal rights activism, we must assume that she closely followed political news and discussed contemporary issues with her socially prominent activist friends, the Grimkés and the Fleetwoods. She must have felt deep disappointment, if not betrayal, when the Supreme Court, in 1883, declared the 1875 Civil Rights Act to be unconstitutional. Like her friends Dr. Alexander T. Augusta, Reverend Francis Grimké, and Christian A. Fleetwood, she likely joined thousands to attend the Civil Rights Mass-Meeting at Lincoln Hall in 1883 to protest the decision and hear the speeches of Frederick Douglass and Robert G. Ingersoll.[25] During the mid-1880s, she and her mother participated in the women's suffrage movement, met several times with Susan B. Anthony, and attended the eighteenth convention of the National Woman Suffrage Association, held in Washington in 1886.[26] They may also have been among the thousands who, two years later, crowded Albaugh's Opera House in Washington on the first day of meetings of the International Council of Women, where invited guests included Susan B. Anthony, Amy Post, Julia Wilbur, Robert Purvis, and Ednah Dow Cheney—all personal friends of the Jacobses.[27] Louisa continued to be involved in women's rights and was active in the National League of Colored Women, founded by, among others, her friends (and Genie's cousins) Lottie Grimké and Sarah Iredell Fleetwood.

Louisa's friend Joseph H. Rainey, the first African American member of Congress (1870–1879), boarded with her in 1885 and would no doubt have personally recounted many examples of southern voter suppression and politically motivated racial violence—in particular, the 1876 murder by white Democrats of approximately one hundred African Americans in Ellenton, South Carolina.[28] Another boarder, William H. Chew, Rainey's business partner and an old friend of Louisa's from Philadelphia, successfully sued in 1880 for the abolition of segregation in Pennsylvania schools.[29] His activism was inspired in part by the rigged low grades given to the only two colored applicants to Philadelphia's Girls' High and Normal School in 1878.[30] Through his and others' efforts, one of those girls, Miranda Venning (whom Louisa and Genie knew well and who is mentioned in these letters), would become the first African American graduate of that school and go on to become the principal of the prestigious Joseph E. Hill School. In general, however, schools would remain segregated in Pennsylvania for almost another hundred years, and Louisa would be constantly reminded of that inequity by Genie Webb's schoolhouse stories.

Louisa reacted with horror to the news in December 1882 of white doctors at Philadelphia's Jefferson Medical College conspiring for eleven years with the black superintendent of Lebanon Cemetery to supply the college with stolen African American cadavers. When she learned that distraught mourners had rushed to the cemetery to retrieve their recently buried dead, she responded, "I do not know how people had the heart to dig for their dead with the dread of not finding them. I would prefer the uncertainty, clinging to the hope that they were there."[31] Over and over, hard-fought legislated rights were revealed to have little impact on the harsh facts of American apartheid.

A five-year gap in the letters suggests the Jacobses' worsening financial straits. It coincides with the worst economic depression to hit the United States up to that time. The Panic of 1893–1897, which newly elected president Grover Cleveland blamed partly on the 1890 Sherman Silver Purchase Act, precipitated an unprecedented number of failures: over six hundred banks closed, more

than fifteen thousand businesses went bankrupt, unemployment in New York shot up to 35 percent, the United Mine Workers went on strike and imploded, the Pullman strike shut down much of the nation's transportation, farm mortgages were foreclosed, workers faced wage cuts and layoffs, and large numbers of hungry and homeless people slipped into tramp life.[32] At the time of the panic, Louisa had just begun work at the U.S. Treasury's "Silver Roll," where she made rolls of coins from the millions of ounces of government silver that had been purchased as a result of the controversial act. Her job ended soon after President Cleveland took office and repealed the act.[33] The Jacobses' friend Julia Wilbur succinctly summed up their situation. "They have suffered so much, & now are poor."[34] Louisa's first letter to Genie after the crash speaks the language of economic depression: "A dollar in hand is worth many in prospect"; it is best to "not borrow on the future"; do not "work yourself to death unless there is some profit behind it."[35]

The letters in this collection not only touch on public affairs but also address the private lives of elite African American women, revealing their feelings and emotions and their dedication to carrying on with Christian forbearance in the face of sickness and death. Poor health, fatigue, and lung problems are constant themes in the lives of Genie, Louisa, Annie Purvis, and Charlotte Forten. Harriet Jacobs was chronically ill. Louisa was overworked and dangerously thin. Charlotte endured debilitating headaches and lived an invalid's life. Genie suffered from a heart ailment for which she was treated with torturous chest blisters. Consumption was rampant; members of the Forten, Purvis, and Wood

Left: The Colored Women's League of Washington gathered at Frederick Douglass's home on July 18, 1896. Louisa Jacobs mentioned the League's July meetings in a letter to Ednah Dow Cheney, and she probably attended at least one of the meetings held during that week. Eugenia "Genie" Webb's cousins Laura Iredell (Hawkesworth) (52) and founder Sarah Iredell (Fleetwood) (53) are seated on the ground and her cousins Evelyn Durham Shaw and founder Charlotte Forten (Grimké) stand in the back row. [Mary Church Terrell] is standing (in the print dress with balloon sleeves), the second person below Shaw (11). [Anna Julia Cooper] stands below and to the left of Grimké (13).

Standing on the left, from bottom, are Ella Swett, [Josephine Silone Yates], Kate Moten (oo) on her right, Mamie Hilyer, Dr. [Henry Davidson] Fry (4), Andrew F. Hilyer (5), Annie King (6), Dr. Amelia Frances Foy, and [Dr. Rebecca J. Cole]. Lula Love stands below Cole. Pictured in the second row are [Robert Purvis, white beard], [John Love, behind and to the right of Robert Purvis], Mrs. R. M. Collett of Baltimore (043), Mallie Bush (44), Helen Appo Cook (45), Helen Pitts Douglass (46), Mrs. Michaux (47), Mrs. J. Pierre (47), and [Hallie Quinn Brown] on the far right. [Dr. Caroline Still Anderson] stands to the right of the right pillar and Major Charles Remond Douglass (34) stands to the left of it. Seated on the ground are a Miss Jordan or Jackson (52), Julia Grant (54), and Mrs. John Smith (58). [Fanny Jackson Coppin] sits behind and to the right of Mrs. Smith, with her arm in the lap of the lady with umbrella. (Christian A. Fleetwood Collection, Library of Congress; square brackets indicate my identifications) families seem to have been especially susceptible, with Genie and Charlotte losing their mothers, maternal grandmother, two Forten aunts, and several Purvis cousins to the disease. Louisa's close friends, the Lawton family of Cambridge, Massachusetts, lost five members to tuberculosis in five years.[36] Nursing of the terminally ill was built into the responsibilities of being female. Genie, Louisa, and Annie all cared for their ailing elderly parents, and all tended to them at their deathbeds. Death was ever-present, far too much a fact of life to be ignored or denied.

The sheer volume of popular consolation literature in the Victorian era attests to the need for it. Nineteenth-century acceptance of death and loss went hand in hand with religious beliefs that proclaimed everlasting life after death. An 1886 entry in Genie's autograph album inscribed by her friend Lydia A. Bustill repeats Reverend John G. Pike's grim words: "The charms of beauty of manners, of wit, may adorn the young in their hasty journey to an endless world; but religion only, will prepare them for a heavenly home. Those may glitter in the casket, but only this will beautify the jewel."[37] The bereaved were to be consoled by assurances that they would be reunited with lost loved ones in their heavenly home. Louisa, forty-six years old at the beginning of this correspondence, had already lost most of her family: her great-grandmother, her only uncle—abolitionist John S. Jacobs—and her only brother, Joseph Jacobs. Aside from her mother and a young cousin, she told Genie, she had no one left. After her closest friend, Delie Chew, died in late 1879, the well-worn words rolled out easily. "God has seen fit to break the link, and I bow to his behest, looking beyond sorrow and self to that hereafter, where my heart is, there to be united to the lost and loved through the endless ages of eternity." Yet her heart was not in it. "This thought is a help to me and yet it does not comfort me now as it ought."[38]

Louisa was devout enough, a Sunday school teacher at St. Luke's in Washington, well-grounded in scripture and doctrine, a model of Christian piety. But she did not obsess about religious rules the way Genie Webb did, and she had no qualms about questioning church doctrine if it interfered with common sense: "I love purity of Religion yet in spirit I could never be a Puritan."[39] When Genie confided her hope that her dead mother and Delie might be beaming from heaven as they watched her younger sisters being confirmed at St. Thomas African Episcopal Church in Philadelphia, Louisa responded with her usual intellect and pragmatic doubt: "Yet if the departed can behold with the visible eye what effects their dear ones here, how does it comport with the idea that heaven is a place of perfect happiness? For it would not be reasonable to suppose only the fair and beautiful side of existence here is turned to their view. And again, we must suppose the higher the sphere of their being the keener their sensibilities. While we love to think of their being near us, I cannot think they have a knowledge of existence here."[40] Genie had disclosed her innermost feelings of grief to Louisa from within a Christian framework where the thought of continuing bonds with her dead loved ones consoled her. Even Delie's dying was sacramental; nearing her end, she and Genie had taken communion together, thus sealing their emotional bond for eternity.

While Louisa did not agree with Genie about the state of heaven above, both women would have accepted Delie's death through the prevailing view of Mizpah—the belief that an all-understanding God watched over separated friends and preserved their bond. Mizpah was a late-nineteenth-century American and British cultural phenomenon based upon the Hebrew word *Mizpah* in the biblical passage from Genesis 31:49, "May the LORD watch between you and me when we are absent one from the other." The Victorian concept of Mizpah captured all aspects of absence, from temporary separation to final parting in death, its meaning sometimes conflated with another biblical passage, "May the LORD be between me and thee and between mine and thine forever."[41]

Louisa, along with other elite African American women, would have been familiar with Lafayette Charles Loomis's book *Mizpah, Prayer, and Friendship*, first published in 1858 and reprinted in 1871 and 1880, which was dedicated to "those who pray for the loved whom they hope to meet and still love in heaven." Loomis informed his readers, "In this prayer-intercourse of kindred spirits, Religion and Affection, alike, are nurtured up to a purer joy and a nobler life." As well, Louisa and Genie would likely have read Julia Aldrich Baker's immensely popular Mizpah poem that opened with the lines, "Go thou thy way, and I go mine / Apart, yet not afar," and Annie Lanman Angier's poem opening with, "Mizpah! How this gentle word / By lips of Friendship spoken." Early in their correspondence, Louisa alluded to the Mizpah prayer when she wrote to Genie, "The pray itself expresses so much. There is a nearness and strengthening in friendship when friends mention one another in their prayers." Mizpah culture validated women's friendships and, by linking emotional bonds with religious prayer, elevated them. Mizpah not only preserved the close bonds that linked Louisa and Genie to their deceased friend, it also defined their long-distance friendship with each other.[42]

Louisa sometimes needed to step outside her church to resituate herself in her grief, to readjust to an environment without Delie, to become open to other relationships. When she reported that she had attended a Unitarian service, Genie was shocked to her core at the thought that Louisa might stop believing in the Trinity. Louisa, for her part, had gone simply because she liked the music. While working one summer in upstate New York, she was not the least bit apologetic about taking Sundays off to rest instead of attending church, "knowing God understands the situation and will judge accordingly."[43] Louisa was not intellectually intimidated by the great spiritual leaders of her day. When she heard Dr. Alexander Crummell's sermon on the "Greatness of Christ" (later published), she allowed that the subject was "ably handled" but felt that Crummell stuck too closely to his manuscript and lacked "the soft tenderness that melts and bows the heart."[44] Louisa's practical side kicked in when she realized that Genie, whose health was already compromised, would half starve herself during Lent. As far as Louisa was concerned, Genie had privation enough. "God knows all things and does not ask of his creatures any sacrifice detrimental to their welfare. So, dear, be governed accordingly."[45] Similarly, when Genie worried that praying to God for an everlasting friendship with Louisa might be considered a sin, Louisa reassured her, "So we love not the creature better than the creator it is all right."[46] Each woman trusted the other with her innermost religious thoughts, but it was Louisa, twenty-three years older and wiser, who expressed herself with more confidence and certainty.

Louisa's candid comments may show her as a clear thinking individualist, but her letters are also liberally sprinkled with aphorisms and popular inspirational verse. Some of these sentiments may seem trite to readers today but—as with most clichés—they originated in someone's authentic experience. Louisa used poetry as a way to speak from her own heart and offer a pathway forward. One of her favorite and oft-quoted poets, the feminist social reformer Adelaide Proctor, advocated for poor and destitute women[47]—a cause that was dear to Louisa's heart and culminated in her employment at the turn of the twentieth century as matron of Washington's National Home for the Relief of Destitute Colored Women and Children. Proctor's poem "One by One" guided Louisa as a reminder of faith, humility, and hope.

How did Louisa cope in late middle age with no financial security and the negation of the civil rights that she had so hopefully championed forty years earlier? Sixty-two years old in 1896—with no home of her own and no hope of having one, and the sole provider and caregiver for her dying mother—she fell seriously ill herself. Outside her door, autumn election fever and the excitement of the inauguration of President McKinley faded away as she focused on basic survival. Asking for help from the only people she trusted, the Willis family, and receiving it from her friend Ednah Dow Cheney, Louisa felt "grieved and hurt at the necessity of calling on friends for aid." She barely had words for her gratitude. "God recognizes them and gives the reward, and so it will be in this case."[48] Invoking the bond of sympathy that opened their correspondence,

Louisa quoted eighteenth-century playwright David Garrick and reminded Genie that "a fellow feeling makes us wondrous kind." The two women suffered together, although apart, and had entered into their own sacred communion: "I know about the hard struggles the anxious thoughts we pillow at night and that rise with us in the morning. Some lives are so shadowed but the curtain will rise some day, if not here in another land where weariness and care do not enter. So let us be hopeful and never turn aside from the little glimmers of sunshine that meet us here and there on our way."[49] Humbled by the Jacobses' faith, Cornelia Willis wrote to Ednah Dow Cheney. "It is a lesson and a benediction to know them, & walk beside them in this trying time. One realizes what the spirit can do for us. It is not all dreariness & pain in that little home."[50]

Our own walk with Louisa Jacobs is no less inspiring. She teaches us, by example in her letters, to patiently embrace the spiritual potential of suffering. She reminds us that carrying on is a profound act of resistance. She urges us to "not look at the pain alone" but to create, hold, and guard the sacred space between people—that intimate place called community—where both a vision of hope and the reality of resistance can be evoked. Only in the "furnace of affliction," Louisa tells us—at the deepest levels of failure, suffering, and loss—can we be refined.[51] She gives to us, her uninvited readers, the greatest gift that one friend can give another—comfort, encouragement, and support.

Biographical Sketches

The following biographical sketches list the important people in the lives of Louisa Matilda Jacobs (1833–1917) and Eugenie "Genie" Webb (1856–1919), in alphabetical order by their nicknames. These sketches provide essential back-story and help to fill gaps in this collection. Louisa and Harriet Jacobs (ca. 1815–1897) appear as "Lulu" and "Mother" on this list.

"Annie"

Harriet Ann "Annie" Purvis (1848–1917) wrote thirteen of the letters in this collection. She was the daughter of gentleman farmer Joseph Purvis (1812–1857) and antislavery poet Sarah Louise Forten (1814–1884), the niece of abolitionist Robert Purvis (1810–1898), and the granddaughter of wealthy black activists James Forten (1766–1842) and Charlotte Vandine (Forten, 1785–1884) of Philadelphia. Her father was born free in Charleston, South Carolina, to British-born cotton broker William Purvis (1762–1826) and his freeborn mixed-race wife, Harriet Judah (Purvis, Miller, 1783–1869).

Annie received her earliest education privately at the Purvis family estate, "Fairview," in Bucks County, Pennsylvania, in a chaotic home plagued by debt and her father's alcoholism.[1] After Joseph Purvis died intestate in 1857, Annie's teacher-aunt, Margaretta Forten (1806–1875), assumed guardianship of some of the eight Purvis children, and Annie, nine years old, moved back to her Grandmother Forten's home in Philadelphia. Annie considered herself a cousin of Eugenie "Genie" Webb (1856–1919) through their mutual upbringing and cousinship with Charlotte "Lottie" Louise Forten (Grimké, 1837–1914).[2]

Antislavery and equal rights activist, head of the 1830s Vigilance Committee of Philadelphia, and the "father of the Underground Railroad," Robert Purvis was Annie Purvis's uncle. (Collection of the Massachusetts Historical Society)

In 1875, Annie, her mother, and her brother William (1838–1914) lost their Bucks County family farm to debt. Annie worked during the early 1880s in the federal Agricultural Department in Washington, DC, and at the office of Recorder of Deeds Frederick Douglass (1818–1895) in 1884, and then, in late 1884, she returned to the old Lombard Street home to care for her aging mother and grandmother. Both died during the course of this correspondence. After her mother's and grandmother's deaths, Annie worked in a Philadelphia shop making artificial flowers. She and her brother, inventor William B. Purvis, both unmarried, continued to live at the Forten home until 1893, when they moved to a small Philadelphia apartment.[3]

"Delie"

The death of Cordelia "Delie" Sanders (Chew, ca. 1843–1879) precipitated the correspondence between Louisa Jacobs and Genie Webb that is included in this collection. Cordelia died of consumption on November 5, 1879, with Genie Webb by her side. Born in Charleston, South Carolina, the daughter of well-to-do British businessperson Richard Walpole Cogdell (1787–1866) and his enslaved common-law wife, Sarah Martha Sanders (1815–1850), Delie and her family arrived in Philadelphia in 1858, where they were befriended by John Chew (1818–1870) and Charlotte Henson (Chew, 1819–1884), Annie Elizabeth Wood (Webb, 1831–1879) and her niece Charlotte Forten (Grimké), and Louisa and Harriet Jacobs. The Sanderses associated with other well-to-do mixed-race families who had moved from Charleston to Philadelphia, such as the Browns, Joneses, Purvises, Humphreys, Adgers, Vennings, Le Counts, Farbeauxs, and Cattos. During one social gathering at the Sanderses' residence in the spring of 1858, Charlotte Forten remarked, "All were Southerners, save me."[4]

Delie taught in Colored School Number 1 in Brooklyn in the mid-1860s, along with colleague Georgiana F. Putnam (1832–1912) of Salem, Massachusetts, under principal Charles A. Dorsey (1836–1907) of Philadelphia. She may have received at least part of her education in Salem, where she accompanied Charlotte Forten (Grimké) in the summer of 1862. Before she married William "Willie" Herbert Chew (1847–1892) in 1870, she was romantically involved with equal rights activist Octavius Catto (1839–1871), who was later assassinated on his way to vote. She was the mother of two boys, Richard Sanders Chew (1871–1962) and Charles Sanders Chew (1873–1954). During 1875 and 1876, Delie visited Louisa Jacobs in Cambridge, and the two traveled together to Herkimer County, New York, to see Louisa's old friends. Delie invited Louisa to

Cordelia "Delie" Sanders (Chew), 1866, taught school after the Civil War in Brooklyn, New York. Delie was Louisa Jacobs's closest friend. Her death in 1879 precipitated the nearly forty-year correspondence between Genie Webb and Louisa Jacobs. (AWWP)

spend at least one Christmas with her family in Philadelphia. A great admirer of Charles Sumner (1811–1874), Delie wore an onyx ring she had commissioned to be made in Italy featuring Sumner's image carved in ivory. Those who knew her characterized her as "a most beautiful and brilliant woman of executive ability, and a fine conversationalist." When Charlotte Forten first met Delie as a young teen she described her in her journal as an "intelligent, interesting girl—very imaginative, with a great deal of freshness and originality." She found her family "much more interesting than Southerners usually are," and vowed to "*try hard* to convert them to anti-slavery."[5]

Delie's mother-in-law, Charlotte Louisa Henson (Chew), and her father-in-law, John Chew, had been close friends of Genie Webb's mother, Annie E. Wood (Webb), during Annie's girlhood in 1840s Philadelphia. Genie Webb's grandmother Edith "Edy" Wood (1794–1846) had rented rooms from John Chew's father, secondhand clothes dealer William Chew (d. 1857), for several years before her death in 1846. John Chew loved Edy Wood "as a son," and he loved Annie Wood as his "sister in heart." When Edy died, he invited the semi-orphaned Annie Wood to come live with him and his family. He considered himself Annie's "Friend and Brother" and declared that he would "share his last farthing and divide his last loaf with [her]." Thus four generations of the Chew family were intimately connected with three generations of the Wood/Webb family.[6]

"Edie"

Edith "Edie" Louise Webb (1855–1912) was the sister of Genie Webb, the recipient of all the letters in this collection. The eldest of the six children of school teacher Annie Elizabeth Wood (Webb) and barber/farmer John Gloucester Webb (1823–1904), Edie was named after her maternal grandmother, Edith "Edy" Wood (1794–1846), the emancipated innkeeper of the Eagle Inn and Tavern in Hertford, Perquimans County, North Carolina. Edy Wood had maintained a long-term relationship with her white lover, planter James Cathcart Johnston (1782–1865) of Edenton, North Carolina, and it was Johnston, through the agency of Frederick A. Hinton, who settled Edy and their children in Philadelphia in 1833. Their two surviving daughters—Edith's mother, Annie Wood (Webb), and her aunt, Mary Virginia Wood—grew up among Philadelphia's "colored aristocracy": the Hintons, Chews, Willsons, Casseys, Millers, Purvises, and Fortens.[7]

Edith Webb and her siblings were raised in the next generation of this closed society of mixed-race elite. Edith's cousin Charlotte Forten (Grimké) affectionately called her "our little Gipsy Girl."[8] During and after the Civil War, Edith acted as secretary to teacher Sarah Mapps Douglass's (1806–1882) Children's Aid Society and collected clothing and funds for the Freedmen's Relief Society. She graduated from the Institute for Colored Youth in 1872 and read Longfellow's "The Legend Beautiful" at her commencement exercises. In the early 1870s she dreamed of becoming a dramatic reader like her aunt Mary E. (Webb, 1828–1859). In 1873 British actor Boothroyd Fairclough (1825–1911) coached her in stage performance and encouraged her to take lessons from Mr. R. Roberts, "the greatest tragedian in the United States," who had recently performed as Mephistopheles at the Walnut Street Theatre. Fairclough assured Edith that "lecturing" was her "destiny," but sadly, Edith's ambitions were stifled when she was called home to care for her ill mother. She trained as a teacher and taught for many years at the Ferry Avenue Colored School in Camden, New Jersey. In later life she became a private nurse. She did not marry.[9]

"Genie"

Eugenie "Genie" Webb is the recipient of all the letters in this collection and was the sister of Edith Webb. She was the second eldest of the six children of Annie E. Wood and John G. Webb. Their father was the mixed-race grandson of Vice President Aaron Burr (1756–1836), and their mother the mixed-race granddaughter of North Carolina governor Samuel Johnston (1733–1816). Their uncle, Frank J. Webb (1828–1894), published the second novel authored by an African American, *The Garies and Their Friends*, in 1857. It was the first American novel to address the themes of passing and interracial marriage. Webb paints a vivid and realistic picture of northern racism and the plight of mixed-race people living in Philadelphia in the 1830s and 1840s. His graphic depiction of a horrifying race riot continues to disturb readers today.[10]

Genie and Edith were educated in Philadelphia at Sarah Mapps Douglass's school and in their "aunt" Margaretta Forten's classes at the Institute for Colored Youth. After the Civil War the family moved to Corry, Pennsylvania, and in the early 1870s they rented a house in Camden, New Jersey, where Genie and her sister Edith taught at the Ferry Avenue Colored School. In the late 1880s, she and her sister Miriam taught at the Mount Vernon Colored School. All five Webb sisters trained as teachers and taught in Camden while their father and

Eugenie "Genie" Webb, 1870s. (AWWP)

brother operated a barbershop there. The Webb family owned several properties in New Jersey, including a farm in Franklinville that remained in the family for 116 years.[11]

In May 1879, six months before this correspondence begins, Genie's mother died of consumption at the age of forty-eight, leaving Genie and her sister Edith with the responsibility of raising the four younger children.[12] Then, just two weeks before the correspondence begins, the Webbs' family friend, Delie Chew, also died of consumption. Genie had nursed Delie through her final illness and was with her at her deathbed when Delie asked her to consider marrying her soon-to-be-widowed husband, Willie Chew, and to raise her two young sons. Like her cousin-friends, however, Genie chose to remain single.

Genie suffered from various illnesses from which she never fully recovered. She stopped teaching, ran the family farm, and began a jam and preserves business. The absence of her brother, John, from the letters reflects his absence from the family. He struggled with alcohol, depression, and debt, and, at twenty-nine, after abandoning his wife and child in Camden, he wrote, "My race is nearly run so you may all consider me dead unless I should at some time make money and then I will return home, but as that is almost an imposability you will sease to remember me."[13] John applied for a post office job in Florida under the name Juan de Webb, and by 1892 he had re-created himself as a Spanish-born barber, Juan Degonzalez. In 1915 John was arrested and jailed for desertion of his second wife and their two daughters.[14] After their father, John Gloucester Webb, died in 1904, the three unmarried Webb sisters— Genie, Edith, and Cordelia—lived together in Philadelphia. They were listed as white in the 1910 census.

In June 1918, when Genie received a $150 bequest from the estate of her close friend Louisa Jacobs, she would have been in a state of profound need. After suffering for a year from stomach cancer that progressed in her last three months to her brain, she died on November 1, 1919, at the age of sixty-two.[15]

"Father"

John Gloucester Webb was Genie Webb's father. He was born free in Philadelphia to Louisa Burr (Webb, Darius, ca. 1785/88–1878) and Francis Webb (1788–1829). The elder Webb named his son for John Gloucester, founder of the First African Presbyterian Church in Philadelphia. The Webb family emigrated to Haiti in 1824 but returned two years later as part of a reverse migration of thousands of disillusioned immigrants. While in Port au Platt, Francis Webb

John G. Webb, ca. 1890s, was Genie Webb's father and a grandson of Aaron Burr. (AWWP)

had served as secretary on the board of instruction of a joint Episcopal-Presbyterian church school. Previously, he had served as an elder in the First African Presbyterian Church, a parishioner at the African Episcopal Church of St. Thomas, a founding member of the Pennsylvania Augustine Education Society, and secretary of the Haytien Emigration Society. After returning to Philadelphia, Francis Webb worked as the Philadelphia distribution agent for *Freedom's Journal* from 1827 to 1829. He died in 1829 of unknown causes. John G. Webb; his sisters, Elizabeth Susan Webb (Iredell, 1818–1888) and Ann A. Webb (1820–1884); and his brother, Frank J. Webb (future author of *The Garies and Their Friends*), were raised among cousins and with the Amy (1808–1856) and Joseph Cassey (1789–1848) family.

John G. Webb's mother, Louisa Burr, was the illegitimate daughter of Vice President Aaron Burr and the sister of John Pierre Burr (1792–1864), a respected antislavery activist in Philadelphia's black community. Louisa worked most of her life for Mrs. Elizabeth Powel Francis (Fisher, 1777–1855), a prominent white Philadelphia society matron closely connected to the oldest Philadelphia families. Louisa was nurse to Mrs. Fisher's only child, Joshua Francis Fisher (1807–1873), and after Fisher's 1839 marriage to Eliza Middleton (1815–1890) of Charleston she helped to raise their young family. Although she retired from child care duties in 1848, she remained a valued part of the Fisher household for most of her life. When Mrs. Fisher died in 1855, she bequeathed Louisa $100 and half of her wardrobe. Joshua Francis Fisher continued to maintain Louisa with allowances and monetary gifts for the rest of his life, and his will directed his heirs to pay her an annuity of $150 and to give her a "respectable" funeral. Louisa died in her nineties—attended by the Fishers' doctor and relative, Dr. Wharton Sinkler (1845–1910)—and was buried as a "Lady." The Fisher family connection continued into the third generation when, in 1897, Joshua Francis Fisher's son and daughters advanced money to Genie Webb to help her establish a small canning business. In 1909, Joshua F. Fisher's children again came to the aid of the three older Webb sisters and paid their rent during the difficult time leading up to the deaths of Cordelia and Edith Webb in 1912.[16]

John G. Webb attended a private school on Cherry Street (probably the Clarkson School run by the Pennsylvania Abolition Society) kept by Mr. Kelly, a graduate of Dublin University. Other elite African American students at the school were Hans Shadd (1821–1911), David Bustill Bowser (1820–1900), John Proctor (b. 1821), Thomas J. Bowers (1823–1885), William Deas Forten (1823–1900), Thomas Willing Francis Forten (1827–1897), and Richard and Edward Johnson.[17] Through their mutual childhood ties to the Cassey family, John G. Webb and Annie E. Wood began their long courtship in 1849 when Annie was eighteen.[18] Like many free, young African American men of his generation,

John was bitten by gold fever and sailed with Sarah L. Cassey's (1833–1875) husband, Joseph C. Smith (1829–1855), to California in search of fortune. He returned from the goldfields in the early spring of 1854 to propose to Annie, and she accepted, but with some reservations about his restless nature.[19] They were married in Charles Lenox Remond's (1810–1873) Salem home by Reverend Octavius Frothingham (1822–1895).[20]

The Webbs' first daughter, Edith, was born in Philadelphia in 1855, and their second, Eugenie, the following year at their new farm in Gloucester County, New Jersey. Their only son, John Johnston Webb, was born in Philadelphia in 1863 during the Civil War and was named for his white southern grandfather, unionist planter James Cathcart Johnston. Later the younger John's middle name would be changed to Degonzalez, and as an adult he would drop Webb altogether in order to present himself as a young man of Mediterranean descent. Daughter Miriam was born in Philadelphia in 1865 (d. 1942). Daughter Charlotte Cordelia (probably named for Annie's niece, Charlotte Forten [Grimké], and her friend, Cordelia Sanders [Chew]) was born in 1868 (d. 1912) in Corry, Pennsylvania. The youngest, Ada, was born in 1872 (d. 1952) at the family farm in Franklinville, New Jersey.[21]

Times were tough after the Civil War, and John G. Webb left his family for ten years in search of work in other parts of the country. He battled depression and was so humiliated at his inability to provide for his family that he could not see or speak to Annie, but he was not estranged from other family members. He wrote affectionate letters to his children, sent money home when he could, and sometimes sent instructions to his wife through his elder daughters. He wrote Genie from Memphis in the 1870s about Annie's plan to open a seminary in the South with her daughters as the school's teachers. "The white people has the whole control of things here," he said, "and the colord man is bound to be at the foot here like anywhere else." He added, "I know you all have great trouble and your young hearts must bleed But God in his justice has wrought this great trouble upon us if we love him he will yet Bring us out, there is a great work here for the Colord people—But my children build no castles in the air unless they are to labor hard for the attainment of good." John G. Webb eventually returned to Camden to live with his daughters, but by the mid-1880s he was unable to work at all.[22]

"Joe"

Joseph Pierce (ca. 1862–?) was born in Georgia about 1862 and adopted after the Civil War by Harriet and Louisa Jacobs, whom he called "Ma" and "Aunt

Lou." He received his early education in Cambridge, Massachusetts, and worked briefly for the pension office in Washington before being laid off in 1881 and returning to Boston. As a young man, Joe became estranged from the Jacobses and led a wild life. In 1893, when he was employed at the Chicago Gas Light & Coke Company, he wrote an apologetic letter to Reverend Francis James Grimké (1850–1937), expressing his shame for not writing Harriet and Louisa for so many years. He asked for forgiveness and for Grimké to convey to the Jacobses that he was now a changed man "enlisted in the army of the Lord." In 1897, working full time for the Salvation Army in Chicago, he advised Louisa that he could not afford the trip to Washington to visit his ailing "Ma." Harriet Jacobs died one week later. Joe wrote another letter to Louisa after Harriet's death expressing his gratitude for all they had taught him. Louisa marked that letter, "Joe's last letter to me." Nothing more is known of Joseph Pierce except for his possible appearance in the Chicago 1920 census as a widower working as a nurse for a private family.[23]

"Lottie"

Charlotte "Lottie" Louise Forten (Grimké)—maternal first cousin of Genie Webb and paternal first cousin of Annie Purvis—was the daughter of Mary Virginia Wood (Forten) and Robert Bridges Forten (1813–1864), and the grand-daughter of antislavery activists Charlotte Vandine (Forten) and James Forten. Her maternal grandparents were Edith "Edy" Wood and James Cathcart Johnston of North Carolina. After the deaths of her younger brother and mother in 1840, Lottie lived with her father, her maternal grandmother, and her young aunt Annie E. Wood, who was just six years older than she was. She would remember fondly her "childish days" with Annie and Edy: that "dear motherly face," "*more* than mother to me;—I long to see thee again; thee and my *own* mother—the darling brother, *all* the loved ones who have gone on before."[24]

In July of 1843, Robert Bridges Forten presented his mother-in-law with a large catch-up bill for rent and "other claims" at 16 Powell Street, the house where he rented rooms from secondhand clothes dealer William Chew. For the next three years, until her death, Edy Wood would pay the rent directly to Chew. Meanwhile, seven-year-old Charlotte and her father Robert Forten, who was struggling financially, continued to live with Edy through 1844.[25] Then, in 1845, Robert Forten married wealthy, Charleston-born Mary Hanscome (ca. 1817–ca. 1876) and moved to the countryside, taking Charlotte with him.[26]

Edy Wood's death hit Charlotte and Annie hard. Annie, in Philadelphia, copied out a freshly published 1848 poem about an angelic long-lost mother,

Charlotte Forten (Grimké), Genie Webb's cousin, in adolescence. (AWWP)

"The Spirit Teachings," and sent it to her eleven-year-old niece in Hartsville, Bucks County, Pennsylvania, with the note, "I send you these lines, for I know you will admire the style and sentiments." Charlotte would draw on this poem ten years later for her own composition about a long-lost mother, "The Angel's Visit," published by Bishop Payne in his *Repository*.[27]

Robert Forten started a new family, tried farming, ran into financial difficulties, then moved to Canada in 1855 and to England in 1858.[28] Charlotte's education, teaching responsibilities, antislavery activism, poor health, and strained relationship with her father prevented her from joining him in this departure. Following in the footsteps of her aunt Annie, who had been adopted by Amy Matilda Cassey (Remond, 1808–1856) and had trained as a teacher, Lottie stayed with the Remonds in Salem, Massachusetts, while attending high school and teachers college.

Annie Wood set up the arrangements in the fall of 1853 for Charlotte and herself to share two adjoining attic rooms at the Remonds' and pay $2.50 per week—washing, ironing, and fuel included.[29] Annie had been encouraged by her white southern father (Charlotte's grandfather) to have her "mind engaged in some useful employment" and to aspire to "being useful & independent & thereby having peace of mind and health of body." He had backed up this advice by paying for her to attend the Massachusetts State Normal School in West Newton in 1852–1853, and it is therefore quite possible that he also quietly contributed toward Charlotte's Salem Normal School education in 1855, particularly since her own father could not afford to do so. In fact, there was no problem with money flowing from Johnston that year; he sent Annie's new husband $1,000 just four months after Charlotte's financial difficulties.[30]

Charlotte's Salem years, from 1853 to 1860, were stimulating and creative: she published poetry and letters in William Lloyd Garrison's (1805–1879) *Liberator* and in the *National Anti-Slavery Standard* and wrote her private journals (posthumously published in 1951 by close friend Anna J. Cooper [1858–1964]). She attended fairs and antislavery lectures, and socialized with luminaries Garrison, Wendell Phillips (1811–1884), Lydia Maria Child (1802–1880), William Wells Brown (1814–1884), Sarah Parker Remond (1815–1894), William Cooper Nell (1816–1874), and Maria Chapman (1806–1885).[31] But Charlotte's first year in Salem also marked the beginning of a deep and painful sense of abandonment. First she lost her young aunt Annie to marriage and another state; then her father, to emigration and another country; and finally, in August 1856, her "dearly loved mother and friend," Amy Cassey (Remond), to death.[32] At nineteen, she felt alone and desolate.[33]

By the spring of 1858 Charlotte had resigned from teaching at the Epes Grammar School because of poor health and had returned to the country air

of Byberry, Pennsylvania, where she taught her young cousins, the children of
Harriet Forten (1810–1875) and Robert Purvis (1810–1898). She returned to
Salem in the fall of 1859 and enrolled in advanced classes (Latin, French, and
algebra) at the Salem Normal School through the following winter, spring, and
summer sessions.[34] She assisted her friend Miss Shepherd with one class at the
Higginson Grammar School but soon had to give up again for health reasons.
In spite of weeks spent at the water cure in Worcester in the summer of 1860,
her health continued to deteriorate. She was forced to spend a miserable winter
in Philadelphia—made worse still by news of the death of her half-brother in
London—a time so dispiriting that she was not psychologically stable enough
to write.[35] Fortunately by the fall of 1861, she had recovered sufficiently to take
charge of her aunt Margaretta Forten's school, the very school that her young
cousins Annie Purvis and Edith and Genie Webb attended.[36]

Inspired in the summer of 1862 by family friend Harriet Jacobs's accounts
of freed people in the South, Charlotte joined the Port Royal experiment and
traveled to St. Helena Island, South Carolina, to teach them and their children.
She published her "Life on the Sea Islands," in the May and June 1864 issues of
the *Atlantic Monthly*. After the war Charlotte struggled with poor health and her
inability to make a decent living by her writing. Her old friend John Greenleaf
Whittier (1807–1892) tried to have her admitted to a Boston sanitarium and
also appealed to publisher James T. Fields (1817–1881) to find her paid work
translating French literary works. In 1869 Scribners published Charlotte's
translation of *Madame Thérèse*.[37]

Charlotte served six years (1865–1871) in Boston on the teachers committee of the New England branch of the Freedmen's Union Commission. John
Greenleaf Whittier—along with Charles Sumner, poet Ralph Waldo Emerson
(1803–1882), and abolitionists Wendell Phillips and Thomas Wentworth Higginson (1823–1911)—wrote to the Boston Public Library to recommend her for a
position. She did not get the job, but she did succeed—after teaching for a
year (1871–1872) at the Shaw Memorial School in Charleston, South Carolina,
and for another year (1872–1873) at the M Street School in Washington, DC—
in securing an appointment with the U.S. Treasury in 1873.[38] She worked
there as a statistician until her marriage in 1878 to Charleston-born Francis
"Frank" James Grimké, minister of the prestigious Fifteenth Street Presbyterian Church. Grimké's mother, Nancy Weston (1811–1895), moved into the
couple's home and is mentioned in this correspondence by Annie Purvis,
who enjoyed talking with the "Old Lady" about the "old times" in Charleston.[39] In 1880 the Grimkés had a baby daughter, Theodora, who lived just six
months.

Reverend Francis J. Grimké, ca. 1870s, was Charlotte Forten's husband. He led the Fifteenth Street Presbyterian Church in Washington. (AWWP)

The Grimkés accepted a call to a parish in Jacksonville, Florida, where they served from 1885 to 1889, partly in hopes that the climate would improve Lottie's health, but it did not. For her entire adult life she had been plagued with debilitating headaches and respiratory ailments. On several occasions in 1885 Louisa Jacobs discussed with the Grimkés the possibility that Genie Webb, who was also very sick, might join her cousin and teach there; there is no record, however, of her doing so.[40] When Francis Grimké's brother Archibald Grimké (1849–1930) was appointed consul to the Dominican Republic from 1894 to 1898, Charlotte and Frank cared for his daughter Angelina Weld Grimké (1880–1958) in their Washington home. Angelina would become a well-respected author in her own right; she dedicated one poem to her beloved aunt, "To Keep the Memory of Charlotte Forten."[41]

After Charlotte's death in 1914, her husband continued his work for equal rights. Frank Grimké retired from the Fifteenth Street Presbyterian Church in 1928 and then turned his mind to the life and writings of his wife. "Tell me anything you may know of Lottie's early life," he wrote Genie Webb's sister, Miriam, in 1929. "I confess I never thought to ask her while she was living."[42]

"Lulu"

Louisa "Lulu" Matilda Jacobs wrote fifty-eight of the seventy-eight letters in this collection. She was born in Edenton, North Carolina, the daughter of member of Congress and newspaper editor Samuel Tredwell Sawyer (1800–1865) and his mixed-race enslaved mistress, Harriet Jacobs. Most of what is known about Louisa Jacobs comes from her mother's fugitive-slave narrative, *Incidents in the Life of a Slave Girl*, published in 1861, and the *Harriet Jacobs Family Papers*, edited by Jean Fagan Yellin, Kate Culkin, and Scott Korb. Those who knew Louisa Jacobs consistently characterized her as quiet and reserved. Illustrator and journalist Thomas Butler Gunn (1826–1904) recalled her as thoughtful and grave, with a "soft, kind voice, beautiful hair and gentle demeanor."[43] Geologist Bailey Willis (1857–1949) remembered her speaking with "quiet reserve."[44] Boston insurance executive Robert Apthorp Boit (1846–1919) described her as "every inch a lady."[45] And, finally, Ednah Dow Cheney (1824–1904) praised "The dear little thoughtful girl who concealed her knowledge of her mother's neighborhood and the deep longings of her heart, . . . [who] has been the same thoughtful child throughout her long life."[46]

Louisa Jacobs lived in Edenton with her great-grandmother until she was six, and then her father took her North to live with his cousin's family in Brooklyn,

Thought to be Louisa Jacobs. (Permission of Jean Fagan Yellin)

New York. Sawyer paid for Louisa's education in private schools in New York and Boston, including teacher training in Boston, and supported her until his death.[47] Louisa's connections to Boston were strong and long-lasting. When she was ten, she and her mother fled from New York to Boston, where she attended school from 1844 to 1849 and lived for part of that time with the sisters of Nathaniel Parker Willis (1806–1867), Louisa Willis (Dwight, 1807–1849) and Sara Payson Willis (future author Fanny Fern, 1811–1872).[48] In 1849–1850 Louisa attended the Kellogg School in Clinton, New York, and she also stayed with the family of white abolitionist Zenas Brockett (1803–1883), who operated an Underground Railroad station in Manheim, New York. The Bracketts remained Louisa's close friends for the next thirty years.[49]

By the early fall of 1852, both Louisa and her second cousin, Annie E. Wood (Webb), were student-teacher friends of William Cooper Nell and were living in Boston, mingling with the same antislavery activists.[50] In September Louisa served as bridesmaid at the Boston wedding of her mother's old Edenton friend abolitionist George W. Lowther (1822–1898).[51] Lowther would later contribute a testimonial to Harriet Jacobs's *Incidents in the Life of a Slave Girl*. Lowther married Sarah J. F. Logan (1827–ca. 1864), the daughter of William H. Logan (1800–1870), a popular caterer and well-respected abolitionist in Boston. Logan's other daughter, Eliza Logan (Lawton, 1822–1883), wife of equal rights activist Edward B. Lawton (1808–1864), would also have been part of the wedding party—as was Lydia Maria Child, who signed as the official witness. The Lawtons became lifelong friends of the Jacobs family; their daughters, Sarah Virginia (1841–?) and Eliza Marianna (1843–1884), would later teach with Louisa in the Jacobs School in Alexandria, Virginia, during the Civil War. Louisa's uncle, abolitionist John S. Jacobs (ca. 1817–1873), would live with the Lawtons when he arrived from England in 1873, and Harriet and Louisa would live with them in 1877. During the course of this correspondence, Louisa would help to nurse a dying Lawton son.

After the George Lowther wedding, Louisa returned for a second year to live with the Bracketts in Herkimer County, New York. From 1853 through 1854 she lived with her mother in the riverside home of poet and *Home Journal* editor, Nathaniel Parker Willis,[52] and as a governess from 1856 to 1858 with Willis's sister, author and journalist Fanny Fern and her husband, biographer James Parton (1822–1891). British writer Thomas Butler Gunn was a frequent visitor at the Parton household, and Fanny Fern encouraged him to consider Louisa as a possible marriage candidate. He described her as a "protégé" of the Partons and "squired" Louisa and Fern's older daughter on various family excursions, once staying up until sunset with them. It was Gunn who recorded in his diary an account of Fern's "atrocious tyranny" over Louisa. Her abusive rages and unfounded accusations of impropriety with Parton culminated in Fern's attempt to physically attack Louisa in the spring of 1858. Louisa left the Parton household abruptly and moved back to Boston, where she studied dressmaking and worked in an Indian botanical shop, remaining through the early 1860s.[53]

During the Civil War, in 1864–1865, Louisa and her mother cofounded a school for freed people in Alexandria, Virginia. Abolitionists Charles Lenox Remond and John J. Smith (1820–1896) visited her there in early 1864.[54] In 1865 she returned with her mother to Edenton, North Carolina. There she would certainly have heard of the death of James Cathcart Johnston, father of her friend Annie E. Wood (Webb). Louisa's white half-sisters and white New York cousins would make a claim on his estate while Annie's letters to the executor went ignored.[55] Louisa's father, Samuel Tredwell Sawyer, died in Bloomington, New Jersey, in November 1865. Mother and daughter then went to Savannah, Georgia, to open a school (1865–1866).

In early 1867 Louisa joined Charles Lenox Remond and Susan B. Anthony (1820–1906) on an American Equal Rights Association lecture tour to promote women's suffrage in western New York state. In Troy, New York, Louisa delivered a speech that reflected both her own mixed-race heritage and her hopes for an American people united by equal rights. "The events of the last six years have a tendency to melt the American people into one great family. Nature has no laws which work wrong."[56] She made another visit to Edenton in the spring of 1867 to visit family and settle property affairs. In 1868 Louisa and her mother sailed to England to raise funds for a home for women and children in Savannah, Georgia, and after their return to the States, Louisa taught at the Stevens School in Washington, DC.

During the early to mid-1870s, Louisa and her mother ran a boarding house in Cambridge, Massachusetts, that catered to Harvard students and faculty, including the Willis family, who had employed Harriet Jacobs for twenty years and had become her second family. As Louisa later explained to Genie, "We are bound by many ties—I may say obligations to [Cornelia Grinnell (Willis, 1825–1904)]."[57] While in Boston, Louisa received several marriage offers from respectable white men, including a Harvard professor who was hopelessly in love with her, but she later confided to Edith Willis (Grinnell, 1853–1938) that she did not believe in interracial marriage.[58]

Just before this correspondence began, Louisa and her mother had moved to Washington, DC, where they ran another boarding house. Senator Henry Laurens Dawes (1816–1903) of Massachusetts, and members of Congress William

Wallace Crapo (1830–1926) and George Bailey Loring (1817–1891), and Governor William Claflin (1818–1905), who founded Claflin University in South Carolina, were among their boarders.[59] For at least one summer Louisa supervised the thriving canning and bakery business of the E. T. Throop Martin (1808–1883) family at their family estate, Willowbrook, in New York. She began her own jam and preserves business in Washington in 1883 and carried on that business while teaching sewing and cooking in the Girls Industrial School at Howard University. In late 1884, with her mother ill but insistent that they be hospitable to the Willis family, Louisa reluctantly accepted geologist Bailey Willis and his wife as boarders in a new rented house while she continued to run her canning business out of the Swedish minister's residence.[60] It is not known whether Louisa maintained any contact with her white half-sister Sallie Peyton Sawyer (Ayres, 1837–1902), who lived in Washington during the same years, but it is noteworthy that Louisa's mother listed herself in the Washington directory as the "widow of Samuel"[61] and that Louisa told the Willis daughters, Edith Willis (Grinnell, 1853–1938) and Lilian Willis (Boit, b. 1850), that her mother "loved [Samuel Tredwell Sawyer] dearly, called him a good and kind man, and knew no other man."[62]

From the mid-1880s the Jacobses ran a boarding house catering to prominent African American politicians. Former member of Congress Joseph H. Rainey (1832–1887) of South Carolina and Louisa Jacobs's good friend William H. Chew (widower of Cordelia "Delie" Sanders [Chew]) boarded with her in 1885 while establishing a coal business in the District. In late 1886 and early 1887, the Jacobses boarded Recorder of Deeds James Campbell Matthews (1844–1930), who succeeded Frederick Douglass in the position. The next recorder of deeds, musicologist James Monroe Trotter (1842–1892), also lived with the Jacobses in 1887. The following year Louisa managed the household of editor and journalist Charles Nordhoff (1830–1901), the Washington correspondent for the *New York Herald*. She joined her mother on an Edenton visit during the spring of 1889, probably to try to sort out an unresolved dispute over her great-grandmother's property.[63] By this time Harriet Jacobs was showing signs of senility,[64] and as her health declined she needed more help from Louisa. In 1890, the Jacobses lived in the Washington residence of their former boarder Senator Henry L. Dawes of Massachusetts.

The silence in Louisa's record from 1890 to 1895 speaks volumes. During this time she assumed full time caregiving duties for her mother, in addition to letting out two rooms in her rented house and working briefly at the treasury and census bureaus. Harriet suffered from numerous illnesses, including breast cancer, and finally a broken hip and Bright's disease.[65] The strain took a toll on Louisa's health, and by 1896 she was unable to work and too weak to lift her mother. She attempted to cash in her life insurance policy, but the company denied her claim for disability. On her behalf, Cornelia Willis petitioned Ednah Dow Cheney for financial aid for the two women.[66] That summer Louisa reported to Cheney on meetings of the National League of Colored Women, and she likely participated in at least one.[67]

After Harriet Jacobs died in the spring of 1897, Louisa became assistant matron, then matron at the National Home for the Relief of Destitute Colored Women and Children in Washington, DC. From 1903 to 1908 she worked as matron at Miner Hall, at Howard University. She finally retired with a heart condition at the age of seventy-five. She spent her last years in Brookline, Massachusetts, living with longtime family friend Edith Willis (Grinnell), who had been one of the white children her mother helped raise.

"Mother"

Louisa's mother, Harriet Ann "Hattie" Jacobs,[68] was born in Edenton, North Carolina, to Delilah Horniblow and Elijah Knox (d. 1826). Harriet spent her early years with her owner, Margaret Horniblow (d. 1825), and later with her emancipated South Carolina–born grandmother, Molly Horniblow (ca. 1778–1853).[69] In adolescence Jacobs was sexually harassed by Dr. James Norcom (1778–1850). After being refused permission to marry the black man she loved, she defiantly turned to white lawyer Samuel Tredwell Sawyer for love and companionship. Sawyer was a cousin of the father of Annie E. Wood (Webb), James Cathcart Johnston. At the age of fifteen Harriet gave birth to Sawyer's son, Joseph, and in 1833, to his daughter Louisa Matilda Jacobs. Sawyer purchased the children and Harriet's brother, John S. Jacobs, to keep Dr. Norcom from selling them. He turned the children over to their great-grandmother and kept John as his valet, promising to emancipate him at a later date.

To evade Dr. Norcom and to protect her children, Harriet Jacobs went into hiding in 1835; she remained concealed in her grandmother's attic for seven years until her escape in 1842, via Philadelphia to New York, where she worked as a nursemaid for the Nathaniel Parker Willis family. She spent several years in Boston, where she was reunited with her son as well as her brother, John, who—impatient for freedom—had left Samuel Tredwell Sawyer in New York in 1838 and become an eloquent abolitionist. After the Fugitive Slave Act

Harriet Jacobs, author of *Incidents in the Life of a Slave Girl* and founder of the Jacobs School in Alexandria, Virginia. (Permission of Jean Fagan Yellin)

passed in 1850, Harriet's brother left for California, and her son soon followed in 1852. Meanwhile, Cornelia Grinnell (Willis), concerned about Harriet's safety, arranged and paid for her purchase and freedom.

Harriet wrote her autobiography between 1853 and 1858. The account was eventually edited by Lydia Maria Child, with changed names, no dates, no author, and no publisher's name. Harriet sailed for England in May 1858 to try to secure a publishing deal, and in June she presented a letter of introduction from Mr. Webb to Miss Weston, explaining that Mr. and Mrs. Webb "has been so kind to give me and my manuscript so much attention." Frank J. Webb might very well have written this letter and read the manuscript. He and his first wife, the dramatic reader Mary E. [Espartero] (Webb), had recently returned to Philadelphia from a two-year tour of England and Europe, his *The Garies and Their Friends* having been freshly published in London eight months earlier. Who better could have provided Harriet with manuscript feedback, up-to-date information on British publishers, and contacts for an antislavery tour?[70] Harriet did not succeed in finding either a publisher or her brother in London, and after an American publisher committed to publish and then failed to do so, Jacobs published the book herself in 1861. Her brother, John, published his *True Tale of Slavery* in London the same year.

The Civil War both eclipsed the potential success of Harriet's book and spurred sales among abolitionists. In the summer of 1862, Harriet participated in the Longwood, Pennsylvania, Quaker meetings organized to draw up an appeal to President Lincoln to declare complete emancipation. At the behest of William Lloyd Garrison, she left Longwood for Washington and Alexandria, where she would write "Life among the Contrabands," an extraordinary piece of war reporting that was published in Garrison's *Liberator* in September.[71] Representing the New England Freedmen's Aid Society and the New York Yearly Meeting of Friends, she canvassed for funds and relief supplies, then she joined relief worker Julia Wilbur (1815–1895) in Alexandria in early 1863. Despite conflict with the Baptist-minister superintendent of contrabands, Albert Gladwin (1816–1869), who undermined Harriet's and Julia's efforts at every turn, the freedpeople's condition in Alexandria improved under their management: disease decreased, the destitute were clothed and fed, ten schools were established, and hundreds of small cabins were built. Harriet's daughter, Louisa, took charge of the largest of the schools in early 1864; it was later named the Jacobs School.[72] Toward the end of the war Harriet and Louisa made a number of trips back to Philadelphia and even sent their new friend Julia Wilbur there to meet with their friends the Chew family. After the end of the war, Harriet and Louisa returned to Edenton, North Carolina, opened a school in Savannah,

Georgia, and sailed to England to raise funds for a home for women and children in Savannah.

Harriet tended to her former employer, *Home Journal* editor Nathaniel Parker Willis, when he was on his deathbed in 1867. He had declared in 1862 that Harriet, after twenty years with his family, "is as much one of my family as I am."[73] That statement would hold true for the rest of Harriet's life. In the early 1870s, the Jacobses—along with their adopted son, Joseph Pierce, and close Edenton friend Sarah Iredell (1806–1885)—lived with the Willis family in Cambridge while Bailey Willis attended Harvard. In 1881, Harriet and Louisa spent three months in New Jersey assisting Edith Willis (Grinnell) as she cared for her dying young husband-cousin. Throughout the 1880s, the Jacobses visited the Willis home in New Bedford, and Cornelia Grinnell (Willis) divided her time in Washington between the Jacobses' home and that of her son. In 1886, Harriet attended the wedding of Lilian Willis (Boit) in New Bedford as a guest of honor. As Harriet's health declined in the 1890s, it was Cornelia Grinnell (Willis) who repeatedly campaigned for medical and financial assistance for her. After Harriet's death, the Willis children rallied around Louisa and continued to be her family for another twenty years.[74]

Mrs. Fleetwood

Sarah Iredell (Fleetwood) was Genie Webb's paternal first cousin, the daughter of Geoffrey George Iredell (1811–1872) of Edenton, North Carolina, and Elizabeth Susan Webb (Iredell) of Philadelphia. Geoffrey Iredell was Harriet Jacobs's contemporary; although there is no documentation to prove their connection in the north, it would have been next to impossible for them not to have known each other in Edenton. Geoffrey's sister, also named Sarah Iredell, lived with Harriet and Louisa Jacobs in Boston in 1870.[75] Geoffrey Iredell's father had been enslaved and emancipated by the Johnston/Blair/Iredell family, and in 1837 his estate was administered by, among others, Harriet Jacobs's lover, Samuel Tredwell Sawyer.[76]

The younger Sarah Iredell and her sister, Laura Iredell (Hawkesworth, 1850–1909), were born in St. Louis, Missouri, where their father ran a prosperous hairdressing business with Cyprian Clamorgan (1830–1906), author of *The Colored Aristocracy of St. Louis*.[77] Sarah attended Oberlin from 1856 to 1858. By 1860, her entire family had resettled with her Webb cousins in Philadelphia, where she taught in the public school system. Sarah was secretary and a founding member of the Ladies Union Association, organized in 1863 to hold fairs and

Sarah Iredell (Fleetwood), a graduate of Oberlin (1856 1858) and the Institute for Colored Youth (1867), was Genie Webb's cousin. She taught school in Washington and operated a women's underwear business before graduating from the first class of Freedmen's Hospital Nurses' Training School. (AWWP)

raise money to assist sick and wounded African American soldiers.[78] In 1866, she taught as second assistant (pupil-teacher) at the Institute for Colored Youth, along with first assistant Mary Jane Patterson (1840–1894) (her former Oberlin classmate) and fellow teachers Octavius Catto, Fanny Jackson (1837–1913), Ebenezer Bassett (1833–1908), Sarah Mapps Douglass, and John Quincy Allen (ca. 1843–1905).[79] In 1867–1868, she taught at the Roberts Vaux School, and later in Frederick, Maryland, before moving to Washington, DC, to teach at the Island School.

In 1869, she met and married musician, Civil War veteran, and Medal of Honor–recipient Christian Fleetwood (1840–1914). The following year Sarah welcomed her uncle—author Frank J. Webb—who arrived after eleven years in Jamaica to attend classes at Howard University's law school. Webb's classmate, James Malcolm Hawkesworth, would later marry Sarah's younger sister, Laura.[80] The Fleetwoods organized the Mignonette Club theatricals and held Thursday evening literary salons at their home, where they received friends, entertained with music (but no refreshments), and discussed poetry and essays. Christian Fleetwood directed the choir at St. Luke's Episcopal Church, where the Jacobses worshiped.[81]

Sarah Iredell (Fleetwood) was one of nine cofounders of the Colored Women's League in 1892, and in 1893 she entered the first class of Freedmen's Hospital School of Nursing at Howard University, under Daniel Hale Williams (1856–1931);[82] at the same time, her first cousin Frank J. Webb Jr. (1865–1901) attended medical school at Howard University and also worked in the Treasury Department.[83] That was the year of the Panic, and Sarah Iredell (Fleetwood), along with her Burr cousin Evelyn D. Shaw (1850–1919) and various well-to-do families, organized aid for the hungry, cold, and homeless in their neighborhood.[84] Sarah Iredell (Fleetwood) graduated from nursing school in 1896 and eventually became superintendent of nursing at Freedmen's and organized the Freedmen's Nursing Association. Along with Anna Evans Murray (1858–1955), she represented the Colored Women's League at the Congress of Mothers in 1898. She died of diabetes-related causes on February 1, 1908.[85]

Mrs. Hawkesworth

Laura Iredell (Hawkesworth), Genie Webb's first cousin and the younger sister of Sarah Iredell (Fleetwood), was born in St. Louis, Missouri, and graduated from Philadelphia's Institute for Colored Youth in 1869, along with her friend musician Matilda "Inez" Cassey (1851–1916). She married James Malcolm

Laura Iredell (Hawkesworth) was Genie Webb's cousin, an 1869 graduate of Philadelphia's Institute for Colored Youth, a teacher, and school principal in Washington. (AWWP)

Hawkesworth, a law student at Howard University, in 1874, and they moved to Natchez, Mississippi, where they started a family. By 1877 they had returned to Washington, but the marriage was troubled, and in 1883 they separated. Laura left her children with her sister, Sarah Iredell (Fleetwood), and went back to work as a teacher, eventually becoming principal of the Jesse Reno School. She attended St. Luke's Episcopal Church in Washington, where the Jacobses also worshiped.[86]

Mrs. Venning

Julia Sanders (Venning, 1837–1910), sister of Delie Sanders (Chew), was born in Charleston, South Carolina, to white businessperson Richard Walpole Cogdell and his enslaved common-law wife, Sarah Martha Sanders. She married Edward Young Venning (1835–1884), the son of Edward W. Venning (1806–1885) and Elizabeth Nixon (Venning, 1810–1897) of Charleston, who migrated to Philadelphia in 1828. She and her sister-in-law, Martha Davenport (Sanders, 1833–1913), were the mistresses of 1116 Fitzwater Street, the Sanders-Venning Philadelphia home. She raised ten children and taught dressmaking in the night industrial classes of the Joseph E. Hill School.[87]

"Rannie"

Miranda "Rannie" Cogdell Venning (1862–1900) was the daughter of Julia Sanders (Venning) and Edward Young Venning, and the niece of Delie Sanders (Chew), Robert "Bobbie" Sanders (1832–1907), and Richard Edward DeReef Venning (1846–1929). She received her early education under Margaretta Forten at the Institute for Colored Youth. In 1875–1876 she attended Washington Grammar School in Cambridge, Massachusetts, where she studied music and art, and boarded with Eleanor Aspland (Herbert, Jacobs, 1832–1903), the English widow of John S. Jacobs (Harriet Jacobs's brother).[88] She attended the Roberts Vaux School in Philadelphia, under Professor Jacob C. White (1837–1902), before going on to Girls High and Normal School, Philadelphia's teaching college, where she was the first colored graduate. Miranda Venning presided for over fifteen years as principal of the Joseph E. Hill Primary School in Germantown. She served as organist at the Church of Crucifixion in Philadelphia, founded the Philadelphia Treble Clef, and was one of the original members of Samuel Adger's (1850–1892) Young People's Musical Association.[89]

Richard

Richard Edward DeReef Venning was the brother of Edward Young Venning and brother-in-law of Julia Sanders (Venning) and Cordelia Sanders (Chew). Like the Sanders family and their friend and relative Octavius Catto, the Venning family originally came to Philadelphia from Charleston, South Carolina. Richard Venning graduated with Sarah Iredell (Fleetwood) from Philadelphia's Institute for Colored Youth in 1867. He taught "mental arithmetic" in the Institute's Boys' and High Preparatory Schools in 1869. He also taught in Maryland. In the late 1870s he worked as a grocer and clerk in Philadelphia. In early 1881, he was appointed to the pension office by member of Congress Henry H. Bingham (1841–1912) and worked there as examiner for over three decades. While in Washington, he lived for more than twenty years with Charlotte Forten (Grimké) and Reverend Francis J. Grimké in their homes at 1526 L Street and 1415 Corcoran Street.[90]

"Willie"

William "Willie" Herbert Chew was the widower of Cordelia "Delie" Sanders (Chew) and boarded on and off in Trenton, New Jersey, with his mother, Charlotte Henson (Chew). After his wife's death, Willie and his two young sons lived at 1116 Fitzwater Street, Philadelphia, with his in-laws, the Julia Sanders (Venning) family. Chew was active politically and in the summer of 1880 launched a successful lawsuit that challenged school segregation on the grounds that it violated the Fourteenth Amendment. On June 8, 1881, Governor Henry M. Hoyt (1830–1892) signed a bill to end school segregation in Pennsylvania, but the law went unheeded for the next one hundred years. Chew worked as a barber in Philadelphia and, in 1885, operated a coal business with former South Carolina member of Congress Joseph H. Rainey in Washington, DC, where he boarded with Louisa Jacobs. In 1887, after their coal business failed, Chew, armed with a reference from former recorder of deeds James C. Matthews, found a job in the federal printing office. William H. Chew belonged to the elite Diamond Back Club in Washington; other members included James T. Bradford, Hon. John H. Smyth, Christian Fleetwood, William E. Matthews, H. H. Williams, Wyatt Archer, Robert H. Terrell, Daniel Murray, F. G. Barbadoes, Dr. S. R. Watts, and Dr. S. L. Cook. Willie Chew died of peritonitis in Washington, DC, in 1892 and was buried at Lebanon Cemetery in Philadelphia.[91]

Willis Family

Cornelia Grinnell (Willis) was born in New Bedford, Massachusetts, the niece and adopted daughter of wealthy Quaker merchant and member of Congress Joseph Grinnell (1788–1885), and the second wife of poet and *Home Journal* editor Nathaniel Parker Willis. When Cornelia met and married Willis in 1846, Harriet Jacobs had been caring for his young daughter by his first marriage, Imogen (1842–1904), and she had accompanied the father and daughter to England in 1845–1846. The child care arrangement continued with the arrival of Cornelia's children: Grinnell Willis (1848–1930), Lilian Willis (Boit), Edith Willis (Grinnell), and Bailey Willis. In 1852, Cornelia Grinnell (Willis) arranged through the American Colonization Society to purchase Harriet Jacobs, who had been intimidated and driven into hiding because of fears of apprehension under the Fugitive Slave Act. In 1853–1854, Louisa assisted with housekeeping duties at the Willis home, "Idlewild," while her mother took time off to recover from health problems and to write her memoir. Although Harriet Jacobs officially left the employ of the Willis family in 1861, she and Louisa remained close to their second family for the rest of their lives. During the course of this correspondence, Louisa visited Grinnell and Edith in New Jersey, Imogen sent messages of love to Lulu and "Hatty," both Bailey Willis and his mother lived in Washington and saw Louisa regularly, and Louisa visited the younger sisters, Lilian and Edith, in Brookline and Newport. During Louisa's last few years in Brookline, Grinnell Willis sent her a monthly check as a gesture of their friendship, saying, "Old friends grow more valuable each year & dearer."[92]

Louisa Jacobs Family Chart

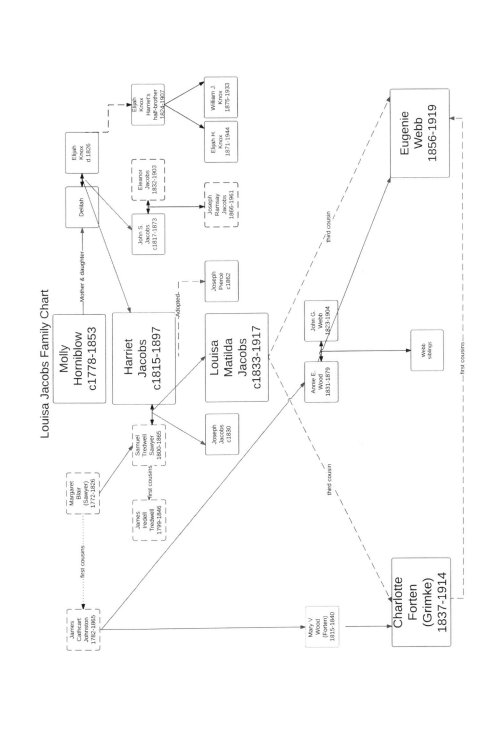

Wood Webb Family Chart

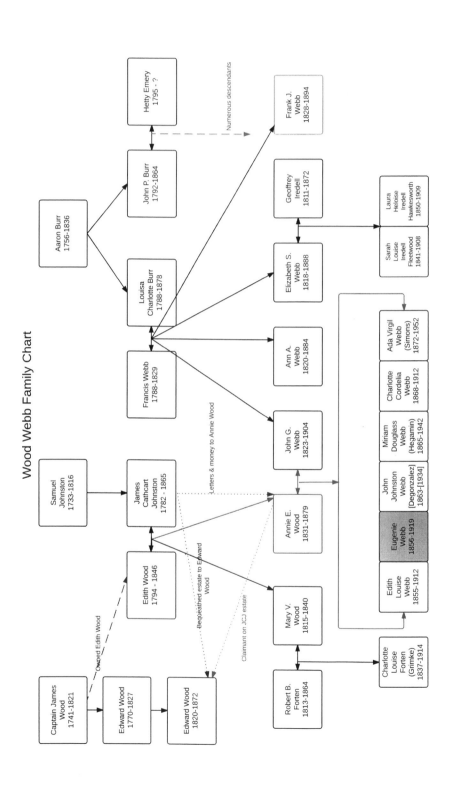

Samuel Johnston
1733-1816

James Cathcart Johnston
1782 - 1865

Aaron Burr
1756-1836

John P. Burr
1792-1864

Hetty Emery
1795 - ?

Louisa Charlotte Burr
1788-1878

Francis Webb
1788-1829

Numerous descendants

Frank J. Webb
1828-1894

Geoffrey Iredell
1811-1872

Elizabeth S. Webb
1818-1888

Ann A. Webb
1820-1884

John G. Webb
1823-1904

Laura Heloise Hawkesworth
1850-1909

Sarah Louise Iredell Fleetwood
1841-1908

Captain James Wood
1741-1821

Edward Wood
1770-1827

Edith Wood
1794-1846

Annie E. Wood
1831-1879

Letters & money to Annie Wood

Owned Edith Wood

Edward Wood
1820-1872

Bequeathed estate to Edward Wood

Mary V. Wood
1815-1840

Claimant on JCJ estate

Robert B. Forten
1813-1864

Charlotte Louise Forten (Grimke)
1837-1914

Edith Louise Webb
1855-1912

Eugenie Webb
1856-1919

John Johnston Webb [Degonzalez]
1863-[1934]

Miriam Douglass Webb (Hegamin)
1865-1942

Charlotte Cordelia Webb
1868-1912

Ada Virgil Webb (Simons)
1872-1952

Sanders-Chew-Venning Family

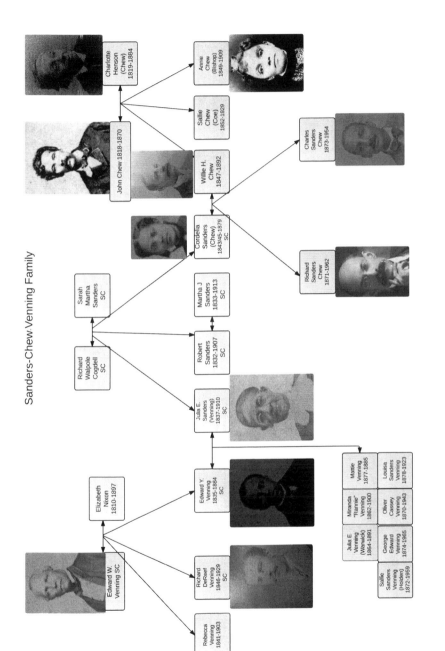

Charlotte Henson (Chew) 1819-1884

John Chew 1818-1870

Annie Chew (Bishop) 1849-1909

Sallie Chew (Coe) 1852-1929

Willie H. Chew 1847-1892

Charles Sanders Chew 1873-1954

Cordelia Sanders (Chew) 1843/45-1879 SC

Richard Sanders Chew 1871-1962

Sarah Martha Sanders SC

Martha J Sanders 1833-1913 SC

Richard Walpole Cogdell SC

Robert Sanders 1832-1907 SC

Julia E. Sanders (Venning) 1837-1910 SC

Elizabeth Nixon 1810-1897

Edward Y. Venning 1835-1884 SC

Edward W. Venning SC

Richard DeReef Venning 1846-1929 SC

Rebecca Venning 1841-1903

Mattie Venning 1877-1885

Louisa Sanders Venning 1878-1923

Miranda "Rannie" Venning 1862-1900

Oliver Cassey Venning 1870-1943

Julia E. Venning (Warwick) 1864-1891

George Edward Venning 1874-1965

Sallie Sanders Venning (Holden) 1872-1959

Forten-Purvis Family

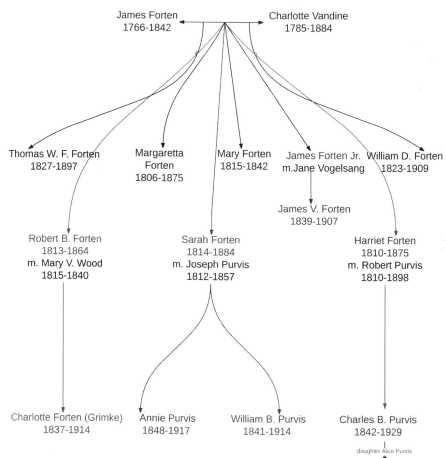

James Forten
1766-1842

Charlotte Vandine
1785-1884

Thomas W. F. Forten
1827-1897

Margaretta
Forten
1806-1875

Mary Forten
1815-1842

James Forten Jr.
m.Jane Vogelsang

William D. Forten
1823-1909

James V. Forten
1839-1907

Robert B. Forten
1813-1864
m. Mary V. Wood
1815-1840

Sarah Forten
1814-1884
m. Joseph Purvis
1812-1857

Harriet Forten
1810-1875
m. Robert Purvis
1810-1898

Charlotte Forten (Grimke)
1837-1914

Annie Purvis
1848-1917

William B. Purvis
1841-1914

Charles B. Purvis
1842-1929

daughter Alice Purvis

Not all descendants are shown on this chart

One by One
the Moments Fall
1879–1880

Forty-six-year-old Lulu Jacobs sends a condolence letter to twenty-three-year-old Genie Webb on the death of their mutual friend, Delie Chew, whom Genie cared for in her last days. Lulu reintroduces herself by asking permission to address her as "Genie" and then by describing her own deep love for Delie. Lulu acknowledges that Genie's faith is stronger than her own, but she agrees that they should mention each other in their prayers as part of their newly developing friendship, forged in grief. She suggests that Genie read Adelaide Proctor's inspirational poem "One by One." As the two women come to know each other better, they exchange accounts of the friends and relatives they have in common: the Vennings and Chews in Philadelphia, and Genie's cousins Charlotte Forten, Annie Purvis, and the Iredells in Washington. Lulu urges the reluctant Genie to reveal Delie's deathbed words, then retracts her request out of respect for the sanctity of such an intimate moment.

[From Louisa Jacobs. Postmarked "Nov. 24, 1879"; addressed to "Fillmore Street, Camden, N.J."]

1419 Pierce Place[1]
Washington, Nov. 21st 1879

Dear Friend

It is evening and I am alone. Your cousin Charlotte and mother[2] having gone to church, and I have come here to speak awhile with you. I am glad you wrote to me. Intuitively I have felt that one or the other would sooner or later write. You were kind in not waiting for me. After our beloved one[3] left us I wanted to write and ask you to tell me of those last days since it was your sad privilege to pass them with her. I would it had been mine too. Then I remembered Genie (for you will let me call you by this name) how your own heart was

53

Cordelia "Delie" Sanders (Chew) with unidentified children, probably her sons, Charles Sanders Chew and Richard Sanders Chew. (Library Company of Philadelphia)

torn, not only by this grief but another so recently passed[4] through how it all came back with a fresh overwhelming force. So I did not ask the boon.

But sometime when your heart is better healed you must tell me all about it. Yes, I loved her most dearly. It was a rare friendship, such as comes but once in a lifetime. God has seen fit to break the link, and I bow to his behest, looking beyond sorrow and self to that hereafter, where my heart is, there to be united to the lost and loved through the endless ages of eternity. This thought is a help to me and yet it does not comfort me now as it ought. Did she speak to any of you before she went—to her children? They tell me she suffered fearfully at the end. Poor darling! I would she could have been spared that. I am glad you cared enough for me to write, for many are the times I have thought of you and been thankful that you were where I could not be, knowing Delie loved you and your presence gave her comfort. My dear Genie I can only take your hand in a oneness of sympathy and love and say, look up, be comforted, your loved ones and mine are at rest. All life's trials for them are over. They rest from their labors. Oh! If our hearts were not so clinging in their selfishness we would not mourn a day. And yet I believe God does not chide us for that since it is not rebellious grief. Your prayer to take with Delie the sacrament you tell me was answered. It must have been a precious comfort and will ever be a precious memory. I would I shared it with you.

I am not yet settled in a home. Give my regards to your sister Miss Edith.[5] I trust all the little people[6] are well, and that you are not working too hard. I wish the distance was less that separates us. Think of me and write as you would to a friend feeling that there will always be a bond of sympathy between us.

Sincerely yours,
Louise

[From Louisa. Postmarked "Dec. 10, 1879"; addressed to "Fillmore Street, Camden, N.J."]

1409 K Street[7]
Washington, Dec. 10th, 1879

My dear Genie

I thought to answer your letter before this. It came the very day we had decided on a house and since each day has found me so busy and the nights too tired and forlorn to inflict on you a stupid letter. We took a furnished house.

You would naturally suppose it in nice order for occupancy. On the contrary it had to be cleaned from top to bottom. I only wish Genie it was the quiet little home that you in your kindness wished me the possessor of. I am afraid I shall never have enough of this world's goods to buy the most modest shanty. And so you had me in mind on Thanksgiving Day, and I thought of you, thought too of the two other Thanksgivings passed with the dear one who now dwelleth where Thanksgivings never end. Ah! Genie I envy you your perfect faith and joy in things beyond this life. I know there is a beyond, and that Jesus is precious to me, but I cannot mount to your heights. I will endever to be faithful to your request. The pray itself expresses so much. There is a nearness and strengthening in friendship when friends mention one another in their prayers. I never forgot darling Delie, and even now the prayer goes on in different form. I am glad you sought me in your sad hour, for such will come struggle we ever so bravely against them. Adelaide Proctor has a pretty little poem called "One by One."[8] If you have forgotten it read it again. And so you would be cared for because you are Genie Webb and worthy of special thought. I think we were mutually attracted in that sick chamber. I saw you a thoughtful tender girl, and loved to remember you as the companion of Delie.

What shall you call me you ask. I am known as Louisa, Louise and Lulu. Make your selection of the trio. I have not hear from Fitzwater Street for several weeks. I hope they are all well. Willie wrote me, if he did not sell out his shop by the first of the year he should close it. I could not regard such a proceeding in the leastwise. I know he wants to be with his children,[9] and it is right he should. But why give up a good business before he finds out what he can do in Philadelphia. He and the children have got to live. Poor fellow! I know he is heart sore and lonely but he has responsibilities upon him such as he has never had and cannot be governed alone by his feelings. You asked me about Lottie. She keeps remarkably well. The event[10] is looked for sometime in January.

I could say many things if I could talk to you. I would you lived near me. Genie dear you and your sister must not work too hard, you know if either brake down how hard it would be for the other. I shall look anxiously for the promised detail letter.

You asked about my health. I have been quite well, if I might except my head which has occasioned me much suffering, and is still full of nervous pain though on the whole better. You must excuse this hurried letter and believe me

Affectionately yours, Louise

[From Louisa. Postmarked "Jan. 24, 1880"; addressed to "Fillmore Street, Camden, N.J."]

Washington Jan., 20th, 1880

My dear Genie

You see I did not as you had hoped write to you on Sunday evening. I was in the place you like me to be. I went to Dr. Crummell's church[11] (did you you ever hear him? His sermon was on the greatness of Christ. The subject was most ably handled. While I always feel the intellectual power of Mr. Crummell he does not touch as much as I am often touched by clergymen of less ability. You feel the truth and wisdom of his words but not the soft tenderness that melts and bows the heart. Then too he is so closely confined to his manuscript and that in my estimation always detracts from a speaker. So you did not quite like my last letter. Intuitively I felt it ere your pen told it. No, Genie dear we can never be too earnest in seeking the souls good. As you justly say we may sometimes in my earnestness overdo in good intention. I know what the ardor is to share with another what we hold most precious. So I am grateful, even tender towards you for bringing me so closely into your inner—your religious life. It proves an interest that finds in me its value.

Beneath the quiet exterior that you know runs another stream that leaps out on occasions and no doubt is too emphatic in expression. So if any of those periods seize upon me in writing to you, you will I hope learn to judge me fairly by them. And so dear you think I am lenient to your wandering thoughts in Church since you gave me a place in them. Be it so. I used to tell my darling Delie I would not shield with a falsehood my best beloved. She knew Genie I was not hard-hearted. You did not answer a question I asked you. Don't you know I am not a little child and can bear to be hurt. The wound might be for my good. Suspense or suppositions were me, while I have ever been able with a knowledge of the worst in store for me to bear it. And so Genie you will answer me. I am sorry enough that Willie is thinking of going to sea.[12] I advised him not to give up his Princeton shop till he could see his way clear to do business in Philadelphia. He urged that it was Delie's request that he should be with the children. I can't think she meant him to break up his shop without something definite before him. I am sure going to sea does not leave him with the children. The children. Poor little things! I think of them daily. They are children that have been greatly indulged, and what they need now is a gentle firm hand to lead them.

Mrs. Venning has so many of her own to look after—their aunt mother and Uncle Bobbie love them and will do to the last for them, but not always wisely.

In 1880 Louisa Jacobs heard Alexander Crummell deliver his sermon "The Greatness of Christ" before it was published in 1882. (Internet Archive)

Charlotte Forten (Grimké) and her baby daughter, Theodora, 1880. (AWWP)

Ah me! How their mamma used to plan for their future. Well, God knows what is best for us all.[13]

I cannot interpret your dream dear. I am not the seventh daughter of a seventh daughter.[14] Do you tell me what meaning you have put to it. Now good night and good dreams. I will finish this tomorrow.

Friday 23rd

If all tomorrows were as long as this has been from the 20 to the 23 it would sometimes be a great joy and at others a great sorrow. Well, Genie if you but knew how busy I have been this week you would not wonder at the interval. To begin with Mrs. Claflin[15] (who is a boarder of ours and the wife of a member in Congress) had a party on Monday evening of 160. Then Tuesday is her regular reception day and she received 180 guests. On Thursday Mrs. Senator Dawes[16] who is another boarder has Thursday for her reception day. After she received yesterday Mrs. Claflin had a dinner party at 7 and a small evening party after. So you see little friend how it has been with me. Oh Genie if you but knew the life of these fashionable women here you feel as I do more than half disgusted with it. It is a perfect round of visiting and entertaining. They go to two and three receptions a day and some to as many parties of an evening. You wonder how they can keep up. I will tell you more of it some other time. And in my next give the required description of Lottie's baby. I am glad you liked the leaves. I will tell next time of a sweet picture should you ever wish to leave one in that place of "Faith." And here I am at last saying good bye and God bless you.

Affectionately,
Lulu

P.S. I did as you bade me kissed and blessed the baby.

[From Louisa. Postmarked "Feb. 20, 1880"; addressed to "Fillmore Street, Camden, N.J."]

Washington Feb. 20th 1880

My dear Genie

Do you think I have tarried long by the wayside? I have since my last letter had many cares and anxieties. In the first place my mother has been very ill, which of course brought not only the household cares upon me but her sick chamber. She was confined two weeks to her room, but now thank God she is up and about again. Do you know that outside of my mother, I have but one relative, the son of a deceased uncle,[17] so you can somewhat imagine my feelings when my mother is ill at her time of life. While Delie lived I felt I had a heart to lean upon should sorrow come to me. I have friends some dear ones Genie. Friends to whom I owe and give love and gratitude yet none come into my life as came that other friend. You tell me dear Gennie I must not ask you to reveal her words of endearment to you. My <u>dear</u> <u>child</u> how little you know me if you could dream I would so desire. The sanctity of some occasions—some words— some thoughts—lose their divinity when shared with another. Moreover dear, I know every word of tenderness her lips could form. So I let it all rest with God. He understands. I suppose you are glad that Lent is here. I am glad too. The fashionable world here make it the time to pause a little in their gayity. It is funny though, just as Lent came in two ladies in the house were taken ill and in the same manner. Both have kept their rooms this week, and both are anxious to be out of them to get back to that life for which they seem to live. What a sin and waste of time giving so much to worldly pleasures.

I heard from Willie since receiving your letter. He did not tell me he had accepted your Church.[18] God grant it may bring him peace and happiness, and bring you comfort dear if you have effected good thereby. We have been having delightfully warm weather, but to day is a touch of old winter. And here I am reminded of that nipping wind that blighted your precious Ivey. Moral don't trust again what is delicate to the mercy of Jack frost. I have the Wandering Jew in water, and trust it will do me the favor to take root. Are you well Genie and the little family too? I told Lottie the other day that you wanted to hear from her. She is very much engrossed with her baby. It is a nice <u>small</u> <u>morsel</u>, half Grimké half Forten. The upper part of the face papa's the lower mamma's. It is to be hoped the present addition will prove both first and last—for what would she do with two babies? It is funny to hear Mr. G tell of their confined management of the young branch of the family. Now I must leave you with all good wishes for your hearts desires.

Affectionately,
Lulu

⌐♦○

[From Louisa. Postmarked "Mar. 25, 1880"; addressed to "1748 Fillmore Street, Camden, N.J."]

Washington, March 21st

My dear Genie

Is this not <u>good</u> of me to write you when you are nearly four weeks replying to my last letter? And I do it because you said, "do not keep me waiting very long for an answer." Now is not this an evidence that I care for you? A proof that I have thought of you more than ordinarily on this day that dates as you tell me the happiest one of your life. Dear child (do you like me to call you child?) I like the word. It is associated with family and tenderness. May that happy occasion never die; but repeat itself in all the years of your life.

As I took my way to church I thought of you and felt that you were happy. The sermon this morning was from St. Matt.—Judas betrayal of Christ. What a lesson it teaches. Ah! Genie darling the world has plenty of Judases now both in and out of the church. Men who profess to love their Master and under cover of greed and selfishness betray Him. I received your postal telling me the little sisters are to be confirmed. I knew then how your thoughts and heart

Ada Webb, 1880s, Genie Webb's youngest sister, taught school in Chicago. (AWWP)

Cordelia Webb, ca. 1880, teacher, was Genie Webb's sister. (AWWP)

Miriam Webb (Hegamin), ca. 1880, teacher, was the only one of Genie Webb's sisters to have children. (AWWP)

travelled to your mother, the mother's friend and your friend and all the yearnings it brought on. You thought dear they might be gazing upon that sacred sceen in the lives of those two young girls. It may be. Yet if the departed can behold with the visible eye what effects their dear ones here, how does it comport with the idea that heaven is a place of perfect happiness? For it would not be reasonable to suppose only the fair and beautiful side of existence here is turned to their view. And again, we must suppose the higher the sphere of their being the keener their sensibilities. While we love to think of their being near us, I cannot think they have a knowledge of existence here. I remember hearing Delie speak of Bishop Hare as being a particular friend of Dr. [W]ise. You and your sister thought his hands lingered longer in blessing on the heads of the two young people;[19] and it is probable they did. You know Genie how the Savior loved the young. You remember how on one occasion while explaining some difficult matters, rather questions some women came through the crowd with their children for Jesus to bless them and he left the grown people notwithstanding the disciples liked it not, and laid his hands in blessings on the little ones heads. And what is sweeter and more blessed than pure children? I have to leave you now but will return ere long.

Thursday 25th

I did not think Genie when I left you on Sunday that to day would find my letter unfinished. But so it is. How near we are dear Genie to Easter—that beautiful season that commemorates a risen Lord. May it find you and yours happy. I was sorry dear for your disappointment. It is indeed hard to dream and long for a thing, to see it within reach, to stretch out the hand and yet not reach it. Comfort yourself, you lost it through duty. God will make it up to you in some other way. I like your quotation on Spiritual friendship. Such a blending and union of heart and spirit must indeed be sweet and lead the possessors nearer to Him whose friendships are so strong, and tender, pure and forgiving. I love purity of Religion yet in spirit I could never be a Puritan.

We shall break up our home in June. Ah me! The thought is not pleasant. What a tramp life! I shall go north and as I pass through hope to see you. The time will soon be here. Do you see them often at Fitzwater Street? I remember some I ought to have answered in your letter but must leave it for my next. What are the many questions I have not answered. Tell me some of them. I saw Lottie a few days ago. She was well and the baby grows finely. My mother has not been at all well this winter, I am hoping she will feel stronger with the coming of the spring. Do you keep well Genie & Take care of yourself dear child. May the cares and responsibilities of your life press not too heavily on your young shoulders is the pray of

Your loving friend.
Lulu

[From Louisa. Postmarked "June 21, 1880"; addressed to "1748 Fillmore Street, Camden, N.J."]

1712 P Street[20]
Washington June 20, 1880

My dear dear Genie

    I never thought to neglect your dear letter for so long a time, and you will believe me though silent I have thought of you again and again. You see when the breaking up time came I was so very busy. I put off writing from day to day, thinking in the meantime when I did write I would be able to tell you when I would be in Philadelphia, but to my astonishment I am still here. We gave up our house on the 5th. On the 7 mother left for Stockbridge, Mass. to arrange for a house we had expected to take for the summer. She has been disappointed in our undertaking, so at present we are adrift.[21] As the season is getting late I do not know, unless we succeed within two or three day that we shall take a house for Summer boarders. We were so sure of the Stockbridge house that I remained behind in the event of there being anything needed in the way of housekeeping which we could supply from our store here. Thus you see child the old lesson goes on; build not with certainty for disappointment lies at the root of all human things. And yet, I would not teach this to the young with their light expectant happy hearts. The knowledge will come full soon enough. I suppose you are about closing your school. I trust dear you will have a restful vacation. I know you and your sister stand in need of it, for you have much care with your duties.[22] I thought darling when I rose this morning I would go to a little chapel near where I am stopping. It is high Church, then tell Genie I was nearer to her to day and not as opposed as she fancies to her church.

    I sympathized with you in the trouble that came to the one you love best. I do not know how it ended but this I know what is right will triumph in the end. Every thing is quiet here now that Congress has adjourned. I shall probably leave some day this week. Will send you a postal and you must try and get to see me. I shall not stop but a few hours a day at most in Philadelphia. I have

had some flowers for more than a week to carry to Delie's grave. How these
Summer days bring her back Dear darling, she is better off in that other home.
I have not heard from Philadelphia for some time. I hope Rannie[23] came off all
right from her examination. She told me how much she missed Delie in her
lessons. Trusting to see you very soon dear Genie.

I am lovingly
yours
Lulu

―◊◎

[Postal card from Sarah Louise Forten Purvis.[24] Postmarked "Aug. 3"
(1880 based on reference to Lottie's loss); addressed to "Fillmore St.,
S. Camden, N.J."]

2nd August

Dear Girls―

How is it that we do not see you anymore? And how is it that you are letting
the vacation slip away without once coming to see Mother [Charlotte V.
Forten]. Annie [Purvis] is still in the country―been there for six weeks―is
well―have you heard lately from Lottie? What a sad loss hers is.[25]

My love to your little sisters. I merely send this card of inquiry―perhaps
you will answer this in person.

Yours ever
S.L.P.

―◊◎

[From Louisa. On enclosed separate slip of paper "Address 46 Market
St Cambridgeport, Mass."[26]]

Boston
August 3, 1880

Genie, my dear dear friend

Do you think I have treated you very badly? Well dear it has not been from
lack of much thinking of you, but some how I have been in every way so unsettled

since I parted from you. I hardly know how the days have gone by. So like a dear childie you will pardon your friend's seeming neglect and take in spirit the kiss I would gladly give in warm tangible form. Perhaps this will not find you at Fillmore Street. You may have gone for the talked of change to Atlantic City. I really hope so for I have thought with dread of the contagious disease in your town and wished you and your little family might be out of the reach of any possible danger. You see, darling I am in Boston, the old home of other days. I am passing a few days at the house of an old friend, Dr. Birmingham.[27] You may have heard Delie at some time speak of him for it was here she stopped with me a few days the last time she was in Boston. And now I sit in the very room we occupied, sleep in the same bed, dream of her but not pleasantly.

Do you know dear there is not a spot I go to that is not, in some way, associated with her so she is an ever abiding memory. You remember I told you my intention of going to some old friends of mine in the western part of New York. When I thought to go a letter came telling me there was sickness in the family. A daughter and granddaughter were ill with Typhoid fever. Both died and now the old people write and tell me to come for they are very lonely.[28] I hope to go about the 15. My old friend here is sick and when I leave here on Friday I shall go to another sick house in Cambridge.[29] Sickness seems to follow in my wake. All this is doleful. I thought of you in church on Sunday morning. Wondered if you too were happy in your little Camden Church. I did not hear good Phillips Brooks,[30] he being in Europe now, but it was a lovely, satisfactory church service. The music never sounded nearer to heaven. As I listen I thought how grand, but how much more so where God is. Tell me of yourself since we parted. Have you been to Fitzwater Street? Do not let anything strange come into your life. You know, Genie, to what I refer. When the time come for you to make a change in your life I want it to be a happy one. I send you the lock of hair you asked for. It is a small bit taken from my front hair. Now, when am I to have your picture?

Do not do as I have done but as Genie Webb ought to do to her friend. Give my love to your sister Edith and the little sisters. I wish dear this will find you <u>resting</u>, getting renewed strength for the Fall work. With God's best blessings.

I am always
lovingly yours,
Lulu

[From Louisa. Postmarked "Little Falls Oct 4th"; addressed to "1748 Fillmore Street, Camden, NJ."]

Brockett's Bridge
Oct. 4, 1880

My dear Genie

I hardly agree with the quotation in your letter that what is denied us either temperally or spiritually is for our good. Privation I know is often good for some selfish natures who have lived alone for self. Then again, others are wrecked because some great desire, some great aspiration—is not fulfilled. And so, darling, you really wanted to hear from me before the letter reached you. It is good of you to think of me and love me in spite of my neglect. I do not know how it would feel to be "annoyed" by any writing from you. Please try it some-time when I have a silent spell upon me. Yes, I know the song you mentioned, and greet you with the, "Would I were with thee,"[31] or rather thou with me on this lovely autumn day. Do you know, Genie, it is just five years this very month since Delie and I in this very spot looked together at the landscape before me now.[32] Wooded hills crowned with the golden tints of autumn, and meadows still fresh and green. And days like this we would wander arm in arm until the stump of some old tree would invite us to rest, and there in the sun we would talk and dream of hopes death has sealed. As I look back I cannot make it seem such a lapse of time. The reality is that she is no more, that she went before the autumn days had ended. I have not yet reached that place where I can resign her wholly to the other world. Nor would I for ten thousand worlds bring her back to this to suffer. Still I so often wish for her, well and happy as I knew her in the long ago. I cannot feel like you that it is sinful that I would bring her from a greater to a less happiness. No, but that our Father had willed that she had staid with us.

I do not question why you have not seen Willie in all these weeks, believing as I do dear that you actuated by good judgement. I am very glad he is testing the school questions for colored children and trust he has come off conqueror.[33] It is just what our dear Delie would have liked him to do. You ask me to tell you something about my present home and its surroundings. In the first place, the master of it is a grand old man.[34] One of God's own. With him lives a young widowed daughter and her only son. It is a double house and in the other section lives a married son, the father of five splendid children. It is a pleasure to be with them, they are such good interesting little chicks. The house is in a valley, pleasantly situated back from the road. All about are long stretches of meadow land and above them hills now gorgeous with the hints of Autumn. To me it is a picture I never weary of. I shall leave here quite soon, probably in two weeks. I hope to see you when I pass through, will let you know at that time. You may be sure my dear Genie that I shall never love you less for having that faith which makes you write to me just as you feel. I am glad you have found pleasant friends in the wife and Pastor of St. Thomas's Church. Such friendships are sunlight on our path. This week takes you into the school-rooms again—trust you and your sister return to it fresh and strong. You will find me improved. I have gained nine pounds and am doing my best to make it more. Give love to the sisters for me and take for yourself a tender kiss and all dear wishes for your happiness and best of all God's blessing.

Fondly yours,
Louise

p.s. You ask me which I like best Louise or Lulu. I am more accustomed to Lulu and perhaps like it best. Use the one you like best. L.

[From Louisa. Postmarked "October 20 from Little Falls, NY"; addressed to "1748 Fillmore Street, Camden, NJ." Written on the side of the letter "Genie you must excuse the mistakes in this. My head is troubling me again. I wish I could get a new one. I know these days are to you like me an incessant reminder of the last year days of this time. L."]

Brockett's Bridge Oct. 19, 1880

My dear Genie

It was thoughtful and loving of you in the midst of anxiety to send me one more greeting in my country retreat. I was relieved that you closed your letter with the assurance that Ada was better and I trust the dear child has ever since been steadily improving. Tell her I asked you to kiss her for me. I can well imagine what your care has been with home, and sickness, and school duties to look after. I trust the worst is over and that you two doing double duty as mother and sister will get restful and happy again. And your father, is he better of the chills? Can you not induce him to wear the "Holman Pad."[35] I have known persons for the same cause to be benefited by wearing it. Do not get sad-hearted dear little friend over your responsible life. Some of the sweetest and noblest women the world has ever known have carried their cross. The victory darling is to carry it patiently and cheerfully. And this is the lesson learned by love to God, or the case or the loved ones for whom the burden is born. Why need I tell you this feeling as I do what I have said is a part of your life and Faith.

This is my birthday. The coldest and most Fall-like of the season. We had a flurry of snow that lasted about five minutes. When I wrote you I expected to leave here about this time but shall not until some time the first of next month.

I think I told you Mother had gone to Washington. She was taken sick at the time and is here with me now will not leave until the last of the month. You may be sure dear I am anxious and unsettled regarding the Washington life this Winter. It is the old story "hope for the best."

The country has greatly changed since my last letter. The meadows have put off their lovely green and the glory of the trees is fast faiding. I went into the woods the other day. It was warm and balmy and every thing was beautiful. I wish you could have enjoyed it with me. My dear child you tell me to remember you in my prayers. I never fail to do it. I am sorry you have to go into hard study but I have no fears of the result. Keep a good heart and I know all will be well. You know dear that whatever you undertake for your good has my interest always. Give love to your sisters. I had a letter from Rannie to day so I know all are well at Fitzwater St. God bless you.

Faithfully yours
Lulu

[Postal card from Annie Purvis to Edith Webb.[36] Postmarked "Oct. 24"; addressed to "Miss Edith Webb, Fillmore Street, South Camden, N.J."]

October 24th 1880

Dear Girls:

I only heard three days ago of the illness of Ada, or I should of been over. I am glad to know she is better. If I am well, and everything favorable I expect to go to Washington on the 1st of November. So my Friends, if you have any message to send Lottie and would like to see me, I will be more than pleased to have you come over Saturday afternoon if you can. With love to all I am yours truly

Annie P.

[Postal card from Louisa. Postmarked "Nov. 18"; addressed to "1748 Fillmore Street, N.J."]

Philadelphia
Nov. 18th 1880

Dear G.

I arrived here last evening and am now wondering if you could come over tomorrow after school. I may leave for Washington on Saturday, but if possible will remain until next week. I am so very glad to hear that the little sister up again.

Love to all.

Yours.
L

[From Annie Purvis. Postmarked "Nov. 30, 1880"; addressed to "Miss Edith & Genie Webb, Fillmore Street, South Camden, N.J."]

1608 R. Street[37]
Washington, D.C.
November 28th 1880

To my dear Friends of Camden:

Greeting, and Love from their distant cousin![38] Washington at times feels as far from Phila as Europe, not that I am not happy, only I feel like seeing my Mamsie[39] once in a-while.

Washington is truly a beautiful City, such wide streets, handsome Houses, and lovely Parks, and last but not least its Public Buildings all combined form a beautiful Picture, and to fully enjoy and understand one must see it—So you Dear Girls must try some day to visit W. especially while such an attractive person as I am here—

I enjoyed reading your letter very much yesterday afternoon, and wish today you girls could just be with me, to enjoy Lottie's Grate fire. I must tell you she has the prettiest, cosiest little House I have ever been in, her Parlors are lovely, furnished in the best of taste, some fine Pictures, great many Books, easy chairs, and best of all is the pleasant spirit over all.[40] Frank uses the back Parlor as a Study, he has a beautiful grate fire. The front parlor has a Latrobe[41] and when the middle doors are open the place is delightful. Lottie is not well today is lying down. F. is studying for tonight, the Old Lady[42] has just gone upstairs, she and I have good times together talking over old times in Charleston. Frank did not think you wrote a nice letter, one of the poorest you have written all because you did not mention him. You know, you ought to on ever line said something about his Lordship.

Now Edie, I must tell you that I did not write before because I was waiting for my work it was not ready when I first arrived, as the Agricultural Dep. is some distance from here. I have to just fly round to reach there by 9 o'clock. I like my work very much. It is only fastening the ends of little bags of seeds counting putting down their numbers, that is we vary the work, as there several departments in the building, sometimes we are changed from one to the other.

So far I have been quite well, — and have been out considerably — met lots of people at a concert at cousin F. church (a concert and Reading with an after chat of good things) — I met L. Jacobs for a few minutes, how well she looks, and her mother too. I will see them soon again I hope. Very many people have called on me, I am feeling rather strange after my quiet life at Grandma's.[43] Now wouldn't you girls like to know the names of all the Gentlemen who honored themselves by calling — well I can't tell you — I know I never saw so many good looking colored people before that is the women, many of them real pretty and how they do dress. I am quite sunk in the shade, in my brown dress and Bonnet.[44] Tomorrow night we are invited to meet, and form a Literary and Musical Society. Then in connection with the Church there are societies to help the poor missionary, which meet at the different houses, to sew for the poor, so there seems to be something all the time. Genie, I will have a private talk with you about the children, though Edie can read it.

In the first place give my love to them everyone, tell John[45] I am glad to hear of his pluck in carrying on two Shops. I hope he will succeed, and Blink and Miriam, I think of as steady little women on whom their sisters can depend in an emergency. Ada I am so glad to hear is getting stronger, I can imagine how tired in heart you Girls often are, and I think you keep up wonderfully.

I took dinner with your relatives the Fleetwoods and Hawksworths, Sara is looking well, she has only commenced going out.[46] Laura and the children are in good health. I wonder if you have such horrid weather as we have. Snow, and rain on top of that, delightful walking for tomorrow. Both of you girls are

<u>commanded</u> to write to me, that is when you have time. I send the love from Frank and Lottie and I think L. will write to you before long.

With love
Ever your friend
Annie

~⫯⊙

[From Louisa. Postmarked "Dec. 6, 1880"; addressed to "1748 Fillmore Street, Camden N.J."]

1413 K Street
Washington Dec. 6, 1880

My dear dear Genie

I know you have expected a letter from me before this. I got Joe (my young hopeful)[47] to send you a postal the day after I arrived here that you might know I reached here safely. I found Mother had taken a house and we had to begin immediately to get to rights. The house had to be cleaned from top to bottom. So each day has found me busy and the nights have found me tired. Your sweet charity will I am sure pardon what seemed like neglect. Things are pretty well shaped now and I take long breaths of relief.

We have a pleasant house. So if you chance to come in the holidays you shall come often and spend the time with me in my little sitting room. I only wish I had a sleeping room to offer that you might be my guest altogether. I hope you did not take cold on that cold Tuesday when you would come and see me off. It was lovely of you but I hated the exposure for you and then the hurry to get back to your school. How constantly we change in situation. Two weeks ago we spent the day together while now long stretches of miles part us. That day and the after-scene recalled so much that is past.[48] Even now it seems strange that I should have knelt there with you. Still dear when we think of it rightly I did what was natural and right in the sight of God. There is but one communion—the Saviour to commemorate. None who profess to love and serve Him should be denied this rite—the precious inheritance of the Christian Church. On that Sabbath morning dear I felt with you that our friendship was linked with a nearer bond. May it never grow less.

I have had only a glimpse of Charlotte Grimké and Annie Purvis. I shall try and get to see them next week. Congress as you know opens tomorrow and busy Washington life begins. If these were the days we read of in our childhood when good faries took the rule and reign of particular individuals I would certainly ask their interceeding grace and so by a silken chain you would feel yourself sometimes drawn from quiet Camden to gay Washington. Would you like it? Is your sister Edith taking care of her cold, and the little Ada[49] still improving? And you my dear child look to yourself. Do not work beyond your strength. I wish you could all come down here and live. Who knows but you may some day. Love to the sisters. God bless and keep you well and happy is the prayer of your loving friend.

Louise

One by One
Thy Duties Wait Thee
1881–1882

The Jacobses' boarders in Washington leave with the old administration. Lulu and her mother travel to Englewood, New Jersey, to assist Edith Willis (Grinnell, 1853–1930), whose cousin-husband is dying. After his death, Lulu stays on through the summer and, in the fall, visits her old abolitionist friends the Brocketts. She returns home earlier than planned because her mother is ill. After another busy winter season she travels to upstate New York to supervise a jam and preserves business at Willowbrook, the Throop Martin family estate.

Genie, suffering from neuralgia in Camden, is exhausted from teaching and caring for her ailing family. She worries that it might have been sinful to ask God to make her bond of friendship with Lulu "a tie for all time." Lulu reassures her that human love is part of God's greater love. Genie offers to care for Louisa should she ever fall ill, and Lulu offers Genie "tender care" in her home—should she ever have one. Lulu finally learns that the dying Delie had asked Genie to consider marrying her soon-to-be widowed husband, Willie Chew, and raise their two little boys. Lulu advises against such a union unless Genie truly loves Willie. Genie takes Lulu's advice.

[From Louisa. Postmarked "Jan. 6, 1881"; addressed to "1748 Fillmore Street, Camden N.J."]

Washington Jan. 4, 1881

My dear Genie

I did not mean to let the old year go out without some word from me but it passed and with a half guilty conscience at my delay I come to greet you with the New Year. May God bless you and your dear in this New Year with its unknown future. May all the hopes and confidences that shall come into it be joys realized. I have thought of you in the holidays and know if they had joys they had shadows too. So come they to me and ever will with memories burdened with pain. I am sure you and your sister Edith united to make them a happy time for the younger ones of your household. I suppose they have before this come to know all about that mysterious and fascinating individual Santa Claus, the dream and joy of childhood. What if we could go back to those days? What a stretch for me. Yet I would make it if there was such a think as time moving backward. Have you been to Fitzwater Street lately? When I last heard from them they were busy preparing a Christmas tree for the children. It would have made me too sad to have been with them on that day. I was with them on that day four years ago.[1] Our loved Delie with her large heart strove to make the occasion happy to all—dear generous loving soul! It is raining to night. I know she does not feel it. And yet the storm hurts me as I think of her grave. We have had such cold weather here and quantities of snow. To night's rain will lessen the pile. There was to have been a carnival this afternoon on Penn Avenue but the rain interfered with the programme.

I must tell you dear how mother and I spent Christmas day and how it came about. She mentioned to Mrs. Claflin (who boards with us) that she had invited an old lady 102 to dine with her on that day and that nothing would give her more pleasure than to invite twenty of the poorest old women she could find to a good dinner on that day. "Do it," responded the lady and I will help to pay for the dinner. This was sufficient. Of course situated as we are we could not on such an occasion brought them into our home without the boarders sanction. Well we went to work and prepared for them in every sense of the word a Christmas dinner. Several friends went out in the byways and found the old people and bade them to this feast. The day was most unfavorable, notwithstanding twelve of them came. They were received into the big dining room. The waiter and I had set a pretty table, I adorned it with bright flowers cut out of paper. Mrs. Claflin the ladies of her family Kate Jenning[2] and myself waited on them. Mr. Grimké came. He made some beautiful remarks and asked a blessing at the table. After awhile the old ladies warmed up and told many things of the war time and their experience in slavery. They were asked to sing. A sister struck up, "My God the Spring of all my Joys."[3] The others joined in. When finished the same old lady said "let us pray." I wish dear child you could have heard the prayer. An ignorant woman uttered it but it was full of faith in and love to God, and then the gratitude she felt for the friends who had brought them together for a happy day. She ended with, "O Lord when you have blessed the big round world then remember poor unworthy me." Each was presented by Mrs. Claflin with a Christmas card and the name was written on it. Then each with a package of tea and sugar one of the flowers off

The Jacobses' white friend Representative William Claflin boarded with them in 1880. (Library of Congress)

of the table and some fruit to carry home with them. Went home happy calling down blessings upon us. Then we had found fifteen poor children we feasted them and sent them off happy. So ended our day.[4]

Now darling a little word more particularly about ourselves. You said in your letter that the altar is the place to carry our heaviest burden and fondest dreams, then why ask me if it was sinful to ask God to make our bond of friendship a tie for all time? Nay Genie He himself is love, and bade but to love one another. So we love not the creature better than the creator it is all right. My dear I can so fully sympathize with your feeling and disappointment in the sister who spoke to you on that Sabbath morning. Let her pass, and if possible all hurtful feelings where Christ and Christianity is concerned. In every church you will find the ungodly spirit. If you have grace to stand it is your victory. Each must be governed in religion by his own needs and convictions looking into God for the right power of action.

Yes, Delie would have been bitter and gone away from the church she clung to to the last. Do not dwell on it Genie. The lesson is bitter but it may have its use.[5]

Is the sewing all out of the way. I am so sorry you have got to study up for that old examination. I wish I could help you out. All I can do now is to say God bless you and remember you in my prayers. Think of my wasting all this time. When you had asked about that cough mixture. Will you forgive me? Here it is:

2 oz. of bloodroot
1 " Paregoric
6 " wine

Dose teaspoon full three or four times a day. Shake before taking. I hope by this Miss Edith does not need it Genie. Love to the sisters and set us a good example by writing very soon.

Always your
Loving friend
Lulu

The M stands for ————— I think I will tell you next time.

[From Louisa. Postmarked "Mar. 25, 1881"; addressed to "1748 Fillmore Street, Camden, NJ."]

1413 K Street
Washington
March 24, 1881

My dear Genie

Life here moves quietly on again after the Inauguration stir though as yet the city is crowded with office seekers, many of whom will go home wiser and sadder men for it is impossible to find places for all who come. Richard Venning[6] has been among the successful applicants.

Inauguration week[7] was a gay, gay season. They tell me Washingtonians have not for years been so gracious and hospitable to strangers as at that time. I only went to one party and was dazzled with the fine dressing of the ladies. I have not much heart in such things. It is all so surfice like. Not that I do not enjoy social life. Yes, very much on a small scale where there are friends, intelligence and heart. You may be sure, my darling my sympathy went out to you as you told me of the sick chamber of your friend.[8] It seemed hard that the old wounds should be touched again by witnessing what had been so hard to bear with other loved ones. Yes, the old sorrow in a measure might have come back to you. You give strong and noble test of friendship to the end standing by and doing for those you love. What can I say to your sweet and comforting offer to me in the event of sickness or trials? I thank you with a full heart, and if there comes a day of need (and such days will come), you shall, if possible, be my good angel. Both mother and I were sick in bed last week with colds. Lottie Grimké has been quite sick and is not well now. And so, little friend, you would not have gone with me to the Unitarian Church, nor would I have urged it if you thought it not well. Genie I am too well founded in my faith and love of Jesus Christ to fear a Unitarian doctrine. I think I understand you dear. It is not fear that I will be influence by the doctrine but a matter of principle that I should go to a church where the divinity of the Son of God is denied. It is sad, unfortunate that a body so large and generous in humanitarian feeling and doing should put from them so precious a truth. Never fear for me child. I have not been since, but may go again for the music is heavenly and does me good.[9] Can you tell what are some of the things you might hope for if I was nearer your age? I am not too old to feel sympathy and an interest in the things and feelings that interest you. Of the prospective home I can say nothing, it is only the hope of the thing that is to be some day.

Are you studying very hard? I wish you had less care and more rest. Do not neglect what might strengthen the shoulders for their burdens. How is the sister's cough? If not well, I will send you what was given to me as a "sure cure." The person saw it tried on a lady who was suppose to be in consumption.

You want to know what the M in my name stands for, not Minerva the wise, oh no, only plain Matilda. Turn it as you will there is no poetry in it.

Our boarders went out with the old administration. As yet, we do not know what we are going to do this summer. I may get something to do here, if so will remain on. Heard from Rannie yesterday. She did not speak of you, so I take it you have not been there lately.

Washington does not yet give much sign of Spring. If I am here in May, I would like to spirit you down for then it will be lovely.

Give love to the sisters. God bless you Genie, and keep life's cares from crowding too much upon you.

Your faithful friend Lulu

—◊◊○—

[Handwritten note from Louisa.]

Washington—April 15, 1881

For dear Genie and Miss Edith, with love to both and a heartfelt wish that Easter may be joyous to you all.

Lovingly yours
Lulu

—◊◊○—

[From Louisa. Postmarked "May 13, 1881"; addressed to "1748 Fillmore Street, Camden, NJ."]

Washington May 13, 1881

My dear Genie

I wonder that I have let so long a time go by without answering your dear welcome letter. If it lessens the neglect to know I have thought of you again and again in the interval then the condemnation will not be quite so great. The lovely Easter card (the kind thought of your sister and self I have placed on the mantle in our sitting room so each day it gives me a loving greeting for which take loving thanks. The mind and heart take in the joy of the new birth. If I might put my arms about you I would draw you down here for a few days of rest. I know you are longing for the vacation. Must you pass through the dreaded examinations? If so I know how busy every moment is. There will be an examination here on the 17 of the month. I hope the neuralgia has left you long before this. If not you must be worn out with your day duties and broken rest at night. Poor child it is all hard. May I trust Easter Sunday brought satis-faction and happiness to you and your household. I thought much of you on the day and of the young sisters deeper and more tender dedication to God. I trust His blessing fell richly upon them on the occasion—a blessing that will follow their steps all through their lives. It is lovely to day Genie—perhaps a little to warm, but then every every thing in nature has such a fresh new look of life; one cannot help be glad and thankful that the eye has so much beauty to rest on while you never the less have to meet trials and to do and sacrifice for those you love. Yours is the Christian spirit, yet I do not believe our Father intends that we should ever quite lose sight of the welfare of self.

Charlotte Grimké is not well. She has been very much troubled of late with her eyes. Mr. G has not fulfilled your commission to me. I went to his house one evening especially to inquire after what you had sent me and why he had not given it to me. I was as innocent as a baby never dreaming of the nature of the promise until Charlotte made some remark about it, and then it dawned upon me. You bad child! All I have got to say is this same gentleman is a man of taste. What he accepted from you was agreeable and sweet and he preferred to keep it for his own. I like good sense, and do not dislike to have it tinctured with a little sentiment. So dear I will have to wait and take it fresh from your own lips. And that is better, some things cannot be done by proxy. I hear Mrs. Bowers has lost her daughter. She must be heartbroken for I have heard the daughter was every thing to her in her not altogether happy life.[10] These trials from God are so hard to bear, yet He knows what is best for us. Give love to thy sister, and tell her to take care of herself. I have not been well of late—am feeling better at present. Tell me of Fitzw— St. when you write. Little Louise[11] had a hard time of it with pneumonia. Write me darling when you have a little time, and remember I always think of you with tender interest. God watch over you.

Faithfully yours,
Lulu

[From Louisa. Postmarked "May 24, 1881"; addressed to "1748 Fillmore Street, Camden, NJ."]

Washington—May 22, 1881

My dear Genie

Do not think I did not pay regard to your request—to remember you on those three said days of last week. Indeed, I fully intended to write and to send you some woods flowers. You know the proverb "Man proposes but God disposes." On Wednesday evening Mother was taken quite sick with dizziness of the head and for several day was ill. She is up and about again for which I am most thankful. You may be sure dear I did not forget you and your sister but each day hoped every thing was going on successfully. Now that it is over, I shall anxiously wait to hear the result though I doubt not that it is satisfactory.

I am indeed sorry you have suffered so much from neuralgia, and then too at a time when you required all your strength and nerve. Have you had the advice of a good doctor? It is something you ought not to neglect. I saw Annie P. yesterday. She spoke of you. She is still hoping to get something to do. Says she has fair promise. Government promises have malleable backbones. Many a poor heart has sickened if not died with the hope long defered. Garfield in his appointments has not done much for colored men leaving only the appointments of Mr. Douglass and ex-Senator Bruce.[12] He has dealt fairly by them. The President must feel just now that this is not treading on a bed of roses what with a very sick wife, the resignation of two senators, one most able and powerful,[13] and other signs of discontent from the people, he must conclude honors are bought at a high price. I suppose you have been to church for the day is lovely. I fully intended to but got up feeling miserable and so lazily stayed at home. I heard from Mrs. Venning the other day. She says she has not seen you for months. How is that? She tells me Willie is looking badly. Poor fellow I do wish he might get a berth on an English steamer. The change would be beneficial. You were a stupid child not to see which Easter card was intended for you. Did you not find the one folding like a book in the little note I wrote? Well, that was thine. I shall be glad my dear little friend when school books are laid aside and you can have some leisure and rest. Mind and do not go to sewing at once but at least rest several weeks first.

You and Edith[14] must pet yourselves sometimes. Life demands it. I would be so glad if you lived nearer me that I might at times be of some small service to you. Life is so full of changes that one cannot tell what the days will bring forth. Fate may in time see fit to turn your steps in this direction. We wait and see. Lottie continues to be troubled with her eyes. Had been obliged to live in a dark room for a week or more.

Your cousin Mrs. Fleetwood has gone into business. Has a furnishing store. Will receive orders for ladies and gentlemen's underware.[15] Now, dear child, I am going to leave you. Wishing you are well and happy, that God will always bless and love you as one of his special children.

Your loving friend,
Lulu

[From Louisa. Postmarked "July 21, 1881"; addressed to "1748 Fillmore Street, Camden, NJ."]

Washington
July 18, 1881

My dear Genie

What has come over you that I do not hear from you? Are you so full of resting that you do not even want to handle a pen? Poor dear child I know you were tired out and in need of all and more than all the rest you will get. Still you must write to me sometimes.[16]

I am glad you have no tiresome examinations to think of for next year, for you and your sister have cares enough without the piling on of extras. I know your thoughts travelled here in search of me when the whole country was startled over the would-be assassination of the President. It was indeed a fearful day. But, thanks to a good God, the skill of physicians, and the pluck and good constitution of Garfield, the nation I trust will be spared the sorrow of his death. Every appliance that ingenuity has and can invent is made use of for his comfort and restoration.[17] Think, Genie, what the hero they will make of the President hereafter! I have great admiration for Mrs. Garfield. She is a brave woman and earnest Christian. In fact they say there exists in the family the most entire harmony and love.

Have you suffered from warm weather yet? We have had some tremendously warm days but, on the whole, I do not know that we ought to complain. To day is delightful (it is Sunday). One of those quiet breezy days, a soul Sabbath that seems to take one nearer to God whether we be in the church or at home. I have not been out. I am not very well, while mother has been ailing for the last three or four weeks. We both need a change, and will probably leave here in the course of two weeks. I had hoped if I went North to stop in Philadelphia a few days, then I could have seen you. Now I think I shall defer it until my return, when I will be in better condition. Just now I look very much like a rail. I am going to Bracketts Bridge where I was last year. How glad I would be if you could be my companion there. Alas! dear life teaches we cannot have in it what we would. We can only make the most of it as we find it.

You remember Joseph, our adopted boy?[18] He was in the Pension Office last week. He suffered dismissal with many others owing to the retrenchment going on in all the departments as Congress did not make appropriations sufficient before adjourning. Of course, it was a great disappointment to him, but he has gone cheerfully to Boston to find work, with assurance of the establishment next December when Congress reassembles.

Have you been to Fitzwater Street lately? I was glad Rannie came all right out of her examination and Julia acquitted herself so well at her graduation.[19] How proud dear Delie would have been could she have lived to see those days. I do not doubt but Willie's agitation of the school question helped to pass the bill in the Legislature for mixed school.[20] We can't but be glad, and yet I fear in time it will interfere with the colored teachers. All we can do is to hope for the best—a change in public feeling. Your cousin Mrs. Fleetwood as you probably know, has opened a nice little store, and she tells me she is full of business. I think you once told me that was what you wanted for your girls. Genie, send me a line before I leave here.

Love to your sister. God bless you dear child.

Lovingly,
Lulu

~⁂©

[From Louisa. Postmarked "September 10, 1881, from Little Falls, NY"; addressed to "1748 Fillmore Street, Camden, NJ."]

Sept 10, 1881
Brockett's Bridge

My dear dear Genie

I have just got here and found your postal and letter waiting for me. You dear child to have sent me such loving greetings. And you will pardon the silence that went on after you so sweetly broke the spell. When I left Wash. I went to Englewood in NJ to Mrs. Willis a life long friend of Mother's and mine.[21] I went with the intention of remaining two or three days, Mother for a longer time. I do not know if I ever told you of a sad and romantic circumstance connected with Mrs. Willis' younger daughter.[22] If not I will relate somewhat here that you may see how it chanced that I was so long in getting here. This daughter married a man who was supposed to be on his deathbed. He was as helpless as a baby and his physicians said he could live but a short time. The marriage took place a year ago last Jan and the husband has lived on until the 21 of last month in a perfectly helpless state and the young lovely wife has had that entire care of him. When I got to Mrs. Willis I found him very ill and they begged me to stay. I was glad to if I might be of the least service or comfort to them. When he passed away they still said "Don't go we love to have you here"; and so dear I remained until now. When I see you I will tell you about those two young people whom God saw fit to part. You will admire the brave woman who loved faithfully to the end. There never was a more faithful and devoted wife. I am so sorry to hear that the two young sisters were suffering from [Malaria] when you wrote. I hope they are much better if not well before this; for truly you have enough on your young shoulders without the anxiety attending sickness. I wish I could have you near me next Winter in Washington in a good position. Perhaps you would not want to leave home even if the chance came. I cannot tell now how it will be with me later on. I am hoping for something but the hope may not be realized.

I trust you went back to your school stronger and somewhat rested. I say somewhat knowing perfect rest could not come to you with your constant thought and efforts to do for your dear ones at home. I am sorry Willie did not come back better. He will probably improve in the next voyage.

My darling Genie I trust you will be too wise to let anything in connection with a subject you spoke of in your previous letter have weight with you. I hold it not right to ask you to accept pledges at such a time when so much is involved—the happiness of a lifetime. What I say dear you know is from interest and love of you. I have not heard from Fitzwater Street for some time. I am wondering to day how the poor President is. One misses the papers so much in these country places. Some one of the household is going to the mail just now, so I must close. With dear love and God's blessings on you. Remember me to the sisters.

Faithfully yours,
Lulu

~∰◎

[From Louisa. Postmarked "October 10, 1881, from Little Falls, NY"; addressed to "1748 Fillmore Street, Camden, NJ."]

Brockett's Bridge Oct. 9, 1881

My darling Genie

Do not think I have not appreciated your kind loving though[t] in keeping me so abundantly supplied with papers, especially during the time of mourning and honors for our late President. What a sad event his death was, Yet I believe out of the loss and sorry great good will come.[23] The whole heart of the civilized could not be so roused and softened without purifying results, particularly to the political parties of this country. If solace can be felt in a great grief, surely

Mrs. Garfield and her bereaved family have it, for never was a man more sorrowed for or honored. I feel great sympathy for his successor for he entered upon his duties under such embarrassing circumstances. The success with which the convention passed off in New York and his (Arthurs) dignified straight-forward deportment will do a great deal towards propitiating the people.[24] I feel sorry too for Conkling.[25] He is a clean handed politician and has been such a power in his party that because of a mistaken step it is now vile of the press (New York in particular) and his countrymen to traduce him as they have. The fickle ingratitude of the multitude is enough to make him a better man.

Let us leave public men and speak of matters more at home. In the first place I hope the little sisters are rid of chills and that your father is strong again. I begin to think Camden is not a healthy place. I noticed when there that many places seemed low and marshy. You were mistaken dear in supposing I had been nursing the sick. The young wife I told you of did all the nursing herself. It was wonderful how for more than a year she bore up under so great a strain. There is truth in the saying, the back is fitted for the burden. I am afraid that September's heat made you almost to wonder if you had had the Summer's vacation. I am sure the little change you got at that time was not sufficient to meet the hard work of the year before you. You must try and save yourself all you can. I am sorry that you were disappointed in making the acquaintance of Owen Meredith in the volume you mentioned of his.[26] There are some lovely things in it. Dear Delie was very fond of the book and it bears as you know many pencil marks of poems and verses precious to her, and ofttimes read to me. I do not like all that Meredith has written, but the special things treasured by our loved one are equally dear to me. You shall see the book some day. I only borrowed it, but if her sister[27] will allow me to keep it, I will gladly put in its place a new volume. She could not value it in the same way that I do. I heard from Rannie when Willie was expected in port. I was surprised to hear of his poor health. I knew he was not well when he started out on his first trip but I had hoped he had been benefited. I trust he came back from the last trip better. I was relieved by your confidence in the matter I mentioned to you. I would have been truly sorry had there been a different state of things. When a change comes in your life I want it to be a happy one, not one to add to its cares.

You ask me when I shall leave here. I cannot tell just yet. I want to stay awhile longer for in the beginning I did not pick up as usual. I was a complete martyr to headaches. I am much better of them now and daily gaining in strength and I believe in weight too. I told you of my mothers going to Newport with intention of remaining several months. She was taken quite sick there and remained but a short time. She is now in New York with our friend Mrs. Willis.

Louisa named little Charlie Chew as a beneficiary in her will. (Library Company of Philadelphia)

I expect you are at Church this lovely Sabbath morning. I am going to a funeral with my friends at one o'clock. It is the third that has occured among these friends since I came here, and I have attended none of them for I like not to go to such places. But this is a particular friend and go out of respect to them.

Does little Charlie Chew grow and does he seem happy? Poor little fellow, he is in my thoughts very often. I pray God will spare the father's life to them both. And so dearie you think my letters grow less in number, be assured my heart does not in affection, and that is more than letters. I rather think Genie is better satisfied with ocular evidence in some things and for that I am not going to chide her being somewhat of a like spirit.

I must say good bye now. Give love to the sisters for me and mind and take care of yourself. God bless you always.

Ever your fond

friend

Lulu

—⁂©

[From Louisa. Postmarked "November 22, 1881"; addressed to "1748 Fillmore Street, Camden, NJ."]

1416 I St.

Washington

November 22, 1881

My dear dear Genie

I know this letter will bring you disappointment as the loss opportunity of not seeing you has given me. I arrived in New York last Wednesday morning with intention of remaining there several days and then to continue my journey South-ward stopping in Philadelphia this week. I had not been in N.Y. more than two hours when the postman came bringing two postals from Mother saying she was ill in bed and would I come on immediately. I took the first southern train and reached here 11 o'clock that night. I found Mother had been very ill with a severe cold. She is much better to day and I think if she is careful she will be able to be out the latter part of the week. You see dear heart in me the proof of neglected opportunity. I could have seen you and the Fitzwater Street friends in my trip northward, but I was not well and the weather was so warm, I longed for the country reasoning I would enjoy the visit so much more on my return trip. Alas, dear we cannot count with any certainty on any thing.

I had anticipated such a pleasant visit with you. Now I must wait I know not how long for the reality. The disappointment teaches me one thing—never to pass through P. again without making good my chance of seeing you. How are you, dear child, and how are the Sisters? I saw Lottie yesterday. She was quite well, although she suffers a good deal at times with her head. Annie has had one of her attacks, but is well again. I have a wretched cold myself. Think I took it coming on. Have been house hunting but have not found the right one yet, and, it will be doleful if we do not in the end. It is comparatively quiet here now, but soon the busy, gay Washington life will begin. How I wish you could come here in the holidays. This idle wishing Delie used to say is foolish. It may be, and if so, few are wise. For who does not picture possibilities and give utterance to desires? Have you been to the Fitzwater St. house lately? I had much to say to you had we been fortuned in meeting. There are things we cannot communicate half as well by pen as by voice. So you must come to me childie, or wait until I can come to you.

Give love to Edith. How is her cough? Take care of yourself, Genie. May God's smile ever be upon you.

Yours fondly,
Lulu

[From Louisa. Undated note, possibly written early in the letter exchange.]

Dec 23

Genie dear

Please give the <u>little</u> <u>sisters</u> each one of the enclosed cards. I am sorry not to direct them but I only know them by their pet name. I hope you are feeling quite well to day. With much love

Yours
Lulu

[From Louisa. Postmarked "Feb. 27, 1882"; addressed to "1748 Fillmore Street, Camden, NJ."]

10 Lafayette Square[28]
Feb. 23, 1882

You are a good darling Genie and I am the opposite. I have meant more times than you have fingers and toes to write. Each day I would say I will try and write to Genie to day. But night's curtain fell and the morrow's sun rose and the curtain fell again, and the deed was not done. Thus you see, childie, you have been in my mind and heart if pen and ink have not told you the same.

We have had a busy time since the Session opened what with dinner parties, day and evening receptions, mother and I are pretty well tired out. I hope Lent will give us a respite. I am so sorry dear to hear that you and Edith are not well. I wish I could do something for you—could lift off some of your cares. What evil spirit put it into the heart of your landlord to change his house at this season of the year!! It is a shame to have to move now and expose yourselves it may be to sickness. Be sure and have fires made in the new house several days before you go into it. If you could have your carpets taken up and put down before you move, you would find it would save you much trouble and annoyance as you could assign each article of furniture where it would belong and in that way be spared extra lifting.

You speak of being worried about Edith. Is her cough worse or is she generally run down? Oh, Genie dear, I wish I had means, I would give you both a long rest, a rest of mind and body. We sometimes get to that place where nothing else can build up but complete rest, stripped of all anxieties.

Lottie Grimké was here to day. I told her about you and she sends love and is very sorry to hear you are not well and of your present troubles. She was quite ill a couple of weeks since and is not well now. I have not heard from Fitzwater St. lately. Wrote to Mrs. Venning last week. I am truly glad Willie has improved in health.

Genie, my child, this is the Lenten season. I want you to listen to me for a moment and do not misconstrue a single word I shall say. In the first place, I want you to remember you are not well and cannot keep to the rules of Lent as proscribed in your church like a strong person. God does not require of you, and you must not let your conscience. Do your duty as you see it—but not beyond the requirements of your present state of health. I know how devotely and tenderly you go onto in feeling to the commands of this sacred season— sacred and to be observed by all who truly live our acknowledged faith. God knows all things and does not ask of his creatures any sacrifice detrimental to their welfare. So, dear, be governed accordingly. You will think me quite wicked when I tell you I have not been to church to day. Mother has been ailing for several days. This morning, I would not let her get up. As I had extras to do, I could not well get out. I met my Sunday school class at 3 o'clock. I teach at St. Luke's. Poor church, it is always in trouble! I cannot help being sorry for Dr. Crummell. They have not treated him right. As for the church, had it not been for him, it would not be in existence now.[29]

With a sincere prayer that all things will work together for your good—
your support—coming in every trial from the love of God. And so darling with
a blessing and a kiss—Good night.

Yours,
Lulu

[From Louisa.]

Washington
April 11, 82

Dearest Genie

What could have been more stupid than my sending you the wrong letter?
It happened this mail. I wrote to you and an old friend in Boston at the same
time. In each letter I enclosed an Easter card. After directing them, I took the
cards and letters out of the envelopes fearing there might be a mistake. Will you
believe me they were all right, but I thinking them wrong changed them. I have
not heard from your letters. Why did you send the card back? You might have
known that it was intended for you. When I directed to you, I could not for the
life of me remember your old number at Fillmore St. As for Webster Street
Miss, how was I to know you lived there? Did you not tell me to direct to the
old home? Of course you did.

It seems poor dear child as if there was always some extra care for you to
shoulder. I am glad you are a Christian darling for it helps you in the warfare.
You can see the sunshine beyond the clouds, the stars that never faid from the
heavens where the dear God reigns and watches over us and loves us to the
end. Tell me whatever you feel to confide in me and be assured you have in me
a friend and sympathizer. Yet, you shall have this letter—should it come back
to me.

Thanks for the pretty card. I trust Easter joys came with your Easter Sunday. I thought of you. You must pardon this little scrawl. God bless you and
yours and give you strength for whatever is before you.

Faithfully and lovingly yours
Lulu

[From Louisa. Postmarked "Sept. 30, 1882, from N.Y."; addressed to "Ferry Road above Vanhook St., Camden, NJ."]

Willowbrook[30] July 23, 1882

My darling Genie

I know you have questioned by day the cause of my silence. When I arrived here I found such a rush of business that I had no time I could call my own, and when night came I was too tired to put a thought on paper. And so dear I took it out in thinking only of you. There is nothing for me to complain of here but hard work. The home is beautifully situated in sight of a lovely lake. The grounds are large and covered with fine old trees. Just the spot to spend the summer months. And then I am treated with the utmost kindness.

Yet I have found it hard. I came before I had time to rest from the Washington life, otherwise I think my strength would have been less taxed. I shall stay as long as I can without real detriment to my health. I feel badly for poor dear Mother to leave her by herself, and yet she wanted me to come. I only trust she may keep well.

Now dearie it is about time I had asked you something about you and yours. Are you well and still intending to go away for awhile? Do not put the going off too long else you will not derive much benefit from it. I was called away so suddenly I had not time to tell you how much I enjoyed the little visit at your home.

God bless you darling for all your kindness. May your love to me and others bring rest and joy to your soul. I suppose you have been to church to day. You will have to pray for me childie for I do not expect to go often while here. I shall take the day to rest in knowing God understands the situation and will judge accordingly. The day is perfect, full of bright sunshine and yet the cool air makes you to wonder if it is warm in other places. I have not felt the heat here save some days in the workrooms where two and three fires are generally going. All the workers are women. I put in a request for a man for all the lifting and pressing is too much for them. So we have had a man a part of the time and ought by right to have one all the time. Have you been to Fitzwater Street since I left? I must try and send them a line to day. My opportunity for seeing you was so short that I now think of many things that went unsaid I had intended to talk to you about. I may see you in the Autumn. Do not take this as a promise, only a possibility. You must pardon this scrawl and write me very soon. I feel that I am a long way from home and friends, thus you see your letter will afford me pleasure and comfort. Renunciation, some one has said is the law of life. No sacrifice! No sacrament! Willing or unwilling we must all sacrifice. Indeed dear we all sooner or later learn the lesson. Give love to the Sister and do you and Edith get all the rest possible. With fond love and a kiss

I am faithfully yours
Lulu

—*illo*—

[From Louisa. Postmarked "Sept. 30, 1882, from N.Y."; addressed to "Ferry Road above Vanhook St., Camden, NJ."]

Willowbrook Sept. 28

My dear Genie

I know you are not looking for a letter from Willowbrook, and you already perceive that your last was received here. I received your note—sent from Boardentown and magnanimously returned you a postal card which I infer from your letter was not received. And now, as to my being here beyond the time mentioned to you. You see dear the combined efforts of a good Dr. and medicine gave me courage and strength to hold on a little longer. But—in very truth I shall leave a week from next Monday—the 10 of October.

Do you see that you send me a letter to Brockett's Bridge by then. This dearie will be only a brief message. It is now 9 o'clock—too late for your old and tired (it has been such a busy week) friend to say little more than how are you? And God bless you. In the final place thanks and a kiss for the dear loving letter. Indeed, I would delight to have you for my companion while at Brockett's Bridge. There would be no lack of employment I assure you. You should read to me each day—talk to me—keep me in good spirits. And then (O! exquisite bliss for you) you might help me to mend my clothes. Could friend be more royally entertained? Never mind dear, if I ever have a home, you shall be tenderly cared for when you come to it. Am I to conclude Genie that Delie's request of you has been regarded? Let it not be unless your heart with true fervor can say amen to it. I loved her with a great love and yet I say this to you. I am fond of Willie, and know he would do his best for the woman he loved. It is a great responsibility marrying a man with two children—So think well of it. I cannot fully answer your letter now. "Unsaid" is a pretty picture of real life.

It is getting very cool here. I have an open fireplace in my room and am fanning a wood fire that is beginning to die down. Good night childie. Give love to the sisters.

Yours fondly

Lulu

⁓∦◌

[From Louisa.]

Brockett's Bridge Oct. 1, 1882

My dear Genie

It was very sweet of you to send your letter in advance of me. I have to admit to you that I staid at Willowbrook beyond my expectation. Not from avarice but because Miss Martin[31] was not well and asked me if I could possibly remain a little longer while she went off for a weeks change. She had been very kind to me dear and I could not say her nay.

Now I am resting and growing fat—I shall not remain long here. Mother is already waiting for me. She is in Washington. I am hoping we shall have a small house this winter. You know darling that Hope is a cheap delusive creature. Nevertheless I thank God for her comforting face and delightful cheap. I was so sorry to hear of your discomfort owing to the hard storm you spoke of. I truly hope it left no bad effects on any of you. If there had been a vacant house anywhere near you it would have been your opportunity for moving since you are not altogether pleased with the present one. And yet it is a good little home, so be satisfied little girl until opportunity brings you what would better please you.

Yes, I am glad you do not cross the ferry alone late in the evening. Of course, I like you to think of my counsel sometimes and to <u>act on it too</u>. You see I am not free of the egotism of being older—more experienced, and on this heavy basis wiser than yourself. I am giving you an insight by degrees into the amiable traits of my character. In defence of your charge of the derangement of my brain and heart, let me state right here that the heart is all right. As to the brain, I admit it does get mixed up sometimes. Nevertheless that postal card was clearly directed to Bordentown. It must have been a great pleasure to you to meet again the young priest whose story and devotion I have not forgotten. Maybe dear we are all better for having some ideal. Some Crusader who embodies, as far as mortal man may Christ. To know such a one must tend to make one more tolerant and tender to the unfortunate and the weaknesses of human nature generally. Thank you dear Genie for the simple candid manner in which you have told your story. It is best that it should be so, and and you justly say, I think she would not have it otherwise. I do pray when the boys are older I may in some way be able to do something for them.[32] Poor dear Delie thought with so much pride of what would or <u>must</u> be their future. How dear is the hand that curtains that future. I in my life have been foolish enough to crave the power to lift it. Not now. I have learned that each days development is sufficient knowledge.

We are having lovely weather. I think it must be our Indian Summer. I may see you very soon—only for a day or so. I wish Willie might be at home. Poor childie, I am sorry the schoolwork is so tiresome. Can't we do something to make a fortune so you may turn your back on the schoolroom? My friend Mrs Feeter[33] has gone off for a few days and I am keeping house for her. I wish you were here to keep me company. It would be very good to you.

Give love to the sisters, and take the same for thyself with the addition of a kiss or two.

God bless you
Ever yours
Louise

[From Louisa. Postmarked "Dec. 13, 1882"; addressed to "Ferry Road above Vanhook St., Camden, NJ."]

1712 P Street[34]
Washington Dec 12, 1882

My dear childie

I ought to have sent you a congratulatory line before this that you might have read in black and white my perfect sympathy and gladness in your and E good luck in getting the night school. You see, I have used the word "luck," but I do not believe it was a chance thing your getting the situation but an acknowledgement of your efficiency as teachers. I only hope the undertaking is not going to be too much for you and that you will not let yourself be over anxious about the result, but take comfort in the words that come to sooth you after your first night in the school. Yea, God will surely give His angel legions to guard and watch over his faithful ones. I believe you to be one of his faithful children. You must rest all you can between school hours. Do not undertake what is not

The Chapel at Lebanon Cemetery, Philadelphia, 1850. Louisa was horrified to learn that African American cadavers stolen from Lebanon Cemetery supplied Jefferson Medical College's dissecting rooms for about eleven years. (Historical Society of Pennsylvania)

necessary for you to do. I hope you do not try to do the hardest work of your household. Let a woman come in once a week and do it for you that you and Edith may save your strength for the many duties that are upon you.

We have not yet secured a house. Expect tomorrow to have a final answer respecting two. I must say this whole thing is most wearing and discouraging. So you would have me promise if I am ever very ill to send for you regardless of school or other occupation. Such an agreement situated as you are would be most selfish. Should I be so placed as to make the request without <u>absolute</u> loss to you, be assured it would be made. I can fancy you a most thoughtful and tender nurse.

I am sorry dear you are not quite satisfied with yourself. I have not the least wish to metamorphose you into a different individual, else I might fail to reach after you, or in any way to keep pace with you and that you know would be disastrous to our friendship. What a stupid world it would be if we were facsimiles one of the other. We would soon weary of each other and of the dull round of existence.

I hope the snow fall cold was as transitory as the substance that produced it. You wanted to pay at "Make me a child again"[35] and was treated as the little dears are who rejoice in that title. Genie were you not horrified at the account of Lebanon Cemetery?[36] Think of a think happening in a so-called civilized country. I do not know how people had the heart to dig for their dead with the dread of not finding them. I would prefer the uncertainty, clinging to the hope that they were there. I hope the criminals will be severely punished. I saw Lottie a few days since, she was well. Write to me soon. You are a dear child far more prompt than I. Love to all, God bless you darling.

Lovingly thine
Lulu

One by One
Bright Gifts from Heaven
1883

The Jacobses board two successive families during the spring, but Harriet is sick and Lulu assumes most of the housekeeping burden, becoming thin and ill herself. Building on her experience at Willowbrook, Lulu decides to start her own jam and preserves business in Washington. Lulu continues to offer words of encouragement to Genie, who is completely run down with hard work and an ongoing dental infection. Lulu believes that the Camden air is malarial and ruining the Webb family's health. By the end of the summer, life has improved for everyone. Genie and her family have returned from the countryside restored, and both she and her sister received promotions in their school. Lulu's shelves are fully stocked with jellies and pickles, and the orders are coming in. She rents a large house in the fall to take in boarders, and in December she lands a teaching job at Howard University, where she and her mother are given comfortable rooms.

[From Louisa. Written along the side: "Sallie is not going to have a wedding, which at least shows some taste under the circumstances."]

Lafayette Square
Washington Jan. 3, 1883

Darling Genie

Your lovely Christmas card was duly appreciated and admired. Thanks my dear childie. I did not mean to pass you by on that occasion Genie. I even got your card (which you shall have some time). Shall I tell you why I did not send it? I felt guilty to remember you and not my dead friends children. Nay, I did not forget them. I have been so worried and perplexed as to lose all heart for the holidays. You know dear how I told you we were on the lookout for a furnished house. After much trouble we obtained one with the understanding that the family who are to board with us this winter would be here the first of January. Imagine our trouble after renting the house and paying the first months rent, to learn the family would not be here until Feb. It was a sore disappointment for we had incured so much expense.

I hope you got a good deal of pleasure out of the holidays and that the New Year will bring you and yours many blessings.

It has been quite gay here in colored society—fashionable weddings and parties. Miss Park and Dr. Shadds was a grand affair.[1] No one was admitted to the church except by card. They had the last wrinkle of the fashionable world viz three bridesmaids and one groomsman. A little girl preceded procession up the aisle bearing a basket of flowers. I was not present but heard that the march up the aile was most funereal. The dresses were very handsome and <u>ought by right</u> to have trailed through broader aisles. I wonder dear if this mind can take in the solemnity of the occasion altered in so much splendor. I mean outward splendor. I am afraid not from remarks I have heard. Mr. Grimké married them with our form of marriage.[2] None other is so beautiful!

Just now a fearful scandal is going the rounds of Washington. I am sorry from my heart that it concerns teachers. I will send you a clipping from one of the papers. They tell me it was nothing to what another (Sunday) paper contained. There is no thought so far as I have heard contradicting the guilt of the parties. Two friends of mine who went from here to spend Christmas in Baltimore knew of their arrival in that city on Sunday morning. The names of the two other teachers have not been made known, but the world with its usual charity has whispered them.

Do you know Sallie Chew[3] is to be married on the 16 of this month? This is in confidence, say nothing about it. Poor girl! I hope she may be happy.

Give love to the sisters. I would kiss them if I could.

God, dear love be with thee.

Thine
Lulu

[Enclosed in the letter is the following newspaper article.[4]]

A Scandal in Colored Society.

**Charges involving a prominent colored church leader and
a colored teacher.**

A scandal, which is expected will soon receive some attention from the board of public school trustees, has obtained very wide circulation among the colored citizens of the District, owing to the social prominence of the parties implicated. It is alleged that Mr. Wm. E. Matthews, a colored Baltimorean,[5] who has resided here several years, holding a position in the Post Office department on the night of the 23d ult. took Euretta Bozeman,[6] a colored teacher in the county, to his room at Mr. I. N. Carey's residence,[7] on 14th Street, between H and I street northwest, and there remained during the night. Miss Bozeman was discovered, it is stated, by Mr. Carey's housekeeper, Mrs. Alexander, when attempting to leave the house the next morning. Mr. Matthews is a prominent official of the 15th Street Presbyterian Church, and, of course, the story, as outlined above, when made public, caused considerable sensation. Friday evening a committee, consisting of Messrs. Frederick Douglass, A.T. Augusta[8] and Rev. Dr. Crummell, investigated the matter and received from Mr. Matthews a denial of all charges of improper conduct on the part of himself or Miss Bozeman. The statement of the housekeeper, however, was taken and involved not only Miss Bozeman, but others.[9]

Mr. Matthews' side of the story.

Mr. Matthews stated to a STAR reporter today that great injustice had been done him in making public the scandal affecting him pending the result of the investigation which was now being conducted, at his own suggestion, to vindicate both himself and Miss Bozeman. He was convinced, he said, and his friends were convinced that the scandal, which was maliciously false, resulted from a conspiracy among certain persons to break him down in the community, he having at various times opposed these persons in their plans. Mrs. Alexander, he said, harbored an enmity against him, which she had now found opportunity to gratify. The whole fabric of the scandal rested on her testimony. The events which, Mr. Matthews says, she has distorted into a serious charge, were substantially as follows: He and Miss Bozeman had been invited to Baltimore to spend the Christmas holidays with friends there, and were to take a train Saturday night. Mr. Matthews was expecting a valuable fur-lined overcoat, which he had ordered from Canada, and which had not arrived. He made several inquiries at the telegraph offices to get word concerning the coat, and almost at the last moment determined to go once more to his lodgings to see if anything had been heard of it. On his way he met his two brothers, who had just come from Baltimore to spend Christmas with him and attend to some business here. The arrangement was then made that one of the brothers should return to Baltimore with Miss Bozeman, and the other should remain here overnight with Mr. Matthews. So one of his brothers went home with him, slept with him and went with him to Baltimore, leaving the house at 5 o'clock in the morning and arriving in Baltimore in time to breakfast with his friends.

His brother, being an <u>invalid, wore a waterproof cloak. Mr. Matthews</u> said, and Mrs. Alexander, in the dark in the morning, mistook him for a woman. [Words underlined by the reader.] Mr. Matthews remained in Baltimore till Christmas day, when he received a telegram from Mr. Grimké, his pastor here, to return at once. He returned and was made acquainted with the scandal against him.

He says that Mr. Carey expressed himself satisfied with the explanation made and retracted statements he had made, but subsequently, under the influence of other parties, insisted upon reopening a case. Thereupon the committee of investigation was selected. When the committee met, Mr. Matthews says, a number of the persons who were exceedingly hostile to him were present, despite the protest of his friends. Mr. Matthews said the committee decided to communicate with his (Mr. Matthews') friends in Baltimore to get their version of the affair, and he was under parole not to communicate with them in any way. He expects within a day or two the evidence of these Baltimoreans that will conclusively prove his innocence, and meanwhile asks the suspension of public opinion concerning the case.

The committee awaiting developments.

The members of the investigating committee say that they are unwilling to say anything for publication at present, but are determined to see that justice is done to all. Mr. John H. Brooks has interested himself on account of the names of colored school teachers being brought in, and intends to get at the facts if possible.

[Postal card from Louisa.]

Washington Jan. 22, 1883

Dreamers

All is well with me at present but if you continue to travel in this cold weather through fields of blooming flowers I cannot predict the end. I have been very busy, will write and tell you about it. Love to all.

Yours
Lulu

[From Louisa. Postmarked "Feb. 8, 1883"; addressed to "Ferry Road above Vanhook St., Camden, NJ."]

Washington February 8, 1883

My dear Genie

Have the dreams through flowery field continued? If you had seen me several weeks ago you might have traced a resemblance to your, or rather Ediths vision of me for I was sick and thin. Not badly enough off to send for you. To begin at the beginning of the chapter (which may prove rather tedious to you.) You remember when I last wrote you we were in trouble, our boarders not coming at the time we had expected them. Well, a kind providence did not desert us in the time of need. Mrs. Willis our friend knew how we were situated and set herself about doing what she could to help us. She heard of a party of seven who were coming here on a visit. She recommended our house to them. They applied for board and rooms. We knew of them by reputation, knew them to be moneyed people and very gladly accepted them for the two weeks. On finding our regular family were not coming until Feb, we made up our minds not to try and get the house in order until the latter part of the month. The weather was cold and the house large (16 rooms) for economy we were not going to have the servant until it was necessary. So when the application came we were not ready for the people and had but five days to get things in running order, and not least among our troubles was that of getting three servants.

To make a long story short, we go[t] through. The people came, had a nice time, and expressed themselves delighted with their accommodations. I had worked so hard that by the time they left I was completely tired out and sick enough to go to bed for several days. You would hardly credit how thin I grew in the short time. Now we are regularly settled with the family who are to remain with us until May.

I am feeling much better and anticipate a large growth in flesh. You always tell me to write about myself, I think I must have done it this time to your entire satisfaction. I am surprised on looking at your letter (the one that crossed mine) to find how far it dates back. Notwithstanding childie you have not been lost to memory. I need not tell you that marriage of mine of which you informed me, and of which I knew nothing about, was most surprising. I cannot imagine what gave rise to the report unless it was our looking for a small house for our own use. Tell me who told you, and if the unfortunate mans name was given. Will I tell you, you query beforehand should this more than doubtful event take place in my life. Most assuredly, would even bespeak you for bridesmaid, but I am too old for that. I was glad dear that Xmas spiritually was a happy season to you, and that your hearts desire is answered and satisfied in the new Church. Were it possible I would gladly accompany you to it sometimes, for I must own I am fearfully neglectful of my church and lacking in your deep devotional earnestness. I would I were as spiritually happy as you. I hope dear Genie you are rid of those troublesome teeth, you have suffered so much with them. Thanks for inquiring about the sets. I shall try and hold on to mine as long as possible. And so you think me very practical. Well—has not this world need of such people? They help to balance the visionary ones.

I do not like to anticipate future evil dear child but since some things belong alike to us all. I promise not to forget your generous and loving offer should sickness come to me. You do not fail to study the happiness of all in your household as the little surprise party to your father proved.[10]

My mother's birthday is on the 11 of this month.[11] I trust the next (God sparing her life) may be spent very differently, in a comfortable little home. She is far from well, seems so weary and worn. I gave her your love and you will accept hers in return. You will meet each other some day. I hope and feel the import of the message. I hear Charlie Chew and Louise have been sick. Have you been to the house lately? I suppose you have learned that the unfortunate report I mentioned in my last was only too true. You probably know the parties are married. Do you know they sent out invitations to the wedding and have since had a party. Only two attended it (the party). He went to church last Sunday for the first time with his bride. The church (Mr. Grimké's) was packed as if in anticipation of some unusual event. It was late when they arrived. Mr. M—[12] tried to go into his old pew, but it was full, so they were marched up to the very front of the church. Can you understand how she bore the battery of so many eyes of criticism and condemnation? If they had taken their disgrace with some show of humiliation, one might feel pity for them.

Mrs. Hawkesworth[13] is trying to have friends take her children that she may break up housekeeping. She thinks she would find work to do. Hers is a sad case. Strange to say, she still clings to her husband and speaks forgivingly of his misdeeds. Could you, would you, love like that? I am not made of such tender material. And so little Sallie Chew is married and settled in her new home. I can only hope it may satisfy and make her happy. I am sorry for her mother. She is in poor health and will be very lonely now.

Do you find yourself bearing without breaking your double duties?

Do not heed the grammar of the last sentence. I have not a bit of fresh news to tell you as I have not seen any of my friends for more than two weeks. Here I end with a good night, a good kiss and our Fathers dearest blessing. Love to the girls. And do you and Edith take very good care of yourselves for you are valuable people.

Lovingly,
Lulu

~⫯◎

[From Louisa. Postmarked "Mar. 19, 1883"; addressed to "Ferry Road above Vanhook St., Camden, NJ." Written on the top left corner "Burn this up."]

4 Lafayette Square
Washington March 19, 1883

My dear Genie

I was truly glad to get your letter and was on the point of sending a postal of inquiry when it came. You poor childie how sorry I am that your teeth cause you so much suffering. There will be I am afraid no permanent relief until you can have them thoroughly attended to. Received your paper and note last week.[14] Such an organ ought to be tared and feathered beyond all resurrection.

Sometimes you find a paper with a debasing love for Scandal but there will be something readable in it. The main price gives you nothing, only makes you ashame of your identity with a people who meet to scandalize each other and whose occupation according to the editors drawing is only that of hotel waiters of whose doings colored people are delighted to hear. The day is gone by for that sort of thing. I know we are poor and have not the wherewith to compete with the other race, for that very reason a colored man who undertakes to edit a paper should make its tone high and elevating, imbue it with a spirit of self respect that will make his readers reach out and struggle for something better than the old life. A life that circumstances have made possible, I will not say easy to improve.

I am truly sorry for the lady in the case. From things I have heard I am afraid the trial (should it take place) will be detrimental to her. The provication was great I admit; she remembered how her own sister had been treated. It is hard to have our loved one misused without retaliating when the chance comes. Christ did not so teach us I know. The poor human being are so slow and weak in our endevors to be like Him. I went to a Confirmation last evening where the class was 105. The dear old bishops voice grew tired and faint before he finished.

Louisa named Richard "Dick" Chew as a beneficiary in her will. (Library Company of Philadelphia)

Do not fear dear child that I shall influence you to think yourself better than you are. Where is the Christian who does not have to battle for the victory over self. I believe you are conscientious and strive to do what is right—who can do more? I saw Charlotte a few days ago. She has not been well for several months, very much troubled with a sore throat. You asked me about a certain lady having a party.[15] I do not know of anything the kind except an entertainment given to the "Art Club" which met at her house. She has two of her sisters children. I think her husband most kind to her relatives. He has even had some of the brother-in-laws debts to pay.[16] Dear childie you must not think I am in any way overworked. We always keep three servants, and the washing is put out except the towels and napkins. The trouble is in getting competent help, and the want of it leaves so much care and responsibility on me. Mother has been very miserable all winter and I have not been well. We are both better now. Poor little Louise I hope she is well again. I was sorry Dick[17] had in his grandmams absence to go to Fitzwater St. There are so many children there. To day is mild, really spring like. I was glad to hear that night school was over. You two children have had much to do. I wish by some mysterious turn of fortune's wheel we could all get some money. Idle wish! You must think of me sometimes this week. It is a solemn and and sacred season. Give love to the sisters and take a friendly hug and big (several) kiss for yourself.

Always lovingly yours
Lulu

[From Louisa.]

Washington, April 24, 1883

My dear Genie

I know you think me the very worse of correspondents. I did not mean that your dear letter with its fragrance of flowers should so long be neglected. I have not even thank you for the lovely Easter card. I was glad your Easter was a bright happy day. I wish that all clouds in your life might pass without any deeper shadow than the one that threatened your Easter morning. Tell you about my Easter you say, there is little to tell childie. A quiet walk on a lovely morning to a pretty church (not St. Lukes) where many flowers lifted their pure heads as if in joy and praise of the day. The singing was fine. I cannot say that the sermon touched me greatly. The holy sacrament carried home its lesson and I felt the divinity and blessed humanity of our dear Saviour. I love to dwell on the humanity of his character. His sensibility to human feeling makes Him so precious to the heart. His love is universal to all the race and yet his sympathy makes it seem particular to each one of the race. "Majesty of character meets in this with beauty of character." I am sorry to learn you are one of the bad children who want your bread buttered on both sides and even then ask for a sprinkling of sugar. As to that long ago letter it went to ashes, and then the picture, why child, I have not had any taken. When I do you for possession shall stand first on the list. I would liked to have seen you in bridal robes, hope some day to do so in a real sense. Your prince has not yet come. Of course he must be somewhere, in all probability getting together material to build his castle. I trust I do not trespass on his generosity by expressing the hope that said castle will will have a spare chamber that I may sometimes abide with you a day.

Much to my surprise I received a letter the other day from Willie Chew. I wrote him last though he seemed to think he had been neglected. I suppose he is at home now. It is better for the boys but his own health may suffer through it. I wish there was some good opening for him where he might make money. I can well fancy dear the weary monotony of the school days now. Keep a good heart. The rest is not so far off. In a measure I agree with your friend with regard to children and flowers. They are most lovely when you can select them to your taste. To test his fine sentiment let him teach for awhile a school like yours and see if his eyes and heart retain the same vision. To day our boarders leave; were to have gone yesterday but for the rain which fell for more than thirty six hours, and the clouds tell us there is more to come. I have nothing of interest to tell you. We shall stay on in this house (cannot say for how long to take charge of it. To me it is forlorn being in a large empty house. I envy you the companionship of a sister.

You cannot tell how as the Spring days come on I miss Delie. She used to say to me (long before she was ill) "Girl you will miss me in my grave." I wish I could plant some Spring flowers above it. Good bye dear heart, try and be kind to yourself. Love to the sisters. The same to yourself with some few kisses which are quite a different thing written from given. In this case the will must go for the deed.

Faithfully Lulu

[From Louisa. Postmarked "June 18, 1883"; addressed to "Ferry Road above Vanhook St., Camden, NJ."]

Washington, June 17, 1883

My dear Genie

It is a lovely Sabbath. I hope it is a happy day with you, that you have been to the little Church around the corner and found spiritual peace and satisfaction. Do you think I have been long answering your letter? I did not intend dear childie that the time should so slip away before I spoke to you again. I have had you in heart all the time and in mind often. I have been quite busy of late making preserves. You remember my telling you I hoped to do something at it this Summer. Not on a very large scale for you know business of any kind requires capital. Still, it will be the beginning for another year if I am spared. The prospect now looks favorable, we have a number of orders and friends who are interested promise their help in getting more. A lady here will introduce me this week to two of the leading grocers; and so I am hopeful of good results. I am very glad dear Genie that your freedom is so near at hand. I wish it was complete freedom from all care and vexations. No needles to ply, no planning to harass.

Will that day ever come to us dear? Not that I would be a drone, but there must be exquisite comfort in folding the hands when the body is tired and crying to rest. When I get a little bit well-off I mean to bring you down here; you shall do nothing but have one entire rest. Are you your sister Edith and the girls going anywhere in the vacation? I hope you will for the sake of change of air. Mattie Shadd and several of the teachers are going in their vacation to North Carolina to teach five weeks in the Normal School; then Mattie will go to Cleveland to see Sallie Coe.[18] I shall not go anywhere this Summer, so there will be no peep at you. I am sorry Genie dear I have lost my good friend Mr. Brockett.[19] He died two weeks ago. He was one of earth's best and has received I know a crown of glory. Thus one more link is severed from human friendship and human love, but I pray I may so live as to meet my aged friend in the hereafter. Have you been to Fitzwater Street lately? That was a sad affair about Miss A—what a pity!

Annie Purvis spent a night with me last week. Lottie and Mr. Grimké attended the commencement at Lincoln.[20] Mr. G. gave the address. Lottie spent a few days in Baltimore with Mrs. Bishop[21] and come home feeling better. She has not been well for a long time. Has Willie found anything to do? I trust he has. We are having very pleasant weather. My prayer is for cool weather for

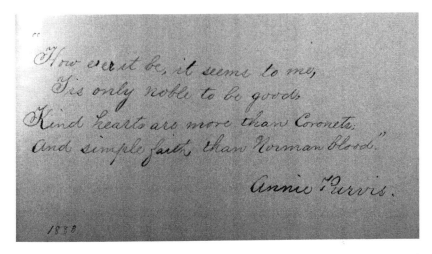

"How e'er it be, it seems to me, / Tis only noble to be good, / Kind hearts are more than Coronets, / And simple faith than Norman blood." Annie Purvis's autograph poem to Genie Webb, 1883. (AWWP)

I have warm work to do. Now dear girl I want you to spend the first week of your freedom in lounging. Carry out the word to the letter, be lazy and make your sisters do the same. Let the girls do the work.

Do not tell on me for fear they might use my rebellions against me. I know of the spirit that dwelleth in the young. I thought of asking Miss Martin (where I was last summer) if she would not like to have you, but I could not bring myself to be so cruel to an already overworked child. With love to all and a dear blessing and kiss for yourself,

I am always fondly yours
Lulu

[From Louisa. Postmarked "July 16, 1883"; addressed to "Ferry Road above Vanhook St., Camden, NJ."]

Washington July 16, 1883

My darling Genie

I am so grieved to hear you are so unwell. I trust that rest and change of air will soon build you up. Get out of Camden at once, at once, and let the others join you. I am afraid you are living in a very malarial part of town. I wish I might point you to some pleasant place to recruit in where loving hearts and hands would minister to you.

Do not get discouraged about yourself dear childie, you are only run down. Rest and change will bring you all right. At the same time you must eat all you can that is nourishing. You and Edith are good nurses. Do not slight the infallible <u>Beef Tea</u>.[22] I wish I was indeed coining money. I would divide with you. Nevertheless I am encouraged, which means hopeful. You know I am not selling any thing now but getting the things ready to dispose of in the Fall. I have had good success in all I have made. I get terribly tired at times. You know it is exhausting to be on one's feet from early morning until near evening, and much of the time over the fires. I feel the dear Father will give me strength to go through with it. Mother does all she can to help me, more than she ought to do. Another year dear I hope to be able to hire help. Now little girl about that picture. I cannot have it taken now but when I can you shall have it.

I have not time to half answer your letter. This is but a poor scrawl to tell you I love you and sympathize with you. Do not fear about Fitzwater Street. It is a long day since I had a letter from them. Miranda is owing me one.

I am glad you found our dear Delie's grave so well cared for. How her memory comes to me in these Summer days. Write me of yourself often if only a postal card. Mother sends love to my friend, and says, "take good care of yourself." Give love to the sisters. God love you dear, keep and strengthen you in the prayer of

Your loving
Lulu

[From Louisa. Postmarked "Sept. 13, 1883"; addressed to "Ferry Road above Vanhook St., Camden, NJ."]

Washington Sept. 11, 1883

My dear Genie

On referring to your letter I find it was written Aug 6, more than a month ago. You probably have thought me neglectful. If you could look in and see all the work I have accomplished this Summer you would say, "Poor old friend depart in peace, I cannot blame or chide you." Indeed dear childie I have worked very hard. Many a time it has been evening before I have finished, and I have been too tired to write. Sometimes I have been forced into writing business letters. Well, vacation is over and you are back in Camden. I hope you all returned renewed in health and strength. I have thought of you many times through the Summer; always with the hope that you were resting and happy, free and easy of all anxieties. I know you dreaded going back to the old school life. I think you told me there was a chance of promotion in your school. I trust it has fallen either to you or Edith. I hear that Rannie and Julia Venning are provided with schools. I am truly glad, and wish that our dear Delie had lived to see the day. I used to believe there was recognition with the spirits of the other world of what befell those whom they had loved here, but somehow the belief has left me. How could it be if Heaven is a place of perfect happiness? No, the discordance and trials of life would distract and disturb happy souls.

I wish childie you could peep into my preserve and pickle room. I have on hand enough to stock a small store. I have of current jelly alone two hundred and forty tumblers. I shall send out the engaged orders this month, and as soon as the rich people come try and get orders from them. I am some times distracted thinking of all I have to do this fall. I want to get as many things as possible off of our hands before the moving time comes. I hope it will not be before the last of October. I hardly think dear we will get into the little home this fall. We think of taking a house large enough to give suites of rooms to two gentlemen, we will breakfast them and they will dine at a hotel. Many live that way here particularly Congressmen. We will furnish ourselves, as we have a good deal of furniture of our own. <u>Next year I hope to do wonders at my business</u>; this is only the beginning of better things.

Mother has been very miserable most of the Summer. I wonder what sort of weather you have to day, here it is like November. There must be a cold wave somewhere. The Summer has been delightfully cool. You can't think dear child how thankful I have been, it has enabled me to keep up and do so much more than I could otherwise have done. I suppose you have seen Annie Purvis. Why is it you never go to Fitzwater Street now? Mrs. Chew[23] wrote us from Cleveland. She is delighted with the place and with Sallie's husband and home. May it ever be thus. Do not work yourself to death, for what will it profit you in the end? I would be glad to hear of your moving into a more healthy neighborhood for I cannot think your present one good. Give love to the sisters. God's dear blessing abide with you, is the prayer of

Your loving
Lulu.

[Enclosure in the above letter.]

Dear Genie

I open my letter to add that yours was received to day. Dear thoughtful and loving friend, I am quite well and wish your rest had given you more strength. Be sparing of it as possible that it may increase. I know you will say the worry of children is not fattening. True. Can't you make them awfully afraid of you? Do something to keep the little heathen under. I wish you had a good husband childie. Look on the bright side, something good will turn up yet.

Yours
Lulu

[From Louisa. Postmarked "Nov. 19, 1883"; addressed to "Ferry Road above Vanhook St., Camden, NJ."]

Washington Nov. 19, 1883

My dear Genie

I was truly glad to hear from you and more particularly so as you had not waited because your first letter was not answered. Genie dear, if you could know how busy I have been you would not chide me a moment for what might seem like neglect. When your first letter came I felt so sorry and worried over your condition, I thought to make time to answer you immediately, but the days came and went and I only thought of you though my heart was full of good intentions to send you a word of cheer and encouragement. I was glad to hear you are somewhat better—glad of your promotion but sorry if it brings you harder work. And the little sister[24] too has gone out an independent worker in the busy world. I am sorry she had to begin so early, but life is hard in its demands if we come into it without the traditional silver spoon. I know you have been miserable since you could not go to the little church. I wonder if you have ever tried hot water for indigestion, if not begin it at once. Sip it as hot as possible. Take a cupful before each meal. Put a very little salt in it (it makes it more palatable) and do not drink while eating. Give up tea and coffee. Drink milk if it agrees with you, but I would be sparing of drink of any kind, confine it if possible entirely to the hot water. Perhaps I may see you shortly, if so I will put you under a <u>rigid system</u> of treatment, and will expect <u>implicit</u> <u>obedience</u>. I have used the hot water with excellent result. It has become a popular remedy for Indigestion.

Well Genie, I have had good encouragement in my work both here and by friends away. I can see in it a good living for us in the future. Next year I shall I trust be able to work to better advantage as I shall be in my own home. This year, every things was unsettled and uncertain. Now, the beginning has been made and the experience gained will count me much another year. I suppose you want to know what I intend doing this Winter. Possess yourself with patience and I will tell you after awhile. I need a little rest and am going to pass a week or so with Mrs. Chew,[25] and the same at Fitzwater Street if convenient. I will try and arrange it so as to have two Sundays there (and will give you, (if you want me) one Saturday and Sunday. Thus you see the dream will in part be true. I think I will go to Philadelphia next week. I have yet a good deal to do. We will move this week, and I am not going to tell you where. I wish it was all over for it is getting Winter-like. Charlotte Grimké was here Saturday. She is still suffering with her eyes and head. She asked me to give her love to all of you when I wrote. I will let you know when I shall be in Philadelphia. In the mean time, begin the hot water treatment and be faithful to it. Give my love to Edith and tell her not to work too hard. She must think of herself sometimes as a duty she owes to that self. God bless you childie is the ever loving prayer of

Your friend
Lulu

One by One
Thy Griefs Shall Meet Thee
1884–1885

Genie is very sick. Her medical treatments include blisters on her chest, which leave her with oozing wounds. Lulu sends her bandage linens and gloves from Washington. Genie's cousin, Annie Purvis, leaves Washington in August to return to Philadelphia to care for her sick mother and for her grandmother Charlotte Vandine (Forten). Both die before the end of the year. Genie's unmarried aunt dies at the end of August, and Lulu assumes the responsibility of notifying Genie's other aunt in Washington. Genie's cousin, Charlotte Forten (Grimké)—almost always ill with debilitating migraines—makes plans to move to Florida, and Lulu suggests that Genie accompany them. Lulu is holding down both her Howard teaching job and the canning business in an effort to save enough money to rent a little house for herself and her mother. Adding to Lulu's burden, family friend Bailey Willis (1857–1949) and his wife ask to board with the Jacobses in the fall. "Bound by many ties," the Jacobses feel they cannot say no. By the end of 1885, Willie Chew and former U.S. senator Joseph Rainey have become coal business partners and are boarding with the Jacobses.

[From Louisa. Postmarked "Jan 6, 1884"; addressed to "Ferry Road above Vanhook St., Camden, NJ." Enclosed in the following letter was a small piece of paper. On one side, it reads, "Genie this letter looks crazy. What you cannot read make into something complimentary to your dear self." On the other side "Louisa M. Jacobs. / Howard University / Washington, D.C."]

Washington Jan. 5, 1883 [1884]

My dear Genie

I am sure you have looked for a line from me before this, and I intended dear child to have sent it sooner, but I know you will readily pardon me under

114

the circumstances. Well Mother and I did not meet until last Wednesday morning. On Tuesday I went to meet her but found she had not come. On Wednesday morning I went to a friends house where we have sometimes boarded, to see if she had been heard from. I found she had arrived late the night before and had gone out to telegraph to me, to learn why I had not met her. It seems she sent me two postal cards, one on Saturday the other on Monday, also a dispatch stating she would pass through Philadelphia Tuesday morning. As you know none of them had arrived when I left the city. In the meantime I was most anxious, anxious to know what detained her and also to get ready for the work. We are not settled yet. The weather is very cold, and the condition makes it so much more difficult to put things in good running order. I shall not be able to begin the sewing before Wednesday. We have been given very pleasant rooms. We have been obliged to remove our furniture which was stored in another building from the rooms first assigned us. I think we shall be very comfortable when we get to rights.

I have been going back and forth each day to the University.[1] On Monday we shall be so settled as to remain altogether. I wish dear you might be allowed to peep in upon us. Some day you will come Genie. Your precious flowers continue fresh and to speak of your dear loving kindness. I have not yet seen Lottie, in fact none of my friends. I suppose Fitzwater Street ended the holidays as merrily as they were begun. This is only a line Genie that you must know I am in the land of the living. I trust you continue to improve. Do all you can for yourself in the way of care taking. I want to know of you as a well woman, and a happy one too as far as possible. Give my love to the sisters. Write soon. Direct to Howard University. God bless you.

Lovingly
Lulu

[From Annie Purvis. Written along the right side "Annie Purvis."]

"Office Recorder of Deeds"[2]
August 3rd 1884
Wash'n D.C.

My dear Genie,

I fully intended my next or rather that this letter, should have been written from Phila, but I will change the old adage, and say that "Woman proposes and man disposes"[3] and it will apply to my case. I thought to have left for Phila.

the past Saturday and enjoyed being with my Mother and Grandmother[4] this lovely Sunday. As two of the Ladies of our Office are away the Deputy has asked me to remain until one of them returns as the work will get behind hand. So I am waiting rather impatiently I must say, as I am anxious to see Mother and I am tired, of writing, I really think I am looking thin and doleful—though I must say I am able to use my tongue yet and laugh too—I hope to leave Washington the middle or last of August, will send you word when I reach Phila.

Tell Edie I enjoyed reading and receiving her letter and think she is a good girl to write such a long one to me, and I am pleased to hear that you all are in so much better health than last summer—and I trust you all will return from your tour much benefitted and strengthened for the School Campaign.

As for Frank and Lottie not a line have they written. I suppose they are so much taken up with each other that they do not care to take the time to write for they both have plenty of ~~time~~ leisure. I find time has run out. Any how I suppose they are having a delightful <u>time</u> in Boston. I hope Lottie will leave her headache's and other troubles in Boston Harbor, or some other convenient spot. The weather here as a whole has been delightful, and Washington is charming as ever—though just now I am very anxious to leave its charms, and fly to "Lombard Retreat"—gaze on its beauties, and be fanned by its invigo-rating Breezes. You know something of this fashionable Resort, so I need not go farther with my description—nevertheless it is the magnet just now how I wish with Edith, that I had the cosey home she spoke about (a Brown Stone) how I would enjoy having you all with me. I do not dispair of having that happiness, and only wish the time did not seem so far off, when it perhaps, will be realized. I will "Hope on Hope ever."[5]

I think I would enjoy your daily routine, reading, writing, sewing, eating and sleeping, what are you reading that is interesting? I have several books to take home with me to enjoy with Mother. I do not get time to do any reading here—so will enjoy it all the more at home—only Grandmother will put rather a damper on my reading as she thinks it a great waste of time.

You have heard I suppose of the little girl who has made her appearance in the Fleetwood home[6]—both are very proud of her. Laura Hawkesworth's little one is well again I hear, and she is (the mother) looking very cheerful. I suppose she thinks her husband will return some fine day.

I have had two or three very pleasant outings, have been down the Potomac to a place called Glymont,[7] about 40 miles from Wash, I enjoyed the trip very much especially as I had such pleasant company. Then I have been to a musical party, where a part of the music was rather poor in my estimation—and last to a Dinner and I enjoyed the feast of good things in the shape of conversation, even more than the ~~seven~~ 12 courses of eatables.

This week I will go to see Mrs. Jacobs and Louisa, it has been a long time since I have seen them. Of course I know L is doing too much and will hardly be able to resume her duties in the fall—but what can one say, she seems to think they must make money—so will go on until she drops down. I know such work as pressing must be very exhausting. She and her mother are doing a good work at the Howard, yet I think that is too much for them. I just wish they could live in a pleasant home of their own—and we could visit once and awhile—Don't you?

Just received a note from Lottie, as she has written to you and Edith I need not say anything more concerning her letter except that I am much pleased to hear how much better her health is eyes and head—growing stronger. Life must be very pleasant to Frank and Lottie away from the Church and its cares—and L does not like the idea I know of returning to Washington.

Last night was to see Louisa Jacobs. Mrs. J has been sick, they are very busy with canning—and are now looking for a woman to help them—L. looks better.

How the time flys, here is the 5th 7th of August and your time with School will soon be opening. I often wish you and Edie would get married and not have that troublesome School work again—still all work has its cares and life seems at times so full of sorrow. Yet there is much that is cheery and bright, and we can gather up happiness and content if we only will. Do not think I am preaching. This letter has been written at odd moments, so is something on the order of the writer—an oddity—I must write to Mother, Lottie, and my little cousin Alice[8] so will have to say farewell for the present. Love to you all, and I hope to see you before long. Write when ever the spirits move you.

With love

I am as ever yours lovingly

Annie

[From Louisa. Postmarked "Sep. 1, 1884"; addressed to "Ferry Road above Vanhook St., Camden, NJ."]

Washington Sept. 1, 1884

Darling Genie

I carried to your Aunt Lizzie the note enclosed in mine. She has been quite ailing for a month or more. I will see that she and the rest of the relatives are notified of your Aunt Ann's death. Poor old woman, I trust she went hopefully to her rest.[9]

Elizabeth Webb (Iredell), Genie Webb's aunt, lived in Washington, DC, with her daughter, Sarah Iredell (Fleetwood). Louisa Jacobs was charged with the task of informing Iredell of her sister's death in 1884. (Library of Congress)

See dear how God in his own appointed time has lifted the burden from your shoulders. I am glad you are stronger and sorry the time has come to take up the strain of the old school life.[10] I am soon to do the same with so much of my other work unfinished.

Mother keeps poorly. I am very anxious about her. I cannot write a letter now but will during the week. Give my love to the girls. God bless you dear childie.

Ever lovingly yours
Lulu

[From Louisa. Postmarked "Sept. 29, 1884"; addressed to "Ferry Road above Vanhook St., Camden, NJ."]

Washington, Sept. 7, 1884

My dear Genie

I wonder if you are not sharing with me this very warm weather. If so, I am sorry as it will tend to diminish the little strength vacation rest has given you. Then to the death bed funeral of your aunt has been another thing to distress you.[11] It is all over now and there can be no sorrow that her life has ended since she suffered much and neither gave or accepted comfort and happiness.

My dear childie, there are no secrets in my business that I would not impart to you. Therefore, I feel rather mean in not writing to you about the jellies in the jelly line. Genie, I was so busy, you must forgive me. But, a word on the subject—as a guide for another year. Perhaps I may see before that time comes and will tell you all I know about it. In the event of not doing so follow these rules.

To all jellies, put one pound of Sugar to a pint of juice.

In making Current Jelly, let the juice come to a boil, then skim it well, having previously put your Sugar in pans to warm in the oven, as soon as you have taken the scum off, put your Sugar in. Stir it until it dissolves, then let it come to a boil and skim it well. I have sometimes found it to jelly on the spoon while scimming it—then I hurry to take it off and put it in the glasses. Current Jelly ~~only~~ only needs to come to a good boil after the Sugar has been put in. Other jellies I boil and scim well twenty minutes before putting the Sugar in and then from five to fifteen minutes after. You can test them by putting a little on a saucer to cool if it jells you may be pretty sure it is done. Do not make up too many good things or you will be giving all the girls Indigestion.

I trust your doctor by this time understands your case and is going to make a new woman of you. Your letter leads me to infer that you are contemplating new duties and if so you must be well and strong to undertake them. I want to see you happy, Genie. You know I am fond of Willie. We have always been good friends. He is a kind, generous-hearted man and I am sure will do his best to make the woman he marries happy. And yet, and yet—my darling there are many things to consider. But, why speak of them to a woman who has made up her mind to accept the conditions. Advice amounts to but little in heart matters. Get well, dear childie, before you dream of taking a husband and two children to take care of. I cannot help being sorry that the new life will begin with the responsibility of a family.

You have not gone through life on flowery beds of ease.[12] My love for you would have the way smoothed and sunned with many joys in the future. Willie's devotion to his boys proves how faithful and tender he can be. I wish he was better in health. I have been meaning for a long time to write to [him]. I sometimes feel badly that I do not write to the children oftener. It is not from want of interest—I trust some day to have more time. Mother has been very miserable all Summer. You can fancy my life has been busy. On the 10 I must go back to Howard with much of my work unfinished, which will have to be done between times. We must move the middle or last of October. The little house has yet to be found. When we are settled, dear, a load will be lifted from my shoulders and heart. Mother will be better I am sure. Rest and quiet is what she needs and cannot get as we are now situated. The doorbell is ringing so, for a time, good bye.

Read this first—
Sept. 28

My dear Genie

I suppose I ought to be ashamed to send you this old letter but I send it that you may see I am not altogether a fraud. Day by day, I thought to finish the letter and what must seem to you like neglect has laid heavily on my conscience. Dear childie—if you could know how pressed for time your friend has been, you would not feel to murmur. You know, I must go to Howard each day[13] and then work after I get home, frequently into the evening, after which I am tired and stupid and can only prove my love of you to myself in secret thought. I am near the end of the preserving and pickling so say nothing about working too hard. I have kept up wonderfully well. I spent yesterday doing up brandy peaches. As the day was warm that and the fire quite used me up, consequently I am not good for much to day, and am just resting. I am so sorry dear child to hear you are not well enough to be in your school, at the same time under the circumstances you wisely gave it up for a time. Lottie says she hopes to induce you to come down here. Do come, Genie. You shall have my shoulder to fall on as much as you want.

If you cannot come now make up your mind to come later. You know I will have a vacation at the Christmas holidays, and I promise to be very good to you if you come. I do not know if this will find you at Atlantic City or home. At all events I will send it to Camden. I believe the air of that town is not good for you, and cannot help believing it not quite healthy where you live. The land about you is marshy and low. The weather is Summer-like here. Rain is much needed.

I wonder what you are doing now and how feeling. Amuse yourself as much as possible. Good cheer is more than medicine for your complaint. My Industrial department will be larger than last year. I am sure you will be tired of reading all this. So, with a kiss, a big hug, and God's blessing, I take my leave.

Ever faithfully yours,
Lulu

~∰◎

[From Annie Purvis. Postmarked "Nov. 6. 1884"; addressed to "Vanhook Street, South Camden, NJ."]

Nov. 6, 1884
336 Lombard St.
Phila.

My dear Genie,

I have just heard from Uncle Thomas[14] that he met your father and he said you were not so well, I have been thinking about you every day and only wish I could be with you and try to cheer and strengthen you—

Though I must admit I am hardly in a condition to do much for others, the spirit is willing but the flesh is weak. So forlorn and miserable do I appear and seem to others beside myself that I am really ashamed. And, every day I say I will be brave and strong to day and still there comes the feeling of oppression and my strength of body and mind seem to leave me—

If I can get out in the air I am sure I will grow stronger and be able to see you all. Your comforting note and Dear Edies presence were indeed a great help to me Sunday—and how many willing hands and warm hearts have I not been surrounded with how beautiful to me is this Love and sympathy, and truly the burden seems lighter and the way brighter for so much affection—

I wish, dear Genie and Edie I could do something to help you, as it is I find I cannot be with you, and even if I was strong I see the work is marked out for me just here. Grandmother does not seem strong and is feeling Dear Mother's absence[15] more and more—and she looks so to me failing. So I must try to give what strength I have to her—

If you do not feel as if you could write to me—I hope Edie will as I am anxious to know just how you are. I am with you all often and I say over and over again how good the Dear Girls are to me. I am trying to be very brave and hope some day I will say He doeth all things well—"

Let me hear from you soon. I have received several letters full of love and sympathy—and I am better for their coming—my eyes are troubling me, and arm paining so I can't do much writing. Give much love to all the Dear Ones, and I trust you will soon be better—Is the wish and love of

Your Friend and Cousin
Annie

[From Louisa. Postmarked "Dec. 22, 84"; addressed to "Ferry Road above Vanhook St., Camden, NJ."]

2125 L Street[16]
Washington Dec. 21, 1884

My dear Genie

I know you think yourself an ill used childie. If you could look within my heart you would reverse your judgment. Scarcely a day has passed that has not brought some thought of you and self-reproach at what may have appeared like neglect to you. Genie dear if you could but know just how I have been situated you would not wonder at my not writing. To begin at the beginning of this chapter (and I will endeavor not to make the story too long).

You know how busy I was in the Summer, and how I had to go back to my Howard work long before the other work was completed. When I left one occupation it was to go to another, and many times continue it late into the evening. Mother did all, and more than she ought to help me. She was feeble, and the responsibility of the work was upon me. To add to our care the son of a family of whom you have heard me speak—I mean the Willis's came here in the Summer for orders, having secured an appointment from the Government in the Geological Survey.[17] We are bound by many ties—I may say obligations to his mother. When he heard we were going into a small home he said we must take him and his wife to board. To me this was not a welcome suggestion. I was tired of the boarding house life and wanted a quiet home of our own. I was sure Mother would not refuse him. He left us with the understanding of returning in November with his wife and we were to be in the home. The second week of October they wrote they were ready to come, were we ready for them. At this time we had not been able to find a small house such as we could afford to rent in a nice locality. Moreover I had not sent out one of my orders and knew it would be a great undertaking to move the things to another house. I advised Mother to write them we had not found a house, that if they must come then it would be best for them to board until we could find a house to settle them in. She thought it best to let them come to the Conn Avenue house,[18] that we might soon be able to find a house. Of course I felt this to be a bad arrangement, Mother not well and with so much to do, added to the additional care of two boarders. They were with us nearly three weeks before a house was found, and that not what we wanted. At all events we are here and must make the best of it. I did not move my Preserves and Pickles but went each day back and forth to the two houses, and slept at the former house nights. At last dear old girl I got so desperate over the conditions of things (after keeping up that kind of life for nearly four weeks) I had every thing moved here and gave up the keys. I could not have remained as long as I did had the house been taken. It has since been taken.

See how selfishly I have talked only of myself. I am truly glad to know you are improving and pray that the good work begun will go on until a complete cure is made. I regret you must go back to your school so soon. Oh! Genie what slaves necessity makes of us. I wish your old friend had means. You should not work for at least a year. I have been fearing you might conclude you could not come here for the holidays. It is too bad! Try and keep a good heart childie. Who knows what good things the future may bring you.

We have been having a few very cold and stormy days. After next Tuesday I shall have a short vacation for which blessing I shall be most grateful. I so much feel the need of a little rest. I wish dear I could spend a part of it with you. Genie you must not have that picture framed. I will frame it. I know you are under much expense and do not darling spend any thing for me. It is not right to. When you are rich you may bestow all you want to on me.

Get all the pleasure you can get out of the holidays. I have not heard from Fitzwater Street for a long time. It is my fault I have not written. I intend to this week. Give my love to the girls. And take much for your dear little self.

May you grow better each day, resting in Faith in the dear Fathers arms who is able as you know to help us in all our needs.

Good night, with blessings and kisses.

Always lovingly
Lulu

This is a poor scrawl, but I could not wait to do better.

Lou

⁓∭©

[From Louisa. Postmarked "Feb. 10, 85"; addressed to "Ferry Road above Vanhook St., Camden, NJ."]

2125 L. Street
Washington Feb. 9, 1885

My darling Genie

Am I never to write you a letter I think I have you now more quietly to yourself? I know it seems and to you needing love and sympathy that I do not come to you oftener. If the spirit might speak you would find me invisibly present again and again.

I am so sorry dear child that while you are gaining it is not faster. You must be of good cheer. The battle is not always to the swift. Yours I trust is the steady march eradicating the long seated disorder that is to make you a well new woman. I received the note sent to Howard and was relieved at hearing from you and was so sorry your poor body had to be tortured with horrid blisters. I wish dear I might beat up your pillows sometimes, sooth you, read to you, do anything that would give you comfort and pleasure. Space is a barrier to so much the loving willing soul would do.

I can hardly imagine you back in school. You are not fit for it. It is working against nature. It is so much better to give up entirely now while you have the strength to battle with your disease than to hope being better, and losing all the while. I was sick at home all of week before last but am quite well again.

This is not a letter dear but I know you would rather have it than no word from me. I promise you, and on good faith too to write oftener though it be but a line. If I can do any thing for you at any time, love me well enough to ask me. Give love to the sisters. God bless you dearie and give you strength of body and ease of mind.

Always lovingly
Lulu

─✥○

[From Annie Purvis. Postmarked "March 2, 1885"; addressed to "Vanhook St. near Ferry Road, Camden, NJ."]

336 Lombard St.
March 1st 1885
Phila.

My dear Genie—

Every day the past week I have looked for your bright smile—but no Genie appeared. Then I thought how tired you are after visiting the Doctor so I concluded to forgive you this time—.

I would have been over to hunt you, only unfortunately I caught cold. Was in bed Two days and not feeling very strong—move round in a rather forlorn way—

Wm. stopped to see Lizzie[19] last night Carrie was not well and Lizzie's neck and Foot are troubling her.

Hasent the weather been cold—I thought of you very often those very cold days and wished you did not have to journey across the River—

Maggie was down for a little while Friday and will be down Tomorrow I think—Caroline LeCount[20] I havent seen for some time—nor Inez Cassey[21] either—

Are you still thinking of taking your Baltimore trip—I wish you would and then go on down to Washington—Lottie and I would be delighted to have you—and I am sure the change would do you good. Perhaps you are preparing for the Inauguration Ball and wish to captivate the incoming President[22]—now do not be too gay—and do remember not to flirt too much—or some one near home may not like it—

My Uncles[23] are well and my Housekeeping goes along nicely—my woman so far has turn out excellant so everything is serene—My Brother Will[24] is not so well—has a cold as most everybody has—

I hope my Dear to have the pleasure of seeing you soon—if you are not well send me word and I will get over to see You this week—

Love to Edie and the Girls. Why don't they stop in and see us sometime—any how send a card telling me just how you are. With Love

Thy
Friend, Annie

[From Louisa. Postmarked "Mar. 3, 1885"; addressed to "Ferry Road above Vanhook St., Camden, N.J."]

Washington ~~Feb~~ March 1, 1885

My dear Genie

Are you getting stronger? I am so sorry you do not mend faster. <u>Take</u> heart dear, Spring is coming and will bring to you I trust new life. Your letter to me arrived shortly after mine had started. Do forgive me for not sending sooner the linen.[25] Poor child I am afraid you suffer much under what seems to me very severe treatment. I cannot bear to think of it unless the end is to justify the means. It seems to me you have given it a fair trial, if you have not improved under it, why continue it?

I heard a queer story the other day but do not give it the least credit. Mrs. Parnell[26] told me a young widower a barber was reported to have married in Camden and for some reason the marriage was kept secret. She said she and Mr. Venning thought it must be you and Willie. I told her I was equally certain it was not. I considered you too wise to marry in your present state of health. Is it not funny how one is arranged and disposed of by outside parties? You get well my childie and I will dance at your wedding. Genie I wish I had money. You should go to Florida and be at rest in mind. To express such a wish seems folly and yet with the foolishness comes some comfort to know there is the will and loving desire.

Washington is fast filling up with strangers to see old Cleveland[27] and his troops pass through. I fear the next four years will be turbulent years for the country.

Did you hear of the death of our young Greek (colored) professor at Howard?[28] He was ill only a week. When I see you I will tell you about him.

With the linen dear are a pair of gloves. They are not much. They were cheap but too small for me. Perhaps you can make use of them. Send me a line soon.

Love to the girls and dear Annie. I have been meaning to write to her. It was so sad the loss of her mother.[29] God bless you darling as always & my prayer. Faithfully

—◦◦◦—

[From Louisa.]

Easter evening
Washington April 5, 1885

My dear Genie

I hope you have been able to enjoy this lovely Easter Sunday. I was glad to be told in your letter that you are improving and pray you may go on from good to better. I had hoped to send this greeting to you in time for Easter but I could not dear childie. My mother was so ill last week I had my hands more than full, in fact I may say my heart too. She is improving and I think it will all be right with her. A week ago to day she was dangerously ill, and now on this beautiful day I am filled with gratitude that it is as well with her as it is.[30] I am glad dear you have a handsome Dr. His face may help you to bear with patience the torture he puts you to.[31] I cannot answer your letter now, and you will have to excuse this poor little scrawl. Give love to the sisters. With blessings and a kiss for yourself think of me always.

Yours faithfully,
Lulu

[Folded into the same letter is the following note.]

Monday morning

My darling Genie

Do not think I am not remembering and sympathizing with you. I have been so full of work my poor sick child. This is only a line as I am about to start for Howard. I will write this week. God bless you dear.

Lovingly yours,
Lulu

—◦◦◦—

[From Louisa. Postmarked "Apr. 21, 85"; addressed to "Ferry Road above Vanhook St., Camden, N.J."]

Washington April 20, 1885

My dear Genie

I hope the anxious time is over with you and the little sister is all right again. I have thought of you daily knowing your care. Poor dear children! It does seem hard that any additional care should come to you and Edith. There is a purpose in all of God's dealings yet their mystery puzzles our poor brains. I hope the Spring time will bring strength to you all and that your gain through watching and nursing will not be loss. You must try and go somewhere for the Summer. I wonder if it is entirely healthy where you were last Summer. Pray do not go back unless it is going to benefit you. Mother is much better yet far from being well. As for myself I am very tired and will be truly glad when my time at Howard is up. Not that I shall have so much rest but the strain will be less. We have to move in June. You know what that means. This is only a line dear that you may know you are with me in memory and love. God bless you.

Lovingly
Lulu

[From Annie Purvis.]

June 18th 1885
Phila. Pa.

Dear Eugenia,

Your card just rec'd, and I must tell you how sorry I am to know you are suffering so intensely from face ache. Have you tried Hope, and other warm applications?

I am feeling very much inclined to step over and see you, and if I could would be with you Tomorrow or Saturday. I chief bother is that Cathererine has decided to leave me, as she wanted to get a house, she expects to take her departure Saturday, and as I have so many things to look after, and not feeling just as bright as I would like to, I find my visit will have to be postponed and as you are going to be at home for an indefinite time I will hope to smile upon you the coming week. This afternoon Maud[32] came down and she and I took a walk on Chestnut St. to see the windows, then to her home. Mrs. C[assey] is still thinking very seriously of giving up her position Tomorrow—and how they will manage I can't see.

As I was coming home had the pleasure or rather uneasiness of seeing your Dr. driving Landau.[33] Love to the Girls—and do come in whenever you can. I hope your face is better. Lottie sent a note last week—she is still full of aches and pains.

Yours with love
Annie

[From Louisa. Postmarked "July 6, 1885"; addressed to "Ferry Road above Vanhook St., Camden, N.J."]

2119 K Street
Washington June 25

My dear Genie

I do not expect you have thought any very loving thoughts of me, nor could I blame you dear. I have been ashamed of myself. In the first place I never thanked you for the pretty lace you sent me. Please take my tardy thanks now, three kisses and a big hug. I am much pleased with it (it was so kind of you to make it.) I shall put it on a nice skirt.

I thought to write to you as soon as I finished at Howard. We moved just before school closed and when I was through there I had so much to do straightening things out at home, so I fell back on that dreadful putting off for tomorrow and tomorrow, all the time feeling my guilt. Nor am I going to write a letter now Genie, only a few lines as I am going to run down to Baltimore to-morrow and I cannot leave Washington without sending a word to you. I am going to B to look for jelly tumblers. I had some sent me from New York. They are not at all what I wanted so I had to send them back. I have been told there is a glass factory in B and if there is not I think I can get them cheaper there than here. I shall spend a part of tomorrow and the night with Annie[34] and do my business in B on Saturday and return home.

Willie was there last week but must have left before this. I am really happy at the thought of getting out of Washington even for a day. I so long for a little change. I hope dear you are trying to arrange to go away. I thought of you so much in those warm days, knowing how they taxed your strength. I have many things to say to you, and mind (truly) I will send them all to you in a letter next week. And now forgive me and love me as of old. And know that I am ever and ever your faithful and loving friend

Lulu

[The following letter is enclosed in the same envelope.]

Washington July 5, 1885

My dear Genie

I scrawled you a note on the evening of the 25th of June and the next morning as the note states left for a day or so at Annapolis. On leaving I said to Mother, "please mail these two letters for me," meaning yours and a business letter. I was gone longer than I expected, until Monday afternoon. When I came back I found I had sealed but not directed your letter and of course it did not get mailed. On Tuesday I went hard to work on Cherries and was busy all the week. You said at one time dear Genie you hoped I was not going to continue the business. I wish I need not, but it is an necessity and I must go on until I can do better. We are in a little home at last but rent day never fails to come. I hope you will be able and that very soon to come and see me. Mr. Grimké and Lottie were here Friday evening. You know he has a call to Florida.[35] I would be very sorry to have them go, yet I could not help thinking of you and feeling if they went it would be your opportunity. If change of climate is to help you I pray that the chance for it may come to you. It was sad about little Mattie[36] but the child is better off. I had written to Mrs. Venning before your letter came. I found Richard Chew looking well and in some ways improved. It is a blessing he can be with Annie.[37] He gets better care and better discipline than it would be possible in the crowded busy house in Philadelphia. I suppose Willie told you of his peep at Washington and how much he liked it, so much so that he thought it would be nice to come down here and go into business. I am sure he would not make a success of his business, there are already too many shops. This is a city where there is little to do outside of government work and teaching. I sympathize with the men and women in the Departments so many have lost their places. It is well enough for young men who have life before them, but is hard on elderly men with families who do not know where or how to turn.

You do not say anything more about moving. I hope you have not given it up. I am persuaded it is not healthy where you live. Have your father dear find you a better locality. How nice it would be if you could all go away and find yourselves on your return traveling another way to another home.

Ah! If fairy times would but come back. Are you forced dear childie still to have those horrible blisters? Do you need more linen? I can send it if you do. Tell me what the Dr sa[id] about you. Does he please you as much as ever? I never knew before that a man's handsome face could so impress you. I am going to enclose in this the stale small note that your heart may relent a little toward me. I never forget you dear Genie notwithstanding my neglect of writing. If there is any comfort in that believe it and know me always as your with sincere love

Lulu

~∰◦

[From Annie Purvis. Postmarked "Phila., Aug. 17, 85"; addressed to "Franklinville,[38] Gloucester Co., N.J."]

Sunday
August 16th, 85

My dear Genie,

I returned from the Country last evening found several letters awaiting me. Yours midst the number was gladly received. I was sorry to learn how poorly you have been feeling, hope the good fresh air will strengthen you.

I feel provoked to think of my not receiving your letter before so I could have sent the Envelopes—my Brother Will did not send my letters as he expected to see me come in every day this week.

I had a very pleasant time with the Sheble's and Cryers. Mrs. Wardle,[39] Daisy, Maud and I were the party that left Broad St. Depot (Thursday two weeks ago) for the Shebles. Mrs. W staid one night the children untill the next week, when Maggie took them home—

My Home—folks I found well, and much pleased to see me. I brought just one of the prettiest little kittens with me named after Uncle Tom. Today I have been trying to get my room in order the dust is over everything. It is pleasant to see Wm. Purvis again, and the old faces and places. The Uncles perhaps would not like to have me speak of their faces as old.

I would like very much to see you, and hope when you come in to see your Dr. again you will come to me too. Did you derive much benefit from the blister? You know we much suffer pain to enjoy the gain, and so I trust you will have health and wealth after your seige of medicines.

My love to all the Sisters. I hope they are in good health, and are resting and gaining health for the Fall work. Are you doing much reading? I have been so busy talking that there was no time to read—

You have no doubt heard from Lottie ere now so know how pleasantly she is located in Freehold L.I. I received a very pleasant letter from her. I am tempted to send it to you—she and Frank stopped only a few hours in Phila. on their way to N.Y. and Lottie's head was in a splitting condition so she was not able to go anywhere. I have not read the Abbies Temptation yet, as it is still at Carrie Cassey's. I shall no doubt enjoy and be benefitted by the "Sermon," especially if you commend it—as a whole Sermons are not in my order or liking—Now you will give up Annie P. and think her a heathen and I think if you do you will be in the right, for that at times is my opinion of her.

I am glad to hear that L. Jacobs and Mother are settled in a cosy home, yet fear Louisa will break down over those everlasting Preserves. My love to them both—

(Monday) I hope my dear you are feeling better this bright morning—the air is so fresh and I am feeling well—so am nearly happy. I wished myself back in the Country to day. I am satisfied even with Phila.

It is too bad to inflict such a letter on you, and fear it will not cheer you up much—its very looks are against it. Nevertheless—it comes from your Friend

Annie

Let me hear from you soon.

[From Annie Purvis. Postmarked "Sept. 7, 1885"; addressed to "~~Franklinville~~, Glouster Co., N.J." Written in pencil below the address "Kaighns Ave Camden Care John Webb, Hair Dresser."]

Sunday

Sept. 6th, 1885

Phila., Pa.

Dear Eugenia,

You have heard I suppose from Lottie, so know of their visit to our City. They stopped at the Jones.[40] Frank preached for Mr. Reeves Sunday morning & evening. They spent five days in Town. Lottie is looking better than she has for a long time and Frank looks well too. They regretted very much not seeing you—sent love to all.

The entire week has been a very busy one to me and pleasant too—only to day I begin with a headache but nevertheless I am going to talk with you—

I must first ask after the state of your health. I hope you are feeling better. I am wondering if you will remain in Franklinville now that the days are so cool.

I am afraid it will be too lonely for you. The Plaster I trust has put the heart in the best of order—

Now I will tell you why I have been busy. Thursday morning the Two Miss Somervilles came, and as Martha had gone to Atlantic City to be away untill the next day and I had a <u>thin</u> Dinner I had to fly round to add to my store. They remained with me until Saturday afternoon. We went out to see the City and enjoyed ourselves ever so much; they were much pleased with Phila. and I only wish I could have kept them longer their going has made me feel so lonely—

Mrs. Cassey sent my Trunk home yesterday. I intended going to see her but my head prevents my getting out of the House today—

You have heard of Julia Venning's marriage?[41] Her Mother I hear is much grieved over her marrying the way she did. I do not know any of the particulars, but feel so sorry for the poor Mother. I wonder why girls act so queer—

I am thinking of so many things just now that I can't write all I would like to—

I am wondering just now if you are in Camden with the Girls, for I know they, or rather think they are there so as to be ready for School Monday. How glad I am to think of the number of teachers who love to teach the young ideas. I know I am one who would not like it, teaching, in any shape—

Love to all the home folks. All are well with us. Uncle Wm. is in Altoona for three days. With Love and hope of hearing from you before long I am yours.

Lovingly

Annie

[From Annie Purvis. Postmarked "Oct. 9, 85"; addressed to "Ferry Road below Webster, Camden, N.J."; return address is "Mayor's Office, Philadelphia." Enclosed in the envelope is another envelope postmarked "Oct. 7, 85" from Washington, DC, addressed to "Miss Eugenia Webb, care Miss Annie Purvis, 336 Lombard St., Philadelphia, Pa." The envelope is open, but no letter is enclosed.]

Oct. 9th ~~18~~

Oct. 5th 1885

Phil,

Penna.

My dear Genie,

I enclose a letter from L. came the day after you were here. I am indeed sorry to have missed you each time you have stopped.

I have had a most charming time visiting the two Exhibitions,[42] of course I came home with a tearing headache—but a night's rest built me up—

I asked lots of questions concerning you of Uncle T. and Wm. B.[43]—they told me you said you were better. I fear your Dr.[44] has placed a verdict on the Teaching plan. Is it not so? He knows better than you, perhaps knows just how much you can stand. Did you stop at Mrs. Cassey's? I am going up there now to see how Joe[45] is. He has been ill. When you think of coming again do send me word for I am very likely to be out—

Love to all the Folks. Our carpets is down now and Kitchen stove up hope you did not catch cold in our cold Parlor—

Write when you can to Friend

Annie

Perhaps Lottie's letter has cheering news in it.

—◦

[From Louisa. Postmarked "Dec. 25, 85"; addressed to "1662 Ferry Avenue, Camden, N.J."]

Washington Dec 20, 1885

My dear Genie

Many have been my self condemnations for neglect in not writing to you, for writing only, not for thinking of you which has been much and frequently. I cannot explain to you dear how busy and how fraught with care my time has been for the last six months. True, the Sundays came when there was less to occupy me. I rose on many a one with full intention to write you before its close, but alas, it came and went, and you know the rest. Foolish child, to judge thy friend so <u>foolish</u> and narrow. I am neither too grave nor yet too old to give and to take a joke. I am sincerely and hopefully glad that you can give a better health account of yourself. The times have been hard with you dear childie. Let us pray that the gray cloud has passed and the tinge brightening sky will increase each day. Mr. Grimké, Lottie and I talked your case over before they left, and they both said they would try and find something for you to do in Florida. I am sure you ought not to teach for sometime to come, but if you could have a light occupation and the air of that climate, I am certain great good would come to you through the change. I speak of occupation because I know you would be more independent and it would serve to take you out of your self. I only trust something of the kind may come about.

Louisa Jacobs's friend Representative Joseph H. Rainey of South Carolina boarded with the Jacobses in 1885 1886. (Library of Congress)

Of course, you know Willie is boarding with us. Mr. Rainey and he are encouraged in their business.[46] It takes time to establish a business. Willie went to Annapolis this morning and will not return until to morrow morning. He will spend Christmas and a few days in Philadelphia. I will have a weeks vacation. I wish you could be with me.

May the season be peaceful if not altogether happy with you. Mother and I will pass the day quietly together. The thronged streets and gay shop windows bespeak holiday times. On the whole festive days are not very joyous with me, they waken so many memories of days gone by. Mine is not the one experience of the world. Few are the hearts that have not their sad corners, but the shadow should not mar the lovely Christmas fete. The day that brought so much of love and hope into the world. If all things work for good you will go to Florida, otherwise spend the holidays with me.

I may next year not return to Howard another year. I find the two occupations a little beyond my strength. I have not been well this fall, am much better and stronger now. You cannot think how much we miss Lottie and Mr. Grimké. They seem to be doing well in their new home. Give love to the Sisters. May the little rest so near at hand benefit all. Take good care of thyself and never doubt the interest and love of your old friend even if her stupid pen speaks but seldom to you. Good night and a good kiss.

Faithfully
Lulu

[Enclosed in the same envelope is the following note.]

Dear Genie

I mislaid your last letter and was afraid you might not get mine if I did not have the right address. To day I found it—the letter. I send a little basket with my love in it to you to day by Express.

I hope dearie you will have a Merry Christmas. I will think of you on that day.

Lovingly yours
Lulu

So Each Day Begin Again
1886–1887

Although she is not entirely well, Genie returns to teaching school in May 1886. In the spring of 1887, Lulu, who has been a tardy and apologetic correspondent, writes for the first time in almost a year. She acknowledges her error and Genie's right to not write first, but she feels it is not "as it ought to be between friends." She had intended to use funds invested four years earlier to give Genie a vacation in Washington; she had wanted to "act the fairy Godmother" but the investment failed. She writes of the serious illness of her boarder, James Monroe Trotter (1842–1892), the recorder of deeds. There is no evidence that Genie responded to this letter and there are no more letters for the next three years. During this time Louisa and Harriet manage the household of journalist Charles Nordhoff (1830–1901) until 1889, when they visit Edenton, North Carolina. Harriet, by now, is showing signs of senility.[1]

[From Louisa.]

Washington
Jan. 11, 1886

My dear Genie,

Have I not been long thanking you for the lovely calendar. Of course, dear—I take it that you sent it—though no line came from you to tell me so. Thanks childie with kisses. But, ought you to have sent; you who have so many expenses to meet?

Did you have a pleasant time on the holidays? I passed them quietly with mother. Willie went home to spend the time with his boys. I was hoping he would see you, but he said he was so busy negotiating for coal, each day part of going until his time was up. Did you get a little basket of jellies from me for Christmas? I sent you a New Year's card misdirected so you may not have received it. Cannot tell just the number now. I thinked I reversed your number 6162. You see how stupid I am. I am afraid you are having fearfully cold weather, it is very cold here and has been for three days. There is quite a deep snow on the ground. Oh! Genie, how the poor suffer at such a time as this. I feel to say so often—may God and good people help them.

I hope you are not trying to teach. Since you are better—Save yourself this Winter and by the Spring, you will be far better prepared for work. Do you have much time to read? I must look up something for you. Other peoples thoughts will direct you from thoughts of yourself.

I wish, dearie, that God's best blessing may rest upon you in this His New Year.

> "Do not look at life's long sorrow;
> See how small each moment's pain;
> God will help thee for to-morrow,
> So each day begins again.
>
> Every hour that flits so slowly;
> Has its task to do or bear;
> Luminous the crown and holy,
> When each gem is set with care."[2]

And now, good night. Sleep well and, if possible, dream of me sometimes.

Always lovingly thine
Lulu

~❦☉

[From Annie Purvis. Postmarked "Phila. Apr. 6, 1886"; addressed to "1662 Ferry Road, Camden, N.J." Written along the side at the top of the letter "Have you heard from Lottie? I haven't—Corrinne has her other child with her I heard."]

Sunday afternoon
April 4, 1886

My dear Eugenia,

I was just selfish enough to wish you had staid over the night with me, for I was one rather forlorn Annie Purvis Friday night—and felt how much good your presence would have done me—I was indeed sorry to have missed you, and sorry too I was to hear how your eyes have been troubling you. Martha thought you were looking better—but I know how much better you often look than you feel—and that is just my condition just now—I have just looked in the glass to see if my face doesn't look haggard but I find it rather round. All night and day I have had pain in my stomache. I was in Bed all day yesterday and slight diarrhea symtoms—and I must tell you how I think I was affected.

You know I have been going to learn the Flower work in the mornings—I noticed every day I would feel sick at my stomache. I thought being in a room with others or the glue used in some of the work hurt me, but on Thursday I found the sewer was out of order—and the air full of it. I told Miss Briggs it was dangerous for all them and the quicker they got out of the house the better—So I have left untill they get into another house—if I had not of left I would have been down with some kind of fever—a little Baby in the house has Gastric Fever—the Dr says comes from the sewer—I am so glad you did not commence the Flower work for you would have been ill in Bed. I like it so far very much and Miss Briggs said I got along nicely—

My Love to Edie, how is her finger. Well I hope. I thought if she was coming over to the Dr's, she would stop in to see me—I hope the Girls are well love to them. And when you can come and see me I have as usual much to talk about or rather to hear you—You must send me word when you are coming or I may be out—every bright day and I am well I am always out—Send a few lines if you can soon. Thanks for the Books lent and returned. I will take care of Mr. Tupper. What a dreary day, snow, rain & hail.

Ever thine
Annie

[From Louisa. Postmarked "May 3"; addressed to "1662 Ferry Avenue, Camden, NJ."]

Washington
May 2, 1886

My darling Genie
Here is only a line that adds God bless you and give you strength for to-morrows undertaking. I will indeed remember you in prayer. I am only sorry you feel you must go back to the school. If you have the strength to stand it, you

may not find it hurtful, you have been living alone in yourself and your thoughts too much.

If the children are not too bad, the change may not be altogether a bad one. Keep up your courage dear childie and our loving Father will help you through the trial. I have been sick in bed to day, hope to be all right by tomorrow. With a fond kiss and a heartful of love and sympathy, think of me always as

Your faithful and loving friend
Lulu

~𝄞◦

[From Annie Purvis. Postmarked "May 19, 1886"; addressed to "1662 Ferry Road, Camden, NJ."]

May 10th 1886
Phila. Pa

Dear Friend Eugenia

I have had you in my thoughts all the past week and wondering if you had the strength and courage to take up your School life last Monday—and if you did how you are progressing.

I would have written before only I was trying to get Mrs. Cassey to decide on going with me to see you the past Sunday. She was here Thursday night and I was to see her Saturday but the rain prevented my seeing her—Some bright Sunday we will pay you all a visit. It seems a long time since I saw you. or any of the Girls. I think they ought to stop in and see me sometime when they are over—

Just received a letter from Lottie. She has been ill. she says her head has been in a fearful condition—somthing like a rush of Blood to her head.

Frank is very enthusiastic over the new Church that is going to be commenced for him next month, he has raised considerable money[3]—and the people all seem to be united in doing all they can to help him—

I haven't seen anything of Corinne or the Saunders[4] for long time—

I do not know if this weather affects you. I seem to be depressed and headaches most of the time. I hope I won't get into Lottie's chronic state of aching—When the weather gets settled I am sure we all will feel better—I must really stop writing or I will give You the blues I am writing so dismally.

If you were here I would talk to you without ceasing, but I cannot write—So you will please take this as a suggestion of a letter—yet with Love and hope that all is well with you. Love to all.—

From
Friend
Annie

If you can do send a line telling me how you are.

[From Annie Purvis.]

May 19, 1886

Dear Genie,—

After writing to you, I placed my letter in the stand drawer instead of in the letter Box—so that is the reason you haven't heard from me.

I hope you are bearing up, and strong in your work, that is if you are Teaching—

We have had so many rainy Saturdays that I haven't been able to see you. Love to the Girls and do send a line saying how you are. This is only another suggestion of a letter—

I was out to the Park Yesterday. The mantle of green was lovely, the air delicious.

Ever your Friend
Annie

[From Louisa. Postmarked "Dec. 31, 86"; addressed to "1302 Broadway, Camden, N.J." Undated, not in envelope.]

My dear Genie

Put the contents of the little box on your beadroom mantel. Next week I will send you a small basket with some jellies. Thanks for your dear letter. God bless you. Excuse this bit. In haste.

Your loving friend
Lulu

[From Louisa. Postmarked "Mr. 24, 87"; addressed to "1302 Broadway, Camden, N.J." Written across the top left corner "Pardon the many mistakes of this."]

2119 K St.
Washington March 20, 1887

My dear Genie

I suppose you will not send me a line until you receive one from me. I do not know that that is as it ought to be between friends, but this I know I ought to have written before this. You see with me it is the old story of neglected duty and love. I have apologised many times for this bad quality of my nature, and so will not weary you with a repetition. There is no time when I think of you more than at present—the Lentent season. Though you cannot be so active as formally at this season yet I know the devotion of your heart is the same. You may feel the lack of the music and the inspiration that the church seems to inspire, but dear, one can get very near to God without either if the love and faith be there.

Are you not better Genie? This is a trying month for those who are not strong and well. Mother was very ill last month with congestion of the lungs. For several days her case was critical. She has not recovered her strength yet.

Genie I have been nursing some pleasant plans with regard to you, but like most anticipated joys they will prove a vision without substance. I made an investment some four years ago with sanguine hope. It prove a failure at the time though there were bright features about it that promised success some day. Stockholders were called together the beginning of the Winter and encouraged to believe that their investment was coming out all right, in fact would be in operaíion before the end of the season. But the end came without the fulfilment. Nor do I know that it will ever amount to any think. If it had proven as I had hoped it might I was going to try and induce you to come down here for a couple of months this Spring. Though I have not room in my home to accommodate a friend, I intended to find a pleasant boarding place for you where I could see you every day either at my home or yours, and I dear was going to act the fairy Godmother.

But alas! Alas! We are full of anarchy at present as we have a very sick gentleman in the house. Mr. Trotter[5] the new Recorder of deeds. He came to us as a boarder last Thursday evening. He was taken ill that night, and has since been very ill with pneumonia. He has a trained nurse which is of course a great relief to us. Then his wife who had been telegraphed for arrived yesterday. You know what an insinuating disease pneumonia is. The patient was better this morning but not so well to-night. I trust it is not going to be fatal. It seems so hard. He has had his position only a few weeks, has a wife and three children. You probably know from the newspapers what a fight there has been over the office of the Recorder of Deeds. The President was determined a colored man should have it. They would not accept the first man of his choice and so he gave them a second.[6] My prayer is that this man may live.

I saw Willie this evening. After he and Mr. Rainey failed Mr. Matthews the former recorder got him a place in the Government printing office, he is there now. Richard seems to be getting on very well at Howard.

It is a stormy night. I just stopped a moment to answer the door bell. I found the ringer an offensive newspaper reporter. They are certainly impudent and annoying.[7] Genie dear send me a few lines and do not be hard on your poor old friend. If you lived with me or near me you would never have cause to complain of lack of love in me nor would you if you could only read my heart at this distance you would be satisfied with it though it does not greet you often by way of letters, yet is it live and loving. Give my love to your Sisters, and take much for yourself dear childie.

Lovingly
Lulu

Hours Are Golden Links
1890–1911

Although it is likely that Lulu and Genie visited each other between 1890 and 1894, there is only one extant letter from Lulu. In it she tries to comfort Genie with thoughts of God's love. This lacuna coincides with Harriet Jacobs's health problems—pneumonia, breast cancer, lameness, and senile dementia—and with Louisa's difficulty in finding work during the Panic of 1893–1894. Letters from her Texas cousin Frank J. Webb Jr. (1865–1901), a medical student in Washington, both support and urge against her inclination toward self-sacrifice.

By 1895 Genie is living in Philadelphia and has mortgaged the Franklinville, New Jersey, farm that she had possibly purchased from her father. Just as Lulu did, she is managing a canning business. She sends farm vegetables to Lulu and appears to be in better health, although all of them—Genie, Lulu, and Annie Purvis—are in dire financial straits. There are no letters from 1896 until 1900—after Harriet Jacobs has died and Lulu has obtained a position as matron at the National Home for the Relief of Destitute Colored Women and Children.

In 1901 Lulu travels to North Carolina to try to settle a nearly fifty-year dispute over the property that had once belonged to her great-grandmother Molly Horniblow, who died in 1853. That property had been subsequently occupied, and was presumed to be owned, by Molly's son Mark Ramsey, who died in 1858. Mark's wife, Ann Ramsey, continued to live in Molly's house but the white executors Molly had appointed legally owned it: Josiah Collins (1808–1863) and Dr. William C. Warren (1800–1871).

In 1859 Harriet Jacobs had asked Josiah Collins about the legal status of her grandmother's property, and he responded that he and Warren would renounce any "copper" of the estate and that he believed that Molly had intended her property, now encumbered with debt, to go to her son. Collins mentioned the "question of an unadjusted exchange of Land" that might require "some interference" on his part. Molly Horniblow's will would not actually be proved until

144

the fog of war was lifting in December 1865. Harriet Jacobs visited Edenton in the fall of that year and visited once again in April 1867, presumably both times to establish ownership of Molly Horniblow's property. Harriet described her grandmother's place to Ednah Dow Cheney: "I felt I would like to write you a line from my old home. I am sitting under the old roof, twelve feet from the spot where I suffered all the crushing weight of slavery." Six months later she told her friend Julia Wilbur that she owned the Edenton property but had "no desire to make her home there." In 1870, in a murky transaction with no record of a dated deed, the property was purchased in the names of the three older children of Robert G. Mitchell (1835–1904).

In late 1888 a new deed was issued to the Mitchell children. Harriet and Louisa Jacobs returned to Edenton in early 1889, perhaps pursuing their interest in the property. In 1890 an undated deed to the Mitchell children was discovered and offered for probate and registration, and then in 1901 the Mitchell family moved from Edenton to Elizabeth City, North Carolina. The 1901 divestment of the Mitchells' Edenton assets might have precipitated Louisa's final visit to Edenton and her last effort to recover her great-grandmother's property.

In her late sixties by now, Louisa's bitter indictment of the white South is all the more scathing considering that she had lived her beliefs with tolerance, faith, and hope. The woman that the Willis family had always known—that "peaceful, quiet, cheerful, sweet, refined, intelligent" lady who passed "simply on without a murmur at the injustice of man"—returns from Jim Crow Edenton feeling the full force of the South's injustice.[1]

In 1903 Lulu changes jobs and becomes matron at Miner Hall at Howard University. She spends summers with the Willis family in New England, and after her retirement at the age of seventy-five, she moves to Brookline, Massachusetts, to live out her final years with her dear friend Edith Willis (Grinnell).

[From Louisa.]

1900 R St.[2]
Washington, April 4, 1890

My dear Genie

Why is it you never send me a line nowaday? I do not look for long letters knowing they are wearisome to you, but a line, two or three lines would suffice that I might know I was not shut out from your thoughts and love. I know my darling your way has been made hard through sickness. Do not look at the pain alone. To you who might teach me lessons of Christian fortitude and devotion to the cause of Christ let me quote to you. "Behold I have refined thee, but not with silver; I have chosen thee in the furnace of affliction."[3]

> Be patient suffering soul, I hear thy cry.
> My trial fires may glow, but I am nigh.
> I see the silver, and I will refine
> Until my image shall upon it shine.
> Fear not for I am near thy help to be;
> Greater than all thy pain, my love for thee.[4]

Dear heart strive to let the thought of mighty love comfort you. You have had a strange uncertain winter which has not been cheering to one not well. I hope as the spring advances it will bring fresh courage and strength to you. I called on Lottie the other day and found her suffering from one of her bad headaches. She was much better for a long time after her treatment in Philadelphia. I hoped she was mending permanently. I trust the sisters are all well. I will think of you lovingly on Easter. May it be to you a day of peaceful hope, free from pain filled with the glory of a dear loving human Savior whose divinity is shaping us I trust for an eternity with bliss in the hereafter.

Ever lovingly yours
Louise

~∭©

[Frank J. Webb Jr. to Eugenie Webb, from Genie Webb's autograph album.]

To My Northern Cousin

The Highest Law tells us many things, but it tells us one very plainly. If we seek happiness in making others happy we most surely attain our aim. Your life exemplifies this law—the self-sacrificing are the happiest after all. As the years roll by may they bring a fuller and more complete realization of your most youthful dreams.

Yours
Frank J. Webb Jr
Texas
Howard
Washington 1893

[Frank J. Webb Jr. to his Webb cousins.]

Treasury Department [stationery]
Office of the Third Auditor
Washington, D.C.

Sept 1st 93

Dear Cousins:

Hope you all won't measure my general courtesy by the delay. I am or rather was compelled to [unreadable] in writing you all. Have only just returned to the city and am writing you all the first thing. Hope you all enjoyed still the blessings of health. Am so sorry I could not return to Camden and bid you all good bye before I returned to Washington. I so missed my two cousins who did not come to the depot.

Tell Mr. Bollivar[5] I was very sorry I failed to meet him. Trust to have better luck next time. You all, dear cousins must excuse this brief [conjoint] epistle, but time will not permit otherwise. The many little loving kindnesses I experienced at your hands you can now rest assured will not soon be forgotten by

Yours Affectionately

Frank J. Webb, Jr.

I sincerely trust that, at least one of you will drop me a line soon.

[Frank J. Webb Jr. to Eugenie Webb.]

Washington
January 18th '94

Dear Cousin:

Your very kind Xmas letter together with its contained pleasing remembrance were welcomed gratefully. Such unmerited evidences of your esteem and thoughtfulness is most heartily appreciated by your Texan cousin. Am at best a poor hand to make Xmas gifts. It is always too much trouble to select suitable presents even when one has a bank account sufficient to meet the requirements of an aristocratic taste—which has come to me naturally I reckon. Am sure it—no not one iota of it (a sentiment in which I am sure I am joined by my cultured cousin "Blink"[6])—has not come to me by cultivation—or from my Texas environments.

Sincerely trust the New Year has opened auspiciously for you and yours. Again it is my hope that you all may prosper during all this and succeeding years as you all have never prospered before. I wish you health and strength and all the blessings of earth, dear cousins.

If you let every dawn of morning be to you as the beginning of life and every setting sun be to you as its close, you will be astonished at the wonderful happiness you will experience. If you do this, everyone of these short lives will leave the sum record of some kindly thing done for others—and some strength or knowledge and something worth having for yourselves. None of us can live and prosper alone by ourselves. Again it is true that a constant life of self sacrifice is not what is required in this workaday world of ours. At this moment Shakespear comes to my rescue and in his language I quote:

"To be or not to be: that is the question. Whether it is nobler in the mind to suffer the slings and arrows of outrageous fortune. Or to take up arms against a sea of trouble.

And by opposing end them? etc. etc."—you can read the rest. They bring out my idea. While it may be good and charitable to endure the ills of life uncomplainingly I can never see it. My grief can never be like my sorrow—silent and uncomplaining. Others must hear me. All I can I'll make the [wel———] ring. Well, I can't say just exactly <u>what</u> word has caused me to scribble the foregoing. If it is intelligible make the most of it—am sure its all true.

Our Xmas here was passed reasonably well. I can't complain: wouldnt if I could: it wouldnt better it I am sure. Got 15 or so pretty remembrances. Gave eight principally to those who remembered me the first Xmas I spent here and a few of those who have been kind to me since I came here a stranger. My slender purse would be totally inadequate to even partially reward <u>all</u> of those upon whose kind friendship I've come to rely. It is, even to me, more than passing strange that I seemingly am so surrounded with people who I gladly call friends. I am sure I am very quiet and reserved as a general thing—not given to prepossess those who are merest acquaintances, yet I count those as friends only who to me are satisfactorily so—have proved it someway sometime.

Am going to write your Father[7] soon. Am sure he owes me a letter, but as I wish to hear from him very much again I'll write next week. Is he at Reading? How is dear Mame[8] and her babies? How I would like to hear from her or her husband occasionally.

Rev and Mrs. Grimké are both well—at least she is as much so as customary. She complained of not hearing from Blink when I last met her—I think it was at a reception at Sadie Gaskins during the Holidays. I passed creditably my midwinter examinations most fortunately for me. By passing my Chemistry I secured entrance into the Senior Labratory—something a considerable number of my classmates did not do—much to their discomfiture and my sorrow. Outside of that excitement and a housewarming at Gov. Pinchbacks[9] there was nothing of notable interest transpiring here during the Xmas. I called on New Years—made about 35 calls—all I had time to make and spent a reasonably enjoyable day.

Heard from Mother yesterday.[10] She was well and doing prosperously. How is Ada[11] getting along? I trust well. Why dont she take some of those civil service examinations? As she knows her Congressman, there would be but little difficulty in getting a tolerably lucrative position here in some of the departments. If she desires to take her examination tell her to write me and I'll fix the matter up for her as best I can.

[unreadable] write me soon. Tell me the news—all about yourself and the girls, about Uncle John,—how he progresses, his health and activity—how Mame is and dear little fat Webb and Pudge—sweet, rebellious bossy "Pudge"—and her genial Papa.[12] Remember me most kindly to Mrs Hinton[13]—the dear old soul to say so many nice things about such a degenerate son of a noble sire[14]—but who redeems quite a lot of his discrepancies by being Your Loving Cousin,

Frank J. Webb, Jr.[15]

—◊◉

[From Louisa. Postmarked "July 17, 1895"; addressed to "~~803 S. 20th Street.~~ 920 S. 16th St., Philadelphia, Pa."]

1538 Pierce Place[16]
Washington, July 17 [1895]

My dear Genie

I really and truly am ashamed not to have answered your dear letter before this. Oh! Childie I am very bad and you must just make up your mind to keep on forgiving me. And to make matters worse I have mislaid your postal and so do not know how to address this. I must venture on the Phil. address trusting it may find you. My first duty is to congratulate you on being a real estate owner. It has its charms, likewise its burdens. I hope the investment may prove of value and the way open to you to pay off the debt without great anxiety. I am so situated dear that a change would be quite impossible for me now. I intend this Summer to do a little at my preserving. I cannot speak for the fall.

I begin to find it wise to live each day and not borrow on the future. Enough without anticipation will come at the time to worry and perplex. Have you any boarders? Does it pay? It is hardly worthwhile child to work yourself to death unless there is some profit behind it. I hope you have not given up your cash work. It would be most unwise it seems to me. A dollar in hand is worth many in prospect. The farm may not give you a living at first, and even if it should the debt you must keep before you and lay by for. Lottie and Mr. Grimké have two weeks for their vacation. They will go to the western part of Massachusetts. I long to go somewhere too but alas! Mother continues feeble. This is a mean little letter but if I wait to write more it might not go to day. Give my love to dear Genie. I meant dear Edith, but here is love for both. May each grow strong and their country home prove an advantage and blessing. Write and tell me how matters go with you.

Always your loving friend
Lulu

⤳∰◎

[From Charlotte Forten Grimké. Postmarked "Aug 26, 1895"; addressed to "Miss Eugenia Webb, Franklinville, Gloucester Co. New Jersey."]

1524 Lombard Street[17]
Philadelphia, Aug 26, 1895

My dear Genie,

We have received your letter, and are very glad to hear from you at last. It has been a long time since we have heard from you. I have not known what to make of your long silence. But I know you are not well, and I am so much of an invalid myself that I can sympathize with others who suffer. I have had to give up much of my own correspondence. In regard to your request that Frank and I, or at least Frank, —if I could not,—would come down and see you, I will say that we wish very much that we, or he, could do so. But I will tell you, frankly, dear Genie, that he really cannot afford it. He has not the money to spare. We have been at a great deal of expense this summer for while we have been boarding up in the country in Mass., we have been at the same time keeping up the rent on our house in Washington, (we have no parsonage,) and also paying some one to take charge of it in our absence. It has been more than we could afford but our health imperatively required a change. It has left us very much straitened financially;—for Frank's salary is paid so irregularly, that we cannot place much dependence upon it. We are very sorry but that is the true statement of the case. And Frank wishes me to ask if you will not write to him in regard to the matter about which you wish to consult him, and he will gladly give you whatever advice or information may be in his power. You had better direct your letter to Washington.—1526 L St. N. W. as we shall be obliged to leave here Thursday afternoon or very early Friday morning. Frank is obliged to be at the church next Sunday, and must have a few days at home before.

I hope you and Edie are as well as usual. I should think it would be much too lonely for you down there in that dreary place, and hope you will come to town, where your friends are, as soon as it gets a little cooler. We shall be glad to have you and Edie make us a visit in W. when ever you can come. Just let us know, and you will have a warm welcome.

Frank is pretty well; but my little vacation in the country has not benefitted me as much as usual this year. My head has ached constantly. Yet the air was delightful, and the scenery, among those Berkshire Hills, most lovely. I must stop now.

Frank joins me in a great deal of love to you and Edie. We shall hope to hear from you very soon.

Ever your affectionate cousin
Lottie

[From Annie Purvis. Postmarked "Nov. 19, 1895"; addressed to "Franklinville, New Jersey."]

3045 Fontaine Street[18]
Phila., Pa
November 18, 1895

My dear Genie,

We, that is William, Lizzie, and I, are sitting around the Table this evening. W. is getting over one of his sick headache's. L.C.[19] has just returned from her trip down Town, and as she was away several days, we were more than glad to see her.

Your letter was read with much interest, and Mrs. Cassey and I decided you must indeed be a Hustler from the amount of of work you have managed to get through with, and I am so glad Edie keeps well. Give my love to her. How very much Lizzie and I would like to walk round the Farm with you Girls and, of course, have a chat with the Justice. I fear he would be much disappointed when he looked upon my not very bonny face. I am glad he is better.

You are very good to want to come down and if I could come, what a real good time we could have, but I fear it can't be, our money affairs are still in a tangle, when they will get out I can't say. Yet, I do not want to burden you with my many vexations, all just now due to that important thing called money. They say that all things come to him who wait's. I feel at times as if I had waited a hundred years allready.

So Dear, If I can't come to you, Why you must come to me, bring your Baggage along and Gentle Annie will see what she can do in the way of nice little Dinners and Teas to soothe your tired spirit—for tired you must be, body and mind, has been, I know, going at a great pace this Summer and a rest will be the thing most needed.

Was'ent you surprised to find all New Jersey Republicans? I do not know what party gained in your neighborhood. You are, I expect, so superior to many of the men round your way that they would all like you to run for Justice against your old Friend.

I haven't seen Blink or Ada since I last wrote. I really haven't been anywhere's. Have you heard from Lottie lately!

Mrs. Cassey joins me in love to Edie and you, and she hopes you will both come to the City before the cold weather sets in. Did you receive the little fashion paper I sent. I cant write more tonight. With love to you both, I am as ever your affect,

Annie

[From Louisa.]

1538 Pierce Place
Washington, Sept 27, 1896

My dear Genie

A more faithful tender-headed forgiving soul than you cannot be found. I have been ashamed of myself at the neglect of your many kind thoughts of me.

But Genie dear I am the same Lulu in heart as of other days. Work and care have made me stupid at letter writing. Not from one moment has my silence been from indifference or want of affection. When Laura[20] brought your donation of vegetables, I could not help laughing and saying, "That is just like Genie Webb." It was sweet of you to send them and most kind of Laura to bring them. I enjoyed them and pronounced you a good farmer. I hope dear you will be able to sell all your product and thereby make some money.[21] I know you are having a hard pull and I need not tell you my sympathy is with you. A fellow feeling Genie "makes us wonderous kind."[22] I know about the hard struggles the anxious thoughts we pillow at night and that rise with us in the morning. Some lives are so shadowed but the curtain will rise some day, if not here in another land where weariness and care do not enter. So let us be hopeful and never turn aside from the little glimmers of sunshine that meet us here and there on our way.

Mother is improving, but slowly. I doubt if she ever walks again.[23] If she could read or do anything to amuse herself her condition would not be so hard. How much longer will you remain in the country? Now that your health is better I wish you might get back to teaching. Have you ever made application? Perhaps when we have a new administration you might know some one who will be in power who could help you to get a government place.

I have two rooms to rent and daily live in hope of some one wanting them. I saw Lottie yesterday. I never saw her looking better, though she was not feeling quite well. Mr. Grimké is getting a great deal of pleasure out of his Bicycle. Lottie is learning to ride. I think it a good thing for her. I hear that Edith's health is better. I am glad you have the comfort of having her with you in the country. Are you able to meet your payments on the place? I am interrupted now so I must leave you for a time.

Wednesday evening

Dear Genie

I began this three days ago, each day I seemed not to have had the time to finish it. Last night we had a terrible wind storm.[24] The city is sad to behold. Many houses were unroofed, business places suffered damage and the streets are blocked with broken trees, many of them uprooted. I could not live in some of the states that are subject to terrible storms. The people must always be apprehensive of sudden danger. And now dear childie I wonder if you are resting from labor. Yes, you must be for it is near nine o'clock. No doubt you are tired and so am I, and in mind we will reach out hands and say, good night, and I will give you a kiss. Give my love to Edith. To you I say never doubt me. No matter how silent may be. I am always your true and loving friend

Lulu

~∅©

[From Louisa. Postmarked "Nov. 27, 1900"; addressed to "920 S. 16th St., Philadelphia, Pa."]

Washington, Nov. 25, 1900

My dear Genie

I think I hear you say, "Well Lulu goes from bad to worse." I cannot dispute you since I must be honest enough to acknowledge the charge. I was glad to hear from you to know that the caps were a success which should have been made manifest by immediately sending the money for them. I supposed you you received a package from me last week. I hope dear childie you will be able to make use of the things. I thought the black material would make you a warm every day dress. The gay skirt had been laid by for a long time. I had an over dress like the poplin on the skirt, it was not made to suit me. I wore it twice and gave it away and kept the under skirt thinking some day I would match it and make me a suit. Now since over skirts are being worn it can easily be done. The other dress is one I began to fix for myself and never finished. I sent it dear hoping it might be of some service to you near Spring. I wish I had had the time to put it in complete order.

I hope dear the world is using you well, that business is brisk and that the tide runs in the right direction every way. No, Genie I did not write to the Jones.[25] I ought to have done so. I do not know their right address thought I might have got it from the Dr. Tell it to me when you write. This is my Sunday off.[26] I have a cold and am not going out but just resting. Dear Annie Purvis must think me mean. I have not sent her a line. Oh dear! When will all my wrongdoings be righted??? Well any how the presidential election went right and we are settled for another four years.[27] Hope the president and his party will do something in the interest of the colored man.

I hope Blinkie[28] is quite well again, also your father. I am sorry you are not going to move. Do try and make yourself comfortable. Did you go to the farm again? This is a typical November day though we have had lovely days this month, sunny and Summer like. And now dear with a kiss and a God bless you I will say good night.

Ever yours
Lulu

~∰○

[From Louisa. Postmarked "Dec. 3, 1901"; addressed to "920 S. 16th St. N.W., Philadelphia, Pa."]

Washington Dec. 1, 1901

My dear Genie

The day is lovely. I have seated myself for a little talk with you and you no doubt think it high time I had sent you a line. It is my day off of duty and I ought to go out for fresh air and a little change, but I do not feel like it, I am both tired and sleepy. I had so much to do getting ready for Thanksgiving, baking and so on that I am not yet rested from it and of course I must have a cold at the same time. Ah me! We must all go through just so much before the journey ends.

And how are you dear? I now know your rounds of duty and busy days. My visit to North Carolina was to no purpose. I do not feel that the matter was finally settled. If I had money I would prosecute it to the bitter end though I gained not a cent myself. The South never did anything for me and to know that white Southern men have the benefit of my great grandmother's labor is too unjust to bear quietly. Dr. Cole[29] was in Philadelphia to the day nursery anniversary. I had hoped she would see you. Poor child! I suppose you were busy with your own affairs.

I hope you enjoyed your visit to the farm. I wish some one would make you an offer for it. You have cares enough without that worry, and to hold on to it I fear will never bring about the result you once anticipated, so why encumber yourself with unnecessary debt.

I wish you could take a run down here at Christmas time. I would be responsible for the fare one way. Think it over and see if you cannot arrange to come. Genie dear I am not going to send you the money to look out for little things for me for Christmas. I afterwards thought it was a selfish request to make, you have too little time at best for rest. I will pick up little things here. Give my best to the sisters. Lottie has been having a very hard time with her teeth. You know

how ill she was when your sister Ada was here.[30] She is not yet altogether rid of
the face trouble. It may be she will in the future have less headaches.

Send me a line dearie and know that I am ever your loving friend

Lulu

[Enclosed in the same letter is the following note.]

December 3—

Good morning childie

I forgot to mail this yesterday. It is raining hard and it is set in for the day.
Hope all is well with you.

Lovingly
Lulu

—✎◦

[From Louisa. Postmarked "Jan. 7, 1902"; addressed to "920 South
16th St., Philadelphia, Pa."]

Washington, Jan 5, 1902

My dear Genie

I begin by wishing I could take your hand in mine while I wished you a
happy New Year. I know dear it will have its shadows, yes, more clouds and
perhaps eye showers. They that have burdens cannot carry them all in sunshine
and what is His will let us strive to make our will. Now first of all thanks for the
two lovely books you sent. You will have things in <u>pairs</u> but all the world does
not match as well as you.

I hope you have had some pleasure in the holidays. I am sure you have in a
spiritual sense if in no other, and that is the highest. Christmas was not a merry
day with us. I wrote you that we had Diptheria here.[31] Many cases, forty or
more, some very light but necessitating confinement and treatment. We have
lossed two children only. We are under the care of the Health Department.
Daily Culture Labs are sent to it for examination. We have yet a number of
children under treatment. I am pretty well tired out and will be thankful when
it is all over and the school reopens.

Dear Genie I wanted to send you something pretty but really I had not the
time to go out to look up Christmas things, but I will not forget you childie. I
hope you are much better and that the sisters are well and your father also.

Howard University, Miner Hall, 1893. Louisa Jacobs served as matron from 1903 to 1908. (Courtesy of the Moorland-Spingarn Resource Center, Howard University Archives)

Genie when your father requires lifting, pray do not undertake to do it alone, you might strain and hurt yourself for life. One does not easily get over a thing of that kind.[32]

Good night dear, with a heart of love filled with blessing for your

Ever and ever thy loving friend
Lulu

[From Louisa. Postmarked "Aug. 23, 1909"; addressed to "1606 Page St., Philadelphia, Pa." This note was written in a very scribbled hand—unlike those before and the one after it.]

1326 V St.[33]
Washington
August 22nd, 1909

My dear Genie

I feel that I must <u>scribble</u> you a line or two. I was so sorry to hear through your friend that you were not well, and I am wondering if you are down sick in bed.[34] Poor dear, I am so sorry for you, and wish that I were near you and might in some way be of service to you.

I was sorry under the circumstances that I troubled you about the school. The catalogues came very promptly. I had Jennie, the young girl who may go to the school acknowledge them. I am merrily waiting waiting on my eye and dearly hope that the time of operation is growing near. The better eye is growing very dim. Genie dear tell me know if there is <u>any thing</u> I can do for you. I think of you wish and do hope I may soon get a line from you.

With a loving kiss
Always lovingly your
Lulu

[From Louisa. Postmarked "Sep 11, 1911, from [Brookline], Mass.";
addressed to "2416 N. Mole St., Philadelphia, Pa."]

Brookline Sept. 7, 1911

My dear Genie

I wrote to Louise[35] and she replied she would be glad to have me stop over with her. Unfortunately I cannot leave here as soon as I had expected. Mrs. Grinnell[36] had a fall last Monday. She hurt her leg quite badly. At first it gave her hardly any pain. On Friday it became painful. The Dr. was sent for. He proscribed, and she is now in bed and may be for one or two weeks. Of course I feel it my duty to stay until she is up. I hope dear you are feeling better. It grieves me that your life is so full of trial. I hope a change some day may come. Let God's love help you, and may your courage hold out with the hope of a change and better condition of affairs. I will write you before I leave. It is a lovely day. It rained most of yesterday. So the sunshine of to day makes life brighter. With love and all good wishes for you.

Faithfully yours
Lulu

Epilogue
The Pilgrimage Be Done

Louisa Jacobs had been diagnosed with heart problems in 1907 and made out her will that summer, naming her closest friends as beneficiaries: sisters Lilian Willis (Boit, b. 1850) and Edith Willis (Grinnell), whom she had known and loved all their lives; her third cousins Genie Webb and Charlotte Forten (Grimké), whose mothers, like Louisa, were born in Edenton, North Carolina; the grown sons of her beloved friend "Delie" Sanders (Chew), Richard and Charles Chew, and Delie's sister-in-law Martha Sanders; Louisa's half-cousins William (1875–1933) and Elijah Knox (1871–1944) of New Bedford; her old Boston friend Hattie L. Smith; and teacher Loretta Simms (1876–1978), whom she had mentored and who would become, like Jacobs, matron of the National Home for the Relief of Destitute Colored Women and Children.

After retiring in 1908 from Howard University's Miner Hall, Louisa boarded at a house on V Street in Washington. Genie Webb's Washington cousins Sarah Iredell (Fleetwood) and Laura Iredell (Hawkesworth) died in 1908 and 1909, respectively, and Genie's sisters Edith and Cordelia died in Philadelphia in 1912. Louisa regularly visited the Grimké household on Corcoran Street, which included her old friends Charlotte and Frank Grimké; Archibald Grimké and his daughter, the poet and playwright Angelina "Nina" Weld Grimké (1880–1958); and Richard D. Venning. In the summer of 1911, during her first visit to Boston in three years, Louisa wrote concerned letters to Angelina and Archibald Grimké after "Nina" fractured her spine in a train accident. Louisa returned to her V Street apartment in September and would remain there until 1914.

Louisa's last year in Washington sounded the death knell of an era. Charlotte Forten (Grimké) died July 23, 1914, followed the next month by Annie Purvis's brother William and then, in September, by Christian Fleetwood. With death on her mind, Louisa made arrangements in August and September to set foundations and pedestals for the graves of her mother and uncle, who

were buried at Mount Auburn Cemetery in Cambridge, Massachusetts. Her
plan to be buried beside her mother would be carried out by Edith Willis (Grinnell). Suffering from "hardening of the arteries and old age," according to the
diary of Robert Apthorp Boit (1846–1919), Louisa gave up her V Street arrangement in 1914 and moved permanently into the Brookline Street home of Edith
Willis (Grinnell). The Willis family's plan to care for Louisa in her old age had
been set in motion back in 1904 when Cornelia Willis, on her deathbed, asked
her daughter Edith to take on this loving responsibility.[1]

[From Edith Willis Grinnell.]

Brookline
April 5th 1917

My dear Miss Webb:
    Louisa died this morning peacefully and quietly. She failed very rapidly
and it is merciful that it was so. I had not expected it so soon, but she has suffered
much this last winter, and though I shall sorely miss her, I rejoice she is at rest.
Her love has meant very much to me all my life.
    Your letter, with the psalms came yesterday morning. She had then lost
unconsciousness of her surroundings so would not know of your loving thought
for her.
    We shall have the Episcopal service here, by our Rector,[2] some time on
Saturday. We have to consult his convenience.

Sincerely yours
Edith Willis Grinnell

[From Reverend Francis J. Grimké. Postmarked "November 7, 1919,
from Washington, D.C."; addressed to "Mrs. Cordelia Webb Hegamin,[3]
1914 W. Norris Street, Philadelphia, Penn." On the envelope, in
pencil, in a later hand, "Louise Jacobs died prior to Eugenie Webb."]

1415 Corcoran Street, N.W. Washington, D.C.
Nov. 7, 1919

Dear Cordelia:
    I was surprised to learn of the death of Genie. I am sure, while you will miss
her, it must be a great relief to you, in view of her condition both physical and

mental, to know that she is at last at rest. I am sure you did all that you could to make her comfortable and happy. The fact that she seemed never to be satisfied, was no fault of yours, but due purely to her mental condition. I shall always think of her, as I used to know her years ago, before the change came in her condition. I was always very fond of her, and it was always a pleasure to meet her. It is a comfort to feel that she is now with all the dear ones who have gone on before her,—father, mother, sisters, dear Lottie, Miss Louisa Jacobs and others. I know it must have been a happy meeting. How glad I know, it must have been for them all to greet her. Some day we shall all be on the other side, in the beautiful Beyond. I often think of it, and look forward joyfully to the time when the happy reunion will take place. This is one of the blessed anticipations, that comes to us from the religion of the Lord Jesus Christ. Let us, as we think of the dear ones who have gone, reconsecrate ourselves to his service; let us strive more earnestly than ever to so live as to receive from him at last, the "Well done, good and faithful servant."

With a great deal of love for you all and with best wishes, I am,

Yours very truly,

Francis J. Grimké.

Notes

Introduction

1. Louisa finally confided her story to Lilian Willis Boit in 1905, but twelve years earlier she felt comfortable telling the Jacobses' friend Julia Wilbur about "their Slave Life & their life since." Jean Fagan Yellin, Kate Culkin, Scott Korb, eds., *The Harriet Jacobs Family Papers*, 815, 860 (hereafter HJFP).

2. One comparable collection of personal nineteenth-century African American women's correspondence is Farah Jasmine Griffin, ed., *Beloved Sisters and Loving Friends: Letters from Rebecca Primus of Royal Oak, Maryland, and Addie Brown of Hartford, Connecticut, 1854–1868.*

3. Willard B. Gatewood Jr., *Aristocrats of Color*, 97–98.

4. Genie's aunt, Elizabeth Susan Webb, also contributed a school farewell to Mary Ann Dickerson's album. Mary Virginia Wood Album, Francis J. Grimké Papers, Moorland-Spingarn Research Center, Howard University; Amy Matilda Cassey Album, Martina Dickerson Album, Mary Ann Dickerson Album, Library Company of Philadelphia; Mary Maillard, "'Faithfully Drawn from Real Life,'" 271–76; Joshua Francis Fisher to [John] Cadwalader, [1856], box 1, folder 5, Dr. and Mrs. Henry Drinker Collection, Historical Society of Pennsylvania.

5. Rev. Daniel Alexander Payne, Mary Virginia Wood Forten's spiritual advisor, wrote about her July 9, 1840, death in his "The Triumphant End of Mrs. Mary Virginia Forten," *The Colored American*, August 29, 1840; Erica Armstrong Dunbar, *Fragile Freedom*, 128.

6. Autograph album belonging to Genie Webb, Annie Wood Webb Papers, private collection (hereafter AWWP).

7. HJFP, 859–60, 870.

8. Elite black Washington society, sometimes called the "upper tens" or the "black 400," were divided between the "old cits," who had been established in the city for several generations, and the "newcomers," who might be admitted to inner circles with proper introductions or have coequal status from another city (like Genie Webb's

cousins who arrived in Washington with solid Philadelphia-based credentials: Charlotte Forten Grimké, Annie Purvis, Dr. Charles B. Purvis, Sarah I. Fleetwood, Laura I. Hawkesworth, Evelyn Durham Shaw, Frank J. Webb Jr., and Evangeline Webb). Washington elites were not a cohesive group but a stratified, fractured society made up of a number of cliques, differentiated by what historian Willard Gatewood calls "nuances and subtleties." What all the "sets" had in common was their distance from, and sense of noblesse oblige toward, the black masses; a belief that their class would ultimately assimilate; and an emphasis on education, family pride, rules of conduct, and respectability. As the nineteenth century closed, intraracial class distinctions hardened and reinforced what literary historian Andrea N. Williams calls class anxiety, the fear of misclassification within black society. Williams explores in the literary fiction of Frances Ellen Watkins Harper, Paul L. Dunbar, Pauline Hopkins, Charles W. Chesnutt, and W. E. B. Du Bois the "uneasy relationship between racial loyalty and class division within African American communities." Willard B. Gatewood, *Aristocrats of Color*, 38–68; Andrea N. Williams, *Dividing Lines*, 1–52.

9. Louisa Jacobs wrote personal letters (as opposed to freedmen school reports) to the following: her uncle, John S. Jacobs, 1849; Cordelia Downing, 1870; William Lloyd Garrison, 1873; Ednah Dow Cheney, 1896; Bailey Willis, 1903; Angelina Weld Grimké, 1911; and Archibald Grimké, 1911. HJFP, 169, 744, 749, 822, 857, 867, 868.

10. HJFP, 870, 860.

11. Louisa Jacobs to Genie Webb, December 1, 1901, AWWP.

12. Margo Jefferson, *Negroland: A Memoir*, 6, 171–72.

13. Louisa Jacobs to Miranda Venning, July 2, 1877, Miranda Venning Autograph Book, Stevens-Cogdell-Sanders-Venning Collection, Library Company of Philadelphia (hereafter SCSVC). Louisa may have learned this adage as a teen from *The Book of Good Examples Drawn from Authentic History and Biography; Designed to Illustrate the Beneficial Aspects of Good Conduct*, written by John Frost and published in New York and Philadelphia in 1846. She may also have been thinking of Sallie Daffin's essay "Example Better than Precept," published in the May 30, 1863, issue of the *Christian Recorder*. Eric Gardner, *Unexpected Places*, 143.

14. Louisa Jacobs to Genie Webb, January 20, 1880, AWWP.

15. Louisa Jacobs to Genie Webb, March 19, 1883, AWWP. Here Louisa echoes editor John W. Cromwell of *The Advocate* (1876–1884), who focused on the obligation of the colored aristocracy to uplift the masses. Gatewood, *Aristocrats of Color*, 56.

16. Louisa Jacobs to Genie Webb, September 28, 1882, AWWP. Historian Darlene Clark Hine echoes this sentiment when she speaks of "those issues that Black women believed better left unknown, unwritten, unspoken except in whispered tones. Their alarm, their fear, or their Victorian sense of modesty implies that those who broke the silence provided grist for protractors' mills, or more ominously, tore the protective cloaks from their inner selves." Hine, "Rape and the Inner Lives of Black Women in the Middle West," 916.

17. Wedding gift list of Charlotte Forten Grimké, Annie Purvis to Genie Webb, January 6, 1879, AWWP.

18. Annie Purvis to Genie Webb, November 28, 1880, AWWP.

19. Henrietta "Cordelia" Ray (1849–1916) and her sisters, Florence (born ca. 1845) and Charlotte (1850–1911), were the daughters of Henrietta and Charles B. Ray, the editor of the *Colored American*. All three women were trained as teachers. Cordelia distinguished herself as a poet and gained national recognition in 1876 when her poem "Lincoln" was read by William E. Matthews at the unveiling of the Emancipation Memorial in Washington. Her sister Charlotte became the first African America female lawyer. "Henrietta C. Ray," 1880 U.S. Census, New York, New York, Roll 897, 618.

20. William Still (1821–1902) published *The Underground Railroad Records* in 1872. The book consists of secret notes that he kept of his interviews with hundreds of fugitive slaves during the 1850s and 1860s.

21. Louisa Jacobs to Genie Webb, March 19, 1883, and Annie Purvis to Louisa Jacobs, August 3, 1884, AWWP.

22. Louisa Jacobs to Genie Webb, December 21, 1884, AWWP; HJFP, 803.

23. Louisa Jacobs to Genie Webb, December 10, 1879, AWWP.

24. Assassins have killed four U.S. presidents. Louisa Jacobs lived in the Washington area when three were murdered: Abraham Lincoln in 1865, James Garfield in 1881, and William McKinley in 1901.

25. "Proceedings of the Civil Rights Mass-Meeting Held at Lincoln Hall, October 22, 1883. Speeches of Hon. Frederick Douglass and Robert G. Ingersoll," *Colored Conventions Project*, directed by Gabrielle Foreman, University of Delaware, http://colored conventions.org/items/show/1194; "The Color Controversy," *National Republican*, Washington, DC, October 23, 1883, 1.

26. HJFP, 773 [Harriet Jacobs], 784, 786–87, 789.

27. "The International Council of Women," *Friends Intelligencer and Journal* 45 (March 14, 1888): 237–40.

28. Mark M. Smith, "'All Is Not Quiet in Our Hellish County.'"

29. Phillip S. Lapsansky, "Afro-Americana: Family Values, in Black and White," 29; Chew Family Papers, SCSVC; Roger Lane and Benjamin R. Collins, *William Dorsey's Philadelphia and Ours*, 154.

30. "Suspicion," anonymous author of letter to the editor, "Our Schools and Colored Children," *The Record*, July 3, 1878, Philadelphia, Pennsylvania, clipping from SCSVC.

31. Louisa Jacobs to Genie Webb, December 12, 1882, AWWP.

32. Ballard C. Campbell, *Disasters, Accidents, and Crises in American History*, 168–71.

33. HJFP, 809. Coincidentally, the chief assayer of the Bureau of the United States Mint at the time was Louisa Jacobs's white nephew-in-law, Cabell Whitehead (1863–1908), who had married the daughter of her half-sister, Sallie Peyton Sawyer (Ayres). R. S. Harrison, *Nome and Seward Peninsula*; "Cabell Whitehead, Ph.D.," Alaska Web,

http://www.alaskaweb.org/bios/whiteheadc.html; "Called to Turkey: Dr. Cabell Whitehead to Retire as Assayer of the Mint," *Evening Star*, March 10, 1899, 11, https://www.newspapers.com/image/145498047/?terms=bena%2Bwhitehead.

34. HJFP, 815.

35. Louisa Jacobs to Genie Webb, July 17, 1895, AWWP.

36. Eliza Ann Logan Lawton (1822–1883), Edward Willis Lawton (1846–1879), Isaac T. Lawton (1860–1880), Arthur Lawton (1857–1882), Eliza Marianna Lawton (1843–1884). Massachusetts Death Records, 1841–1915.

37. John Gregory Pike, *The Works of the Rev. J. G. Pike of Derby*, 365; Lydia A. Bustill to Genie Webb, July 10, 1886, AWWP.

38. Louisa Jacobs to Genie Webb, November 2, 1879, AWWP.

39. Louisa Jacobs to Genie Webb, March 25, 1880, AWWP.

40. Louisa Jacobs to Genie Webb, March 21, 1880, AWWP.

41. 1 Samuel 20:42.

42. From the mid-1870s through the turn of the century, Mizpah sentiments grew in popularity and appeared in poetry, hymns, sermons, and funerals. Mizpah monograms were applied to Protestant prayer books and gravestones. Greeting cards, bookmarks, calendars, memorial cards, and jewelry carried Mizpah messages of hope and sadness. In 1892, for example, African American clubwomen presented antilynching activist Ida B. Wells with a Mizpah brooch. Indicative of how deeply Mizpah culture had permeated the late-nineteenth-century African American psyche, the last resounding line of J. McHenry Jones's 1896 antiracist novel *Hearts of Gold* echoes both the Mizpah prayer and 1 Samuel 20:42 in the line, "May the Lord be between me and thee and between mine and thine forever." A number of letters in the Annie Wood Webb Papers are signed "Mizpah."

Louisa Jacobs to Genie Webb, February 20, 1880, AWWP; Lafayette Charles Loomis, *Mizpah, Prayer, and Friendship*, v; Julia A. Baker, "Mizpah," in Hazel Felleman, ed., *Best Loved Poems of the American People* (1881; reprint, New York: Doubleday, 1936), 304; Annie Lanman Angier, *Poems by Mrs. Annie Lanman Angier* (Boston: A. Williams Co., 1882), 234–35; Homer Greene, "Mizpah," *Lippincott's Monthly Magazine* 43 (1889), 222; Patricia Ann Schecter, *Ida B. Wells-Barnett and American Reform, 1880–1930*, 19; J. McHenry Jones, *Hearts of Gold*, 272; clipping of Julia A. Baker's "Mizpah," in Christopher Rhodes Eliot, *A Manual for Use at Funerals: Consisting of Scripture Readings, Poems, and Prose Selections from Various Sources* (Boston: George H. Ellis, 1892).

43. Louisa Jacobs to Genie Webb, July 23, 1882, AWWP.

44. Louisa Jacobs to Genie Webb, January 20, 1880, AWWP.

45. Louisa Jacobs to Genie Webb, February 23, 1882, AWWP.

46. Louisa Jacobs to Genie Webb, January 4, 1881, AWWP.

47. Gerald Massey, "Adelaide Anne Proctor," http://gerald-massey.org.uk/procter/index.htm.

48. Louisa Jacobs to Ednah Dow Cheney, July 22, 1896, HJFP, 822.

49. Louisa Jacobs to Genie Webb, September 27, 1896, AWWP.

50. Cornelia Willis to Ednah Dow Cheney, June 30, 1896, HJFP, 820.

51. Louisa Jacobs to Genie Webb, April 4, 1890, AWWP.

Biographical Sketches

1. Joseph Purvis's death certificate listed intemperance as the cause of death. "Pennsylvania, Philadelphia City Death Certificates, 1803–1915," database with images, *FamilySearch* (https://familysearch.org/ark:/61903/1:1:JXJQ-KM1, 9 December 2014), Joseph Purvis, 17 Jan 1857; citing, Philadelphia City Archives and Historical Society of Pennsylvania, Philadelphia; FHL microfilm 1,976,364.

2. Annie Purvis's kinship with the Webbs is expressed in a postcard she wrote to Genie shortly after the marriage of Charlotte Forten to Rev. Francis J. Grimké. "Cousins, Grandmother [Charlotte Vandine Forten] has been confined to her room for two weeks. . . . I have not heard from our cousin Mrs. Grimké. I was told she looked very lovely, and Uncle Robert P. conducted her into the Church. . . . If you don't get over send a line to your forlorn Cousin Annie. I have very much to say to you as usual. My love to Edith and my other cousins." Annie Purvis to Genie Webb, December 24 [1878], AWWP.

3. Julie Winch, *A Gentleman of Color*, 111–12, 120, 233, 310, 366. Margaret Hope Bacon, *But One Race*, 130. Brenda Stevenson, ed., *Journals of Charlotte Forten Grimké*, 233. "Find a Grave Index," database, *FamilySearch* (https://familysearch.org/ark:/61903 /1:1:QV2C-2F5L: 13 December 2015), Harriet Anne Purvis; Burial, Philadelphia, Philadelphia, Pennsylvania, United States of America, Saint James the Less Episcopal Churchyard; citing record ID 63249622, *Find a Grave*, http://www.findagrave.com. "Find a Grave Index," database, *FamilySearch* (https://familysearch.org/ark:/61903 /1:1:QV2C-2F5G: 13 December 2015), William B. Purvis, 1914; Burial, Philadelphia, Philadelphia, Pennsylvania, United States of America, Saint James the Less Episcopal Churchyard; citing record ID 63249595, *Find a Grave*, http://www.findagrave.com. "Find a Grave Index," database, *FamilySearch* (https://familysearch.org/ark:/61903 /1:1:QV2C-239V: 13 December 2015), Sarah Louisa Purvis, 1884; Burial, Philadel- phia, Pennsylvania, United States of America, African Episcopal Church of Saint Thomas; citing record ID 63248192, *Find a Grave*, http://www.findagrave.com. "Sarah Louisa Purvis," Philadelphia, Pennsylvania, Death Certificates Index 1803–1915, FHL #2069872. Annie Purvis to Genie Webb, November 28, 1880; August 3, 1884; November 6, 1884; and April 4, 1886, AWWP. "William B. Purvis," Philadelphia City Directories, 1885–1893.

4. "Pennsylvania, Philadelphia City Death Certificates, 1803–1915," database with images, *FamilySearch* (https://familysearch.org/ark:/61903/1:1:JFDK-4ZZ: 9 December 2014), Cordelia S Chew, 06 Nov 1879; citing, Philadelphia City Archives and Historical Society of Pennsylvania, Philadelphia; FHL microfilm 2,031,903. Chew family records state her death as November 5. Cordelia Chew's birth year is probably 1843. Her marriage record and 1870 Census suggest 1845: 1870 U.S. Census, Philadelphia,

Ward 4, Pennsylvania, Roll: M593_1390, 267A. Her death certificate and the 1860 Census record state that she was born in 1843. https://familysearch.org/ark:/61903 /1:1:MXR8-L37: 30 December 2015), Delia Saunders in entry for Robert Saunders, 1860. "Pennsylvania, Philadelphia City Death Certificates, 1803–1915," database with images, *FamilySearch* (https://familysearch.org/ark:/61903/1:1:JXV6-M38: 9 December 2014), Charlotte Louisa Chew, 13 Jun 1884; citing Philadelphia City Archives and Historical Society of Pennsylvania, Philadelphia; FHL microfilm 2,069,689. "New Jersey, Deaths, 1670–1988," index, *FamilySearch* (https://familysearch.org/ark:/61903 /1:1:FZZ3-8TL: 8 April 2016), John Chew, 08 Apr 1870; citing Trenton, Mercer, New Jersey, United States, Division of Archives and Record Management, New Jersey Department of State, Trenton; FHL microfilm 584,590. Brenda Stevenson, ed., *Journals of Charlotte Forten Grimké*, 294, 297, 310 [Cordelia and Sallie Sanders visited Charlotte Forten on March 30–31, 1858; the *S* has been transcribed as *L* in Stevenson's edition]. Chew Family Papers, SCSVC. William C. Bolivar, "Pencil Pusher's Points: A Cursory Glance at the Various Movements from Charleston to Philadelphia, for Over One Hundred Years," W. C. Bolivar file, Library Company of Philadelphia.

    5. Brooklyn School Board, *Annual Report of the City Superintendent of Schools of the Consolidated City of Brooklyn* (1863, 1865, 1868–72), 87, 95, 122, 129; "Sanders, Cordelia A., teacher," The Brooklyn City Directory (J. Lain & Company, 1868), 539; "Georgiana Frances Putnam (1832–1912)," in Jesse Carney Smith, ed., *Notable Black American Women*, Book 2, 532–34. The sixteen-year-old southern girl transcribed as "C. E." in Charlotte Forten's June 22, 1862, journal entry is probably "C. S.," an abbreviation for Cordelia Sanders. Brenda Stevenson, ed., *Journals of Charlotte Forten Grimké*, 292, 294, 365; Daniel R. Biddle and Murray Dubin, *Tasting Freedom*, 252; photograph signed 1866 by Cordelia Sanders, AWWP; room and board receipts, family Bible records, SCSVC; Louisa Jacobs to Genie Webb, January 4, 1881, October 4, 1880, AWWP; Mabel Elbert Perry, letter to the editor, *Ladies Home Journal*, August 11, 1942, African Americana collection, Library Company of Philadelphia.

    6. "John Chew," 1850 U.S. Census, Philadelphia, Pennsylvania, Pine Ward, Roll M432_813, 321B; rent receipts, AWWP; John Chew to Annie E. Wood [July 1846], AWWP.

    7. Frederick A. Hinton (ca. 1804–1849) opened an account on August 5, 1833, at the Philadelphia Savings Fund in trust for Edy Wood, Mary Virginia Wood (Forten, 1815–1840), Caroline Wood (1827–1836), Louisa Wood (1828–1836), and Annie Elizabeth Wood (Webb), and he collected Edy Wood's 1833–1835 rental payments to Sarah Bass (Allen, 1764–1849), widow of Bishop Richard Allen (1760–1831). Hinton's daughter Ada Howell Hinton (1832–1903) grew up with Annie Wood (Webb) and Charlotte Forten (Grimké), acted as godmother to three of Annie's daughters, and remained close to both women throughout her life. From 1835 to 1836, Edy and Annie Wood boarded with Mrs. Elizabeth Keating Willson (ca. 1791–1847), mother-in-law of Frederick A. Hinton and mother of Joseph Willson (1817–1895), the author of *Sketches of the Higher Classes of*

Colored Society in Philadelphia (1841). Annie Wood stayed with a Mrs. Miller in 1846 who may have been Robert Purvis's mother, Harriet Judah (Miller, 1785-1869), of New York and Philadelphia. Annie Wood was adopted by Amy Matilda Cassey (Remond) and married at the Charles Lenox Remond home in Salem, Massachusetts. "Edy Wood, August 5, 1833," *Historic Pennsylvania Church and Town Records*, Historical Society of Pennsylvania, Philadelphia, Pennsylvania, accessed through ancestry.com; "Ada Virgil Webb," "Miriam Douglass Webb," "Charlotte Cordelia Webb," 1877 baptism records, Church of Our Savior, Stockton, New Jersey (Ada Hinton and Charlotte Forten, sponsors), Pennsylvania and New Jersey Town and Church Records, 1708-1985, accessed through ancestry.com; rent receipts, AWWP; Julie Winch, *The Elite of Our People*, 51, 58-60; John Chew to Annie Wood [July 1846], AWWP; Mary Maillard, "'Faithfully Drawn from Real Life,'" 265-76; Mary Virginia Wood Album, Moorland-Spingarn Center, Howard University; Amy Matilda Cassey Album, Library Company of Philadelphia.

8. Brenda Stevenson, *Journals of Charlotte Forten Grimké*, 329.

9. "Edith Webb, September 10, 1912," Pennsylvania Death Certificates, 1906-1963, #89255, ancestry.com; *The Pennsylvania Freedmen's Bulletin*, February 1867, 5, and April 1867, 7; Institute for Colored Youth, Commencement Exercises, May 17, 1872, AWWP; Maillard, "'Faithfully Drawn from Real Life,'" 265-79; Edith Webb to [Ma], February 1 [1874], AWWP; admission ticket, "Select Readings and Recitations by Miss Edith L. Webb," June 30, 1881, Odd Fellows Hall, Philadelphia, AWWP; Camden, New Jersey, city directories, 1880-1890, ancestry.com; will of Sara Iredell Fleetwood, Fleetwood Papers, Library of Congress.

10. Maillard, "Faithfully Drawn from Real Life," 265-70, 279.

11. Camden, New Jersey, city directories, 1880s and 1890s; J. W. Erwin [attorney for John G. Webb] note re: deed to Weymouth property, March 11, 1862, AWWP; the Franklinville farm was purchased in 1855, probably with funds sent to John G. Webb by Annie's father, James Cathcart Johnston, and it was sold in 1971 after Eugenie Webb's fifty-year estate case was finally settled. James Cathcart Johnston to Annie Wood Webb, July 17, 1855; John G. Webb deeds, AWWP.

12. "Pennsylvania, Philadelphia City Death Certificates, 1803-1915," database with images, *FamilySearch* (https://familysearch.org/ark:/61903/1:1:J6S2-TNR: 9 December 2014), Annie E. Webb, 08 May 1879; citing, Philadelphia City Archives and Historical Society of Pennsylvania, Philadelphia; FHL microfilm 2,031,101.

13. John D. Webb to Edith Webb, July 23, 1881; August 3, 1884; and November 22, 1891. John D. Webb to Genie Webb, December 22, 1886, AWWP.

14. Post Office bond, July 24, 1886, AWWP; postcard to Mr. Juan de Webb, June 15, 1888, AWWP; "Juan Degonzalez," 1892 Harrisburg, Pennsylvania, city directory, 154; "Juan Degonzalez," Greater Richmond Virginia Directory 1907, vol. 43 (Hill Directory Co., 1907), 228; "Juan Degonzallis," 1910 U.S. Census, Richmond, Virginia, T624_1644, Page: 7A; "Accused of Non-Support," *The Evening Journal*, Wilmington,

Delaware, July 17, 1915, 7; "Jaun Degonzalez," 1920 U.S. Census, Baltimore, Ward 24, District 0399, 16B. In keeping with his literary namesake, Don Juan, John D. Webb named his first daughter Haidee, after Byron's exotic Greek heroine.

15. Louisa Jacobs probate documents, Harriet Jacobs Family Papers, Wilson Library, University of North Carolina, Chapel Hill; nursing bill for Eugenia Webb covering expenses for August, September, and October, 1919, AWWP; "Eugenia Minnehaha Webb," Philadelphia Death Certificate, November 2, 1919. Genie's middle name on her death certificate may provide a clue to her racial background: specifically, to that of her North Carolina–born grandmother, Edy Wood. "Minnehaha" was the fictional Native American lover of Hiawatha, the romantic hero of Longfellow's immensely popular epic poem, published the year before Genie was born. In late 1855 and 1856, Mary Webb—the dramatist wife of Genie's uncle Frank J. Webb—performed *The Song of Hiawatha* throughout the northeastern United States. Aside from this death certificate, completed by Genie's sister, there are no records showing that Genie ever used a middle initial during her lifetime. Of the six Webb children's births recorded in the Webb family Bible, Genie is the only child without a middle name.

16. Maillard, "'Faithfully Drawn from Real Life,'" 273–76. Mrs. Eckley B. Coxe [Sophie Fisher (Coxe)] to Mrs. John Henry Simons [Ada V. Webb (Simons)], August 27, 1909; George Harrison Fisher to Rev. John Henry Simons, August 13, 1909, AWWP.

17. William C. Bolivar, "Pencil Pusher," *Philadelphia Tribune*, June 22, 1912, W. C. Bolivar file, Library Company of Philadelphia; "Clarkson Hall," Historical Society of Pennsylvania, https://hsp.org/history-online/digital-history-projects/pennsylvania-abolition-society-papers/pas-board-of-education/clarkson-hall.

18. John G. Webb to Annie E. Wood, November 12, 1849, AWWP.

19. Annie E. Wood to John G. Webb, February 15–16, 1854; March 9, 1854; April [11], 1854; and [April 1854], AWWP.

20. Maillard, "'Faithfully Drawn from Real Life,'" 285–86.

21. Wood Webb Family Bible, AWWP.

22. John G. Webb to Genie Webb, February 27 [1872–1878], AWWP; John D. Webb to Edith Webb, August 3, 1884, AWWP.

23. HJFP, 816, 825, 962. "Joseph Pierce," 1920 U.S. Census, Chicago, Cook, Illinois, Roll T625_316, 9 B.

24. Stevenson, ed., *Journals of Charlotte Forten Grimké*, xxxiii, 144, 210; Maillard, "'Faithfully Drawn from Real Life,'" 265–67; rent receipts, AWWP; Daniel Alexander Payne, "Triumphant End of Mrs. Mary Virginia Forten"; Winch, *A Gentleman of Color*, 2.

25. Rent receipts, AWWP; "Edith Wood," "William Chew," "R B Forten," McElroy's Philadelphia directories, 1843–1846.

26. Julie Winch, *Gentleman of Color*, 340.

27. Mrs. Julia C. R. Dorr, "The Spirit Teachings," *The Columbian Magazine* 9 (1848), n.p. [Google Books ebook]; Annie E. Wood to Charlotte Forten, 1848, AWWP; Charlotte Forten, "The Angel's Visit," www.poetrynook.com/poem/angels-visit-0; Ronald J. Zboray and Mary Saracino Zboray, *Literary Dollars and Social Sense*, 54–57.

28. Julie Winch, *Gentleman of Color*, 343–44.

29. Annie made these arrangements from Philadelphia, where she was visiting the Fortens with Sarah Parker Remond. She had spent the summer in Canada with Sarah L. Cassey (Smith, 1833–1875) and in the spring had been forced by poor health to interrupt her Normal School classes to take the "water cure." Amy M. Remond to Annie E. Wood, October 14, 1853, AWWP; Dorothy Porter Wesley and Constance Porter Uzelac, *William Cooper Nell*, 333, 341, 352.

30. James Cathcart Johnston to Annie E. Wood, November 22, 1847, June 10, 1852, and July 17, 1855, AWWP; Wesley and Uzelac, *William Cooper Nell*, 333; Stevenson, ed., *Journals of Charlotte Forten Grimké*, 130–32.

31. Stevenson, ed., *Journals of Charlotte Forten Grimké*, 19.

32. Ibid., 119, 182, 163.

33. Carla L. Peterson, *"Doers of the Word,"* 185–86. Peterson's entire chapter "Seeking the '*Writable*': Charlotte Forten and the Problem of Narration" is requisite reading for understanding the life of Charlotte Forten (Grimké), particularly Peterson's treatment of her difficulty in finding a "usable past."

34. Catalogues, Salem Normal School, 1859, 1860, American Antiquarian Society, www.ancestry.com; Stevenson, ed., *Journals of Charlotte Forten Grimké*, 362.

35. "Wendell Phillips Forten," July-Aug-Sept 1860, England & Wales, FreeBMD Death Index, 1837–1915, 1b, 83; Carla L. Peterson, *"Doers of the Word,"* 185.

36. Stevenson, ed., *Journals of Charlotte Forten Grimké*, 363. Annie Purvis had moved into the Forten home after her father's death in 1857. When Edith and Genie began school is not known; in 1861 Edith would have been six and a half and Genie five years old.

37. John Greenleaf Whittier, *The Letters of John Greenleaf Whittier*, 3:97, 233.

38. Ibid., 233–34; Stevenson, ed., *Journals of Charlotte Forten Grimké*, introduction; Dorothy Sterling, ed., *We Are Your Sisters*, 285; Eric Gardner, "Charlotte Forten," 408.

39. Annie Purvis to Genie Webb, November 28, 1880, AWWP.

40. Louisa Jacobs to Genie Webb, March 1, 1885, July 5, 1885, and December 20, 1885, AWWP.

41. Stevenson, ed., *Journals of Charlotte Forten Grimké*, 3–55; Carolivia Herron, ed., *Selected Works of Angelina Weld Grimké*, 31–34.

42. Francis J. Grimké to Miriam [Webb], April 8, 1929, AWWP.

43. Joyce W. Warren, *Fanny Fern*, 224; Thomas Butler Gunn Diaries, Missouri History Museum, vol. 10, 135, March 1859.

44. HJFP, 800.

45. HJFP, 860.

46. HJFP, 833.

47. HJFP, 859–60, 870. Robert Apthorp Boit's account is based on details provided to him in 1905 by his wife, Lilian Willis (Boit), and on stories relayed earlier by her mother, Cornelia Grinnell (Willis).

48. Henry Augustin Beers, *Nathaniel Parker Willis*, 284–85; Warren, *Fanny Fern*, 73, 93, 224. Harriet Jacobs, *Incidents in the Life of a Slave Girl*, chapter 37, first paragraph [May

1845]. Thomas Butler Gunn Diaries, Missouri History Museum, vol. 16, 157, 1861; note accompanying newspaper clipping about publication of Harriet Jacobs's book.

49. HJFP, 168, 176, 178, 186, 213; Wesley and Uzelac, *William Cooper Nell*, 342, 352; Louisa Jacobs to Genie Webb, October 4, 1880, AWWP.

50. James Cathcart Johnston to Annie Wood in West Newton, June 10, 1852, AWWP; "Annie E. Wood," State Normal School at West Newton, 1852 catalog, American Antiquarian Society through www.ancestry.com, 23. Louisa Jacobs told Edith Willis (Grinnell) that she had been educated in a "Mass Normal School" and that her father paid for her education and supported her until he died. We do not know for certain if Louisa Jacobs and Genie's mother, Annie E. Wood (Webb), claimed kin through their white fathers (who were cousins from Edenton, North Carolina), but it is likely that they did since both women were sent North, knew each other in Boston, and were supported and educated by their fathers. HJFP, 859, 160; Maillard, "'Faithfully Drawn from Real Life,'" 271.

51. Wesley and Constance Porter Uzelac, *William Cooper Nell*, 307, 333, 341, 354; Mary Maillard, "George W. Lowther," http://www.blackpast.org/aah/lowther-george-w-1822-1898.

52. HJFP, 206, 223; Harriet Jacobs to Amy Post, March [1854], http://glc.yale.edu /sites/default/files/files/HJ%20to%20Amy%20Post%20March%201854.pdf.

53. HJFP, 231, 266. Thomas Butler Gunn Diaries, Missouri History Museum, vol. 8, 28, 41, 133; vol. 9, 20, 128, October 28, 1857; vol. 10, 220, 1859; vol. 17, 43, [44], 1861, http://collections.mohistory.org/search/?text=louisa%20jacobs&q=custom_search.

54. HJFP, 539.

55. "Note admitted to probate at November term 1867 of the County Court," Hayes Collection, Wilson Library, University of North Carolina, Chapel Hill; Maillard, "'Faithfully Drawn from Real Life,'" 265n8, 271.

56. HJFP, 698.

57. Louisa Jacobs to Genie Webb, December 21, 1884, AWWP.

58. HJFP, 863.

59. HJFP, 792.

60. Louisa Jacobs to Genie Webb, December 21, 1884, AWWP.

61. Sallie Peyton Sawyer (Ayres) worked as a clerk in the pension office in the District in 1879 while her husband, Colonel Edward W. Ayres (1837–1902), worked as a newspaper correspondent. 1880 U.S. Census, 1900 U.S. Census, Washington, DC; "Obituary Notes, Col. E. W. Ayres," *New York Times*, January 4, 1902; 1879, 1888, and 1894 Washington, DC, directories.

62. HJFP, 861, 834–35.

63. Louisa Jacobs to Genie Webb, December 1, 1901, AWWP.

64. HJFP, 800.

65. HJFP, 800, 817, 824.

66. HJFP, 819–22, 824.

67. William L. Andrews, "Harriet A. Jacobs," in *The Concise Oxford Companion to African American Literature*, ed. William L. Andrews, Frances Smith Foster, and Trudier Harris, 223; HJFP, 823.

68. The exact year of Harriet Jacobs's birth has not been determined. Mary Maillard, "Dating Harriet Jacobs."

69. Jacobs *Incidents in the Life of a Slave Girl*, 12.

70. HJFP identifies Mr. Webb as Irish antislavery activist Richard D. Webb (1805–1872). Historian Gloria C. Oden, however, posits that the writer could have been Frank J. Webb. HJFP, 249–50; notes from Gloria Oden, Frank J. Webb vertical file, Library Company of Philadelphia.

71. HJFP, 399–417.

72. HJFP, 558–61, 567.

73. HJFP, 420.

74. Louisa Jacobs to Genie Webb, September 10, 1881, AWWP; HJFP 793, 819, 821, 824; Jean Fagan Yellin, *Harriet Jacobs: A Life*, 257.

75. Sarah Iredell (1806–1885) was thus Sarah Iredell (Fleetwood's) paternal aunt. "Sarah Iredell," 1870 U.S. Census, Cambridge Ward 1, Middlesex, Massachusetts, Roll: M593_623, 241; "Sarah Iredell," May 22, 1885, New Bedford, Massachusetts, Massachusetts Death Records, 1841–1915, ancestry.com; Blair/Iredell family Bible, private collection. Of note, another of Geoffrey Iredell's sisters, Annis Iredell (Douglass, 1796–1834), named her son Samuel Tredwell Sawyer Douglass (1832–1906) after Louisa Jacobs's father. St. Paul's Episcopal Church records, Edenton, North Carolina.

76. "Geoffrey G. Iredell," Administrators' Bond, May 1837, North Carolina estate files, 1663–1979, Chowan County, North Carolina.

77. Maillard, "'Faithfully Drawn from Real Life,'" 276–80; Julie Winch, *The Clamorgans*, 140–42.

78. The younger Sarah Iredell's mother, Elizabeth Susan Webb (Iredell), served as vice president. Ladies Union Association, First Annual Report, 1863, Leon Gardiner Collection of American Negro Historical Society Records, Historical Society of Pennsylvania. http://exhibits.library.villanova.edu/institute-colored-youth/their-own-words/ladies-union-association-1863-annual-report/.

79. Objects of the Institute for Colored Youth, with a list of the officers and students, and the Annual Report of the Board of Managers for the year 1866, American Antiquarian Society, through ancestry.com.

80. Maillard, "'Faithfully Drawn from Real Life,'" 276–79; Howard University Catalogue, Law Department, Junior Class, 1870, 1871, American Antiquarian Society, through ancestry.com.

81. William Loren Katz, ed., *History of Schools for the Colored Population*, 257; Willard B. Gatewood, *Aristocrats of Color*, 13; Fanny Jackson Coppin, *Reminiscences of School Life*, 145; *Annual Catalogue of the Officers and Students: Catalogue of Oberlin College for the College Year 1857–58* (Oberlin, OH: James M. Fitch, 1857), 28; Sterling, ed., *We Are Your Sisters*, 430–32.

82. Sharon Harley, "Fleetwood, Sara Iredell," in Darlene Clark Hine, ed. *Black Women in America: Science, Health, and Medicine.*

83. Frank J. Webb Jr. graduated from Howard University Medical School in 1895. Howard University catalog, medical school students, 1892, 11; Howard University alumni catalog, 1896, 23; American Antiquarian Society, through ancestry.com; Frank J. Webb Jr. to Cousins, September 1, 1893, and January 18, 1894, AWWP.

84. Smithsonian Anacostia Museum and Center for African American History and Culture, *The Black Washingtonians*, 124.

85. Harley, "Fleetwood, Sara Iredell"; "Sarah Iredell," 1860 U.S. Census, Philadelphia Ward 2, Philadelphia, Pennsylvania, Roll: M653_1152, page 296, image 300, Family History Library film 805152; Jesse Carney Smith, *Notable Black American Women*, 2:492; Laura Iredell Hawkesworth to Genie Webb, February 1, 1908, AWWP; Sarah Iredell (Fleetwood) birth, April 17, 1841, Christian A. Fleetwood Papers, Library of Congress; "District of Columbia Deaths, 1874–1959," database with images, *FamilySearch* (https://familysearch.org/ark:/61903/1:1:F7Y7-NZ1: 3 December 2014), Sara I. Fleetwood, 1908.

86. Institute for Colored Youth, *Nineteenth Annual Report of the Board of Managers of the Institute for Colored Youth*, 17; "Laura Iredell Hawkesworth," funeral notice, *Washington Post*, February 19, 1909, www.newspaperabstracts.com/link.php?action=detail&id =34232; "Laura Iredell," 1860 U.S. Census, Philadelphia Ward 2, Philadelphia, Pennsylvania, M653_1152, 296; "Laura H. Iredell," 1870 U.S. Census, Camden, New Jersey; "Laura H. Hawksworth," 1880 U.S. Census, Washington, District of Columbia, Roll 121, 109C; "Laura Isedell Hawksworth," District of Columbia Select Deaths and Burials, 1840–1964, FHL# 2115608.

87. Miranda Venning death notice, SCSVC.

88. October 3, 1862, marriage of Eleanor Herbert, cab proprietor, to John Swanson Jacobs, mariner, father Robert Aspland, witnessed by Elizabeth Aspland, London Metropolitan Archives, Saint Barnabas, Finsbury, Register of marriages, 76/BAN, Item 005.

89. Undated obituary notices for Miranda Venning, Box 8, Folder 1; "To the Editor of *The Record*: Philadelphia, Pa., July 3, 1878"; rent receipts; Miranda Venning to Richard DeReef Venning, October, 1875; Margaretta Forten tuition receipt to Julia Venning, October 20, 1871; Daniel Mansfield to Miranda Venning, November 7, 1877; Miranda Venning to Rebecca "Beckie" Venning, January 1, 1875, SCSVC.

90. Institute for Colored Youth, *Nineteenth Annual Report of the Board of Managers of the Institute for Colored Youth*, 17; Commencement Exercises Program, Institute for Colored Youth, May 16–17, 1872, AWWP; Octavius V. Catto, Board of Managers, Institute for Colored Youth, Minutes 1855–1866, Friends Historical Library, Swarthmore College; Coppin, *Reminiscences of School Life*, 148, 153; William C. Bolivar, "Pencil Pusher," *Philadelphia Tribune*, April 13, 1912, in W. C. Bolivar file, Library Company of Philadelphia; "Richard E Venning," 1870 U.S. Census, Philadelphia Ward 7 Dist 18 (2nd Enum), Philadelphia, Pennsylvania, Roll: M593_1420, page: 736A, image: 779, Family History Library film: 552919; "R. D. R. Venning," 1880 U.S. Census, Philadelphia, Philadelphia,

Pennsylvania, Roll: 1170, page: 90B, enumeration district: 121, image: 0362, Family History Library film: 1255170; "Richard D. Vening," 1900 U.S. Census, Washington, Washington, District of Columbia, roll: 160, page: 13B, enumeration district: 0040, Family History Library film: 1240160; "Richard T. Venning," 1910 U.S. Census, Precinct 8, Washington, District of Columbia, Roll: T624_153, page: 2A, enumeration district: 0145, Family History Library microfilm: 1374166; "Richard Venning," 1920 U.S. Census, Philadelphia Ward 30, Philadelphia, Pennsylvania, Roll: T625_1634, page: 5A, enumeration district: 990, image: 970; Boyd's Washington City Directories, 1884–1912; "Richard Venning," Pennsylvania Death Certificates, 1906–1963, # 79519.

91. Chew Family Papers, SCSVC. Anne M. Stewart, "Desegregation of Pennsylvania Schools." Roger Lane and Benjamin R. Collins, *William Dorsey's Philadelphia and Ours*, 154. McElroy's Philadelphia City Directory, 1858, 594. "William H. Chew," 1880 U.S. Census, Philadelphia, Philadelphia, Roll 1168, 481A. "William H. Chew," Mains and Fitzgerald's Mercer County Directory, City Directory, Trenton, New Jersey, 1879, 389, and 1880, 135; Louisa Jacobs to Genie Webb, March 20, 1887, AWWP; "Great Events Last Week," *Washington Bee*, March 16, 1889, 3; "Pennsylvania, Philadelphia City Death Certificates, 1803–1915," database with images, *FamilySearch* (https://familysearch .org/ark:/61903/1:1:JX64-R9L: 9 December 2014), Wm H Chew, 06 Jun 1892; citing 26671, Philadelphia City Archives and Historical Society of Pennsylvania, Philadelphia; FHL microfilm 1,901,686; "Wm H. Chew," Pennsylvania and New Jersey, Church and Town Records, Historical Society of Pennsylvania, Burial at Crucifixion Church, June 7, 1892; "Wm. H. Chew," District of Columbia Deaths, 1874–1961, (https://familysearch .org/ark:/61903/1:1:F7TT-R6N: 3 December 2014), Wm. H. Chew, 1892.

92. HJFP, 180, 221–23, 869; Imogen Willis Eddy to Bailey Willis, December 13 [1886], Harriet Jacobs Family Papers, Wilson Library, University of North Carolina, Chapel Hill; Beers, *Nathaniel Parker Willis*, 285.

One by One the Moments Fall: 1879–1880

1. This was the home of Genie Webb's (Eugenie "Genie" Webb, 1856–1919) paternal cousin Sarah Iredell (Fleetwood, 1841–1908) and her paternal aunt Elizabeth Webb (Iredell, 1818–1888). In 1907, in anticipation of her death, Sarah Iredell (Fleetwood) transferred her rights to this property (presumably to her husband or daughter). Genie's maternal cousin Charlotte "Lottie" Forten (Grimké, 1837–1914) and her new husband, Reverend Francis James "Frank" Grimké (1850–1937), also lived in the home in 1880 and appear to have been living there at the time of this letter. "Francis J. Grimké," 1880 U.S. Census, Washington, Washington, District of Columbia, Roll 121, 146B. "Christian Fleetwood," Boyd's Washington City Directory, 1875, 212; 1876, 224; 1877, 278, 363; 1878, 292; 1879, 192; 1881, 388; 1884, 381; and 1905, 428. "Elizabeth S. Iredell," Boyd's Washington City Directory, 1878, 385; 1879, 427. "Edith Fleetwood," Boyd's Washington City Directory, 1906–1917. Will of Sara Iredell Fleetwood, 1907, Fleetwood Papers, Library of Congress.

2. Harriet Jacobs (ca. 1815-1897) was Louisa Jacobs's (1833-1917) mother and the author of the fugitive slave narrative *Incidents in the Life of a Slave Girl* (1861). She was an abolitionist, founder of a school for freed people in Alexandria, Virginia, and former operator of a boarding house near Harvard University. HJFP.

3. Cordelia "Delie" Sanders (Chew, ca. 1843-1879) died of consumption on November 5, 1879, but her official death record states November 6. Born in Charleston, South Carolina, the daughter of Richard Walpole Cogdell and his enslaved common-law wife, Martha Sanders, Delie had arrived in Philadelphia with her family in 1858. "Cordelia S. Chew," Pennsylvania, Philadelphia City Death Certificates, 1803-1915, FHL 2031903; Chew Family Papers, SCSVC.

4. Genie Webb's mother, Annie E. Wood (Webb, 1831-1879), had died of consumption six months earlier. "Annie E. Webb," Pennsylvania, Philadelphia City Death Certificates, 1803-1915, FHL 1003705.

5. Edith "Edie" Louise Webb (1855-1912) was Genie's sister, older by twenty months. "Edith Webb," Pennsylvania, Philadelphia City Death Certificates, 1803-1915, FHL 1421343; Wood-Webb family Bible, AWWP.

6. Genie's younger sisters were Miriam "Mame" Douglass Webb (Hegamin, 1865-1942), Charlotte Cordelia "Blink" Webb (1868-1912), and Ada Virgil Webb (Simons, 1872-1952). Her brother, John Johnston Webb (1863-1934), later known as Juan or Jaun Degonzalez, worked as a barber. Wood-Webb family Bible, AWWP; "Charlotte Cordelia Webb," Pennsylvania, Philadelphia City Death Certificates, 1803-1915, FHL 1421320; "Ada Webb Simons," Cook County, Illinois, Death Index, 1908-1988, 6083062; "Miriam Webb Hegamin," Pennsylvania Death Certificates 1906-1963, certificate #50668.

7. This address is confirmed by Louisa and Harriet Jacobs's listing in the 1880 Census, Washington, Washington, District of Columbia, Roll 122, 317D.

8. Adelaide Proctor (1825-1864) was a popular mid-nineteenth-century British poet whose works were published in England and the United States, translated into German, and often set to music or turned into hymns. Ian Petticrew, "Adelaide Anne Proctor," Minor Victorian Poets and Authors, http://gerald-massey.org.uk/index.htm.

9. The children of Cordelia Sanders and William H. Chew—eight-year-old Richard "Dick" Sanders Chew (1871-1962) and five-year-old Charles Sanders Chew (1873-1954)—moved after their mother's death into the Sanders family home at 1116 Fitzwater Street in Philadelphia. The home had been purchased when the Sanders family moved to Philadelphia from Charleston, South Carolina, and was now occupied by Delie's brother, Robert "Bobbie" Sanders (1832-1907); his wife, Martha (1833-1913); and Delie's sister, Julia Sanders (Venning, 1837-1910), and her large family.

Willie Chew, widower of Delie Sanders (Chew) and son of John Chew (1818-1870) and Charlotte Henson (Chew, 1819-1884), was trained as a barber in Philadelphia. In 1879 and 1880, he ran a shop in Princeton, New Jersey. McElroy's Philadelphia City Directory, 1858, 594; "William H. Chew," 1880 U.S. Census, Philadelphia, Philadelphia, Roll 1168, 481A; Mains and Fitzgerald's Mercer County Directory, City Directory, Trenton, New Jersey, 1879, 389; Fitzgerald's Directory, Trenton, New Jersey, 1880, 135;

"Richard S. Chew," California Death Index, 1940–1997, SS# 563525763; "Charles S. Chew," *Find a Grave*, http://www.findagrave.com, citing record ID 162626966.

10. The "event" was the expected arrival of the first child of Charlotte "Lottie" Forten (Grimké) and Reverend Francis "Frank" Grimké. Lottie was forty-two years old; her husband was twenty-nine. Theodora Cornelia Grimké (January 1880–June 1880) was born New Year's Day. Brenda Stevenson, ed., *Journals of Charlotte Forten Grimké*, xxxviii.

11. After a twenty-year career in Liberia, Reverend Alexander Crummell (1819–1898) founded the first independent black Episcopal church in Washington, DC, in 1875. St. Luke's first opened its doors two months before this letter, on Thanksgiving 1879. The "manuscript" sermon that Louisa Jacobs heard was published in 1882 in Crummell's *The Greatness of Christ and Other Sermons*. Wilson Jeremiah Moses, *Alexander Crummell*, 199; Leslie Alexander, "Alexander Crummell," in *Encyclopedia of African American History*, 361–64.

12. Willie had signed on for several sailings in 1877 as a barber on the *City of Richmond*, which sailed between Liverpool and New York. "William H. Chew," Liverpool, England Crew Lists, 1861–1919, reference #387CRE/222, at ancestry.com.

13. On a handwritten list of Delie Chew's funeral carriages, someone wrote, "Poor Deley's death made a big change in domestic matters." Julia Sanders (Venning), Delie's sister, had married Edward Young Venning (1835–1884) and had seven children at home: Miranda, Julia, Oliver, Sarah, George, Martha, and Louisa. Robert "Bobbie" Sanders and his wife, Martha J. Davenport (Sanders, 1833–1913), were childless and helped to raise the young Chew boys. By the summer of 1880, the older boy, Richard "Dick" Sanders Chew, was residing in Trenton, New Jersey, with his grandmother Charlotte Henson (Chew) and aunt Sallie Chew (Coe, 1852–1929). Chew Family Papers, SCSVC; "J. E. Venning," 1880 U.S. Census, Philadelphia, Philadelphia, Pennsylvania, Roll 1170, 102A; "Charlotte Chew," 1880 U.S. Census, Trenton, Mercer, New Jersey, Roll 788, 335D.

14. The seventh daughter of a seventh daughter was believed in some folk traditions to have the gift of second sight. Gabrielle Hatfield, *Encyclopedia of Folk Medicine*, 305.

15. Mary Bucklin Davenport (Claflin, 1825–1896) and former Massachusetts governor William Claflin (1818–1905) had moved to Washington after his election to Congress in 1877. An active abolitionist, William Claflin also promoted women's suffrage, helped to found the Massachusetts Republican Party, advocated prison reform, cofounded Boston University and Claflin University, and served three terms as governor of Massachusetts. From 1868 to 1872 he served as national chair of the Republican Party, and from 1877 to 1881 he served as member of the United States Congress.

16. Electra Sanderson (Dawes, 1822–1901) married Henry Laurens Dawes (1816–1903), who had succeeded Charles Sumner (1811–1874) as the U.S. senator from Massachusetts from 1875 to 1892. Like Sumner, Dawes promoted antislavery causes and Reconstruction measures.

17. Louisa is speaking of her maternal relatives. Harriet Jacobs's brother, John S. Jacobs (ca. 1817), had died in 1873, leaving behind a son, Joseph Ramsey Jacobs

(1866–1961). Louisa did have one other, more distant relative: her mother's half brother, Elijah Knox Jr. (1824–1907), who had a son and daughter by his first wife, and two sons by his second wife, Elijah and William, whom Louisa remembered in her will. Louisa Jacobs was also related to Genie Webb and Charlotte Forten (Grimké) through her father, Samuel Tredwell Sawyer (1800–1865): Louisa's white Edenton grandmother, Margaret Blair (Sawyer, 1772–1826), was a first cousin of Genie's and Charlotte's white Edenton grandfather, James Cathcart Johnston. HJFP, lxxiv, chart (n.p.), 864.

18. Genie and Edith Webb were listed as communicants on April 21, 1878, at the Episcopal Church of the Ascension, Gloucester, Camden, New Jerey, and they were members of the affiliated Stockton Church of Our Saviour. Reverend Charles H. DeGarmo served as deacon at both churches. Genie's younger sisters, Ada, Miriam, and Cordelia, were baptized a year earlier at Stockton Church of Our Saviour. Charlotte Forten (Grimké), Ada Howell Hinton (1832–1903), and Edith L. Webb acted as their sponsors. Although William H. Chew was confirmed, married, and buried at the Crucifixion Episcopal Church in south Philadelphia, there is an undated notation in the parish records that he "removed" to another parish. By October 1880, Genie Webb had made friends with the rector of St. Thomas African Episcopal Church in Philadelphia, so it may be that Willie Chew had joined St. Thomas's congregation. Historical Society of Pennsylvania, Historic Pennsylvania Church and Town Records, Reels 868, 637; baptism certificates, AWWP; Louisa Jacobs to Genie Webb, October 4, 1880, AWWP.

19. Miriam Douglass Webb (age 14) and Charlotte Cordelia Webb (age 12) were confirmed March 5, 1880, at the St. Thomas African Episcopal Church in Philadelphia by Bishop William Hobart Hare (1838–1909), who officiated by the laying on of hands. Raised and educated in Philadelphia, Reverend Hare had served as Missionary Bishop of Niobrara in the Dakota Territory from 1872. In February 1880, he returned east to defend himself in a libel suit launched in the New York state court. Confirmation certificates, AWWP; M. A. DeWolfe Howe, *Life and Labors of Bishop Hare*, 6–7, 167, 387; "Clergyman in a Libel Suit," *New York Times,* June 8, 1880.

20. This was a later address of Jacobs's friend Richard DeReef Venning (1846–1929), who worked as a clerk in the pension office. Boyd's Washington City Directory, 1884, 1887.

21. According to the Jacobses' friend, Cornelia Grinnell (Willis, 1825–1904), "Mr. Watson drove too hard a bargain as to his furniture." HJFP, 758.

22. Edith and Genie Webb both taught at the Ferry Avenue Colored School in Camden, New Jersey. Camden City Directory, 1882–1883, 33, 405.

23. Miranda "Rannie" Cogdell Venning (1862–1900) attended the Vaux School in Philadelphia, under Professor Jacob C. White (1837–1902), before going on to the Girls' High and Normal School, Philadelphia's teaching college. Her maternal aunt, teacher Delie Sanders (Chew), had tutored her. Undated obituary notice for Miranda Venning, Box 8, Folder 1, SCSVC.

24. Early antislavery poet Sarah Louise Forten (Purvis, 1814–1884) was the mother of Harriet Ann "Annie" Purvis (1848–1917) and aunt-in-law of Genie Webb. Sarah's brother, Robert B. Forten, had married Genie's aunt, Mary Virginia Wood, in 1836.

25. The infant daughter of Charlotte Forten (Grimké), Theodora Cornelia Grimké, had died June 10, 1880. Eric Gardner, "Charlotte Forten," 408.

26. Address of the Jacobses' friend, Eliza Ann Logan (Lawton, 1822–1883).

27. Dr. Samuel Till Birmingham (1800–1896) was a wealthy mixed-race naturopath, born in Wilmington, Delaware, and a former resident of Pennsylvania and New Bedford, Massachusetts, who operated the Indian Botanical Drug store in Cambridge, Massachusetts. Louisa Jacobs had clerked in his store in 1860. HJFP, 269; will of Samuel T. Birmingham, December 8, 1892, proved April 1896, Massachusetts Wills and Probate Records, Suffolk County; "Samuel Birmingham," 1850 U.S. Census, Bradford, Clearfield, Pennsylvania, Roll: M432_768, page: 327A; "Sam'l Birghminghan," 1880 U.S. Census, Boston, Suffolk, Massachusetts; Roll: 554, page: 145C; "Samuel T. Birmingham," March 5, 1896, Massachusetts Death Records 1841–1915.

28. The adopted daughter of Zenas Brockett (1803–1883), Harriet Brockett (Petrie) (1833–1880), of Cuyler, Cortland, New York, died July 18, and her daughter, Anna B. Petrie (1864–1880), died on her sixteenth birthday, July 12, at her grandfather's home near Brockett's Bridge. Edward J. Brockett, *The Descendants of John Brockett*, 360; Cortland County Death Notices and Obituaries—1880, the *Cortland County Democrat*, www.usgenweb .info/nycortland/vitals/d1880.htm.

29. Louisa and Harriet Jacobs assisted their Cambridge friend Eliza Ann Logan (Lawton), whose twenty-year-old son Isaac died of consumption on September 13. The whole family suffered from the disease: two brothers had died previously, and Eliza, her daughter Mariana, and another son, Arthur, would be dead by 1884. At the time of this letter Eliza Logan (Lawton) served as president of the United Daughters of Zion in Boston, an organization dedicated to assisting sick women of color. The Jacobses' friendship with the Lawtons went back to at least 1852, when Louisa attended as bridesmaid at the wedding of Eliza's sister, Sarah J. F. Logan (1827–ca. 1864), to George W. Lowther (1822–1898), the Jacobses' good friend from Edenton. Harriet Jacobs's *Incidents in the Life of Slave Girl* included a testimonial written by George Lowther. "Eliza A. Lawton," Massachusetts, Death Records 1841–1915, March 14, 1883; *A Directory of the Charitable and Beneficent Organizations of Boston* (Boston: 1880), 79; "George W. Lowther," Massachusetts Town and Vital Records, marriage September 9, 1852; Dorothy Porter Wesley and Constance Porter Uzelac, eds., *William Cooper Nell*, 354; William H. Logan will, January 20, 1870, Massachusetts Wills and Probate Records, 1635–1991, Case No. 50524, image 279, ancestry.com; HJFP, 752, 758; "Eliza Lawton," 1880 U.S. Census, Cambridge, Middlesex, Massachusetts, Roll 543, 376D; "Isaac T. Lawton," Massachusetts, Death Records 1841–1915, GS Film #960218.

30. Phillips Brooks (1835–1893) served as Episcopal rector of the Church of the Holy Trinity in Philadelphia from 1862 to 1869, then took Boston's Trinity Church until 1891 when he became bishop of Massachusetts. Brooks is best known as the composer of "O Little Town of Bethlehem." "Phillips Brooks," *Encyclopædia Britannica Online*, www .britannica.com/EBchecked/topic/81281/Phillips-Brooks.

31. The ballad "Would I Were with Thee," written by Mrs. Norton and arranged by Carlo Bosetti in 1850, expresses love, grief, loss, and longing. The song opens with

"Would I were with thee, ev'ry day and hour / Which now I pass so sadly far from thee / Would that my form possess'd the magic power / To follow where my heavy heart would be." Music Library, University of North Carolina, Chapel Hill, http://dc.lib .unc.edu/cdm/compoundobject/collection/sheetmusic/id/16442.

32. Five years earlier, Louisa Jacobs lived in Cambridge, Massachusetts, and assisted her mother in running a boarding house. Cordelia Sanders (Chew) had boarded in Cambridge with Louisa's aunt by marriage, Eleanor Jacobs, from October 9 to November 20, 1875. Eleanor Aspland (Herbert, Jacobs, 1832–1903) was the English wife of Louisa Jacobs's uncle John. HJFP, lx; board receipts, Chew Family Papers, SCSVC.

33. William H. Chew was part of a lawsuit in the summer of 1880 that challenged school segregation on the grounds that it violated the Fourteenth Amendment. Phillip Lapsansky, "Afro-Americana: Family Values, in Black and White," 29; Chew Family Papers, SCSVC; Roger Lane and Benjamin R. Collins, *William Dorsey's Philadelphia and Ours*, 154; "More Notes," *The Weekly Courier* (Connellsville, Pennsylvania), September 17, 1880, 4, https://www.newspapers.com/image/37121255/?terms=William%2Bh.%2 Bchew; "Blacks in a White School," *The Dallas Daily Herald*, September 8, 1881, 7, https://www.newspapers.com/image/78149073/?terms=William%2Bh.%2Bchew.

34. Zenas Brockett (1803–1883) lived with his daughter Anna Feeter, son Nathaniel, and grandchildren at his farm near Brockett's Bridge, Manheim, New York. Louisa first knew the Brocketts through her uncle abolitionist John S. Jacobs and had lived with them in 1849 and during the winter of 1851–1852, the fall of 1852, and the spring and summer of 1853. Louisa's time with the Brocketts coincides with Zenas Brockett's position as a manager of the American Anti-Slavery Society in 1852–1853. Brockett's cousin remembered, "He not only *said* the black man shall be free, but he took into the shelter of his home fold stray lambs and cared for them. He shielded them from the voice and touch of the enemy." "Zenus Brockett," 1880 U.S. Census, Manheim, Herkimer Co., New York, Roll 837, 291; HJFP, 168, 170, 176, 178, 186, 204, 213; Wesley and Uzelac, *William Cooper Nell*, 320, 342; George Beckwith, Martha Lewis Beckwith Lewis, and Annie Ewell Russell, *Beckwith's Almanac*, volumes 33–41, 409–10; John R. McKivigan, *The War Against Proslavery Religion*, 205.

35. Dr. George Wood Holman (1826–1911) invented the Holman Liver Pad, a medicated pectoral pad worn with straps around the neck and chest, "designed for the quick and perfect cure of a class of Diseases and Symptoms not accessible to other kinds of treatment. Among these are the various forms of LOCAL and SEATED PAIN, and the dangerous manifestations of INTERRUPTED or SLUGGISH CIRCULATION." The Holman Liver Pad was advertised between 1879 and 1882 on Internal Revenue stamps used to show payment of taxes on manufactured goods. "Adjunct to Moulton and Rawlins," https://sites.google.com/site/adjuncttomoulton/the-george-holman-three-senior-junior-and-the-third.

36. Annie Purvis of Philadelphia was the daughter of Joseph Purvis (1812–1857) and Sarah Louise Forten (Purvis). She arrived in Washington on November 1, 1880, to work for the federal Department of Agriculture.

37. Frank and Lottie Grimké had recently moved from 1419 Pierce Place to 1608 R Street. Boyd's Washington City Directory, 1883, 1886, 428; "Francis J. Grimke," 1880 U.S. Census, Washington, Washington, District of Columbia, Roll 121, 146B.

38. Annie Purvis was not technically a cousin of the Webbs; she was a paternal first cousin of Charlotte Forten (Grimké), who was a maternal first cousin of Genie Webb.

39. Possibly her mother or fifteen-year-old Miriam Webb, whose nickname was "Mame."

40. Shortly after her December 19, 1878, wedding to Francis Grimké, Lottie Forten sent Annie Purvis a list of the wedding presents she received. Annie Purvis forwarded the list to Genie Webb. Annie Purvis to Genie Webb, January 6, 1879, AWWP.

41. The Latrobe Stove, also called the Baltimore Heater, was invented in Baltimore by John Hazelhurst Latrobe (1803-1891), the son of America's first professional architect, Benjamin Henry Latrobe (1764-1820). The cast iron, coal-burning stove was round and ornate, stood about two feet tall, and was placed inside the fireplace. Paul K. Williams, The House History Man, http://househistoryman.blogspot.ca/2012/03/thought-your-fireplace-heated-your.html.

42. Francis Grimké's seventy-year-old mother, Nancy Weston (1811-1895) of Charleston, South Carolina, lived with the Grimké family "in her sunny room on the second floor" at the back of Francis Grimké's home. Nancy and Henry Grimké (1801-1852), a widowed Charleston planter, had three sons together: Archibald (1849-1930), Francis (1850-1937), and John (1852-1915). Henry Grimké died when Nancy was pregnant with her third son, and he directed that his white son, Montague (1832-1896), treat Nancy and her sons as family. Montague, however, used his half brothers as servants, hiring them out, and eventually sold Francis. After the war, Henry Grimké's abolitionist sisters, Sarah (1792-1873) and Angelina (1805-1879), discovered their young nephews and arranged for them to attend Lincoln University, Harvard University, and Howard University, where they studied law. Francis went on to study theology at Princeton. Carolivia Herron, ed., *Selected Works of Angelina Grimké*, 425; "Nancy Grimke," 1880 U.S. Census, Washington, Washington, District of Columbia, Roll 121, 146B; Mark Perry, *Lift Up Thy Voice*.

43. The grandmother of Annie Purvis and Charlotte Forten (Grimké), Charlotte Vandine (Forten, 1785-1884) married wealthy sail maker James Forten in 1805. She was an active member in the Philadelphia Female Anti-Slavery Society, along with her daughters, teacher Margaretta Forten (1806-1875), Harriet Forten (Purvis, 1810-1875), Mary Theresa Forten (1815-1842), and Sarah Louisa Forten (Purvis). Her sons were abolitionists: James Forten, Jr., William Deas Forten (1823-1900), Thomas Willing Francis Forten (1827-1897), and Robert Bridges Forten, the father of Charlotte Forten (Grimké). Winch, *Gentleman of Color*, 111-13.

44. There are no known pictures of Annie Purvis. Her white Quaker friend Ellen Wright (Garrison, 1840-1931; niece of Lucretia Mott [1793-1880]) described her as "quite dark & not at all pretty." Annie described herself in 1879 to Genie: "You won't know your plain cousin, so changed will she be." Years later she would speak of her "not

very bonny face." Harriet Hyman Alonso, *Growing Up Abolitionist*, 188; Annie Purvis to Genie Webb, January 6, 1879, November 18, 1895, AWWP.

45. Genie's only brother, nearly eighteen-year-old John Degonzalez Webb worked as a barber in Philadelphia as well as at his father's shop in Camden. Camden City Directory, 1881, 281; 1883, 405.

46. Sisters Sarah Iredell (Fleetwood) and Laura Iredell (Hawkesworth, 1850–1909) were Genie Webb's first cousins: they were the only surviving children of Elizabeth Webb (Iredell) of Philadelphia and Geoffrey George Iredell (1811–1872) of Edenton, North Carolina. Their mother was a sister of Genie Webb's father, John Gloucester Webb (1823–1904), and of novelist Frank. J. Webb (1828–1894). Their father was a brother of Sarah Iredell (1806–1885), who had lived with Louisa and Harriet Jacobs in Boston in 1870. Their paternal grandfather's estate had been administered in Edenton, North Carolina, by Samuel Tredwell Sawyer (Louisa Jacobs's father). Sarah Iredell (Fleetwood) was recovering from the birth and death of her only child at the time, four-day-old Alice Louise Fleetwood, on October 1, 1880, in Rockland, Maryland. The funeral was held in Washington at the home of Sarah's sister, Laura, at 1618 Corcoran Street. The children of Laura Iredell (Hawkesworth) were Malcolm, 5, Conrade, 3, and Laura Heloise, 1. "Sarah Iredell," 1870 U.S. Census, Cambridge, Middlesex, Massachusetts, Roll 593_623, 240B, 241A; "Alice Louise Fleetwood," obituary notice, *Washington Post*, October 2, 1880; "Laura H. Hawksworth," 1880 U.S. Census, Washington, Washington, District of Columbia, Roll 121, 109C; North Carolina Estate Files, Chowan County, Jeffrey G. Iredell, May 7, 1837.

47. Joe is probably Joseph Pierce (ca. 1862–?), the eighteen-year-old adopted son (born in Georgia) of Harriet and Louisa Jacobs.

48. November 5 marked the one-year anniversary of the death of Delie Sanders (Chew).

49. Ada Virgil Webb (Simons) was the youngest of Genie Webb's siblings. Wood Webb family Bible, AWWP.

One by One Thy Duties Wait Thee: 1881–1882

1. In 1876 Delie Sanders (Chew) had visited Louisa and Delie's niece Miranda Venning twice in Cambridge. Both times—two weeks in March and during most of September—she boarded at Eleanor Jacobs's boarding house. Receipts, Chew Family Papers, SCSVC.

2. Twenty-six-year-old Kate V. Jennings from New York worked as a clerk at the Treasury Department and advocated for equal rights. In 1872 she wrote to Charles Sumner and praised his "able and fearless advocacy" of his Supplemental Civil Rights bill, a bill to end all racial discrimination in juries, schools, inns, restaurants, and all modes of transportation. Jennings wrote that the legislation would "fully arm and equip us to enjoy all the rights that make a free American citizen!" "Kate Jennings," 1880 U.S. Census, Washington, Washington, District of Columbia, Roll 121, 239C; the United

States Department of the Treasury, Treasury Register (Washington: 1879), 40; K. V. Jennings to Charles Sumner, Jan. 15, 1872, reel 56, fr. 151, in the Charles Sumner microfilm edition, Houghton Library, Harvard University, with thanks to Beverly Wilson Palmer.

3. Isaac Watts (1674–1748) wrote the words to "My God, the Spring of All My Joys" in 1707. This hymn was probably sung to the music "Richmond," composed in 1792 by Thomas Haweis (1734–1820). http://cyberhymnal.org/htm/m/g/mgspring.htm.

4. This event was recorded by the Jacobses' friend Julia Wilbur (1815–1895) in her diary and was reported a week later in *The People's Advocate*. Julia Wilbur diaries, Haverford College, Quaker and Special Collections Transcriptions; HJFP, 760–63.

5. A possible clue to Genie's disappointment may be found in an undated letter from her mother. "I am very very glad to learn that you are desirous of being confirmed in the faith our Our Blessed Savior. . . . I suppose we ought to consider this point: whether we as a people are perfectly welcome in this little white church—it is a very delicate question yet should be considered." Annie Wood (Webb) to daughters, before May 1879, AWWP.

6. Richard E. DeReef Venning, the brother of Edward Y. Venning and brother-in-law of Julia Sanders (Venning) and Cordelia Sanders (Chew), had secured a clerkship in the government pension office.

7. James Garfield (1831–1881) had been elected president of the United States.

8. This may be a reference to the death of Joseph W. Cassey (1827–1881) on February 9. Cassey, the eldest son of Joseph (1789–1848) and Amy Matilda Cassey (Remond, 1808–1856), was a lifelong friend of both of Genie's parents. "Joseph W. Cassey," Philadelphia, Pennsylvania, Death Certificates Index, 1803–1915, FHL # 2047635.

9. All Souls Unitarian Church, under the leadership of Reverend Rush R. Shippen (1828–1911), was well known for its excellent music. A history of the church attests that "the esthetic sense of the church has always demanded good music as essential in the satisfactory conduct of religious services. . . . The standard then set has been well maintained and the choir of All Souls has always comprised some of the best musical talent of the city." Jennie W. Scudder, *A Century of Unitarianism in the National Capital*, 101–2, 138.

10. Alice C. Bowers (1855–1881) was a Philadelphia schoolteacher and the daughter of Lucretia Turpin (1827–1911) and Thomas J. Bowers (1823–1885). Her father, also known as the "American Mario," was a wealthy Philadelphia coal dealer who attained operatic fame during the 1850s touring with the "Back Swan," Elizabeth Taylor Greenfield (1824–1876). "Alice C. Bowers," Philadelphia, Pennsylvania, Death Certificates Index, 1803–1915, film #2047961; "Death of Thomas J. Bowers," *New York Times*, October 5, 1885; James M. Trotter, *Music and Some Highly Musical People*, 131–37.

11. Louise Sanders Venning (1878–1923), daughter of Julia Sanders (Venning), was about three years old. "L. S. Venning," 1880 U.S. Census, Philadelphia, Philadelphia, Roll 1170, 102A.

12. Frederick Douglass (1818–1895), well known abolitionist, civil rights activist, and journalist, served as U.S. marshal for the District of Columbia from 1877 to 1881,

and was appointed by President Garfield as the recorder of deeds from 1881 to 1886. Blanche Kelso Bruce (1841–1898), a wealthy Mississippi plantation owner and the nation's second black senator, was appointed to be Register of the Treasury. "Frederick Douglass," "Blanche Kelso Bruce," *American National Online Biography*, www.anb.org/articles/15/15-00186.html?a=1&n=frederick%20douglass&d=10&ss=0&q=1.

13. Lucretia Garfield (1832–1918) contracted malaria in early May 1881 and had gone to Long Branch, New Jersey, to recuperate. New York senators Roscoe Conkling (1829–1888) and Thomas Platt (1833–1910), resigned on May 16, 1881, to register their opposition to Garfield's nomination of customs collector. The senators were confident that the state legislature would reelect them, but it did not. Betty Boyd Caroli, "Lucretia Garfield," Encyclopedia Britannica's guide to American presidents, www.britannica.com/presidents/article-9096542; U.S. Senate: Art & History Home, Historical Minutes, 1870–1920, "Both New York Senators Resign," www.senate.gov/artandhistory/history/minute/Both_New_York_Senators_Resign.htm.

14. In addition to teaching, Edith Webb gave public literary readings. Admission ticket, "Select Readings and Recitations by Miss Edith L. Webb," June 30, 1881, Odd Fellows Hall, Philadelphia, AWWP.

15. Sarah Iredell (Fleetwood), an 1858 graduate of Oberlin, had worked for twenty years as a teacher before embarking on this clothing enterprise. She was probably assisted by her mother, Elizabeth Webb (Iredell), who was an accomplished dressmaker.

16. Both Genie's illness and the Webbs' inability to make mortgage payments were confirmed by her brother, John, who intended to send money from his barbering job at the seaside resort "Hathaway House" in Deal Beach, New Jersey. He assured his sister that he had "not touched a drop of any intoxicating drink althoug[h] it is all around me." John D. [Degonzalez] Webb to Edith Webb, July 23, 1881, AWWP.

17. Eleven weeks after he was shot on July 2, 1881, President James Garfield died of infection and complications caused by his doctors' continuous probing of his wound with unsterilized fingers and instruments. One "ingenious" device used to try to find the bullet lodged in Garfield's body was a metal detector invented by Alexander Graham Bell (1847–1922) that malfunctioned because of the president's iron bed frame. The first doctor to attend to President Garfield after he was shot was Dr. Charles Burleigh Purvis (1842–1929)—first cousin of Annie Purvis and Charlotte Forten (Grimké). Amanda Schaffer, "A President Felled by an Assassin and 1880's Medical Care," *New York Times*, July 25, 2006; Margaret Hope Bacon, *But One Race*, 191; Candice Millard, *Destiny of the Republic*, 162–65.

18. Joseph Pierce was born in Georgia about 1862 and adopted by Harriet Jacobs, whom he called "Ma," and Louisa, whom he called "Aunt Lou."

19. Miranda "Rannie" Venning and Julia E. Venning (later Warwick, 1864–1891) were the daughters of Julia Sanders (Venning) and Edward Y. Venning. In 1878 the *Record* reported that Miranda Venning, one of only three colored students who presented themselves for the high school entrance examinations, had conducted herself "very lady-like in manner." But in a discriminatory move that outraged many, school examiners

"failed" the three applicants. By June 1879, however, Miranda Venning and Amanda Bustill had passed the Normal School entrance examinations. Miranda was the first black graduate of Philadelphia's Girls' Normal School in 1882. Colored teachers were required to pass their certification examinations with a minimum average of 70 compared to whites, who needed only 65 to pass. Roger Lane and Benjamin R. Collins, *William Dorsey's Philadelphia and Ours*, 153–55; Megan Atkinson, "More Processing Please . . . ," PACSCL Hidden Collections Processing Project, November 3, 2010, Library Company of Philadelphia; "Miranda Venning," certificate to teach in the Public Grammar Schools of Philadelphia from the Girls' Normal School, Philadelphia, June 19, 1882, SCSVC.

20. William H. Chew launched a lawsuit in 1880 to abolish racially segregated schools in Pennsylvania. On June 8, 1881, Governor Henry M. Hoyt (1830–1892) signed a bill to end school segregation in Pennsylvania. The law went unheeded for the next one hundred years. Chew Family Papers, SCSVC; Anne M. Stewart, "Desegregation of Pennsylvania Schools."

21. Cornelia Grinnell (Willis) was the second wife of poet and editor Nathaniel Parker Willis (1806–1867). She had employed Harriet Jacobs for many years as nurse to her children. She purchased Harriet's freedom in 1852, encouraged Harriet to write her autobiography, and contributed to Harriet's care in her later years. Cornelia was staying at this time with her son, Grinnell Willis (1848–1930), in Englewood, New Jersey. Grinnell Willis, like his siblings, considered Louisa a close family friend who grew "more valuable each year & dearer." He provided a monthly allowance for Louisa in her old age. "Grenelle Willis," 1880 U.S. Census, Englewood, Bergen, New Jersey; Roll: 770, 225B; HJFP, 869; "Death List of a Day," *New York Times*, March 27, 1904.

22. The younger Willis daughter, Edith (1853–1938), married her dying cousin, Lawrence Leslie Grinnell (1851–1881), on April 7, 1880. A few weeks later, Harriet Jacobs came to assist the Willis family and stayed three months. Edith Willis (Grinnell) did not remarry after her husband's death on August 20, 1881, and remained a close, lifelong friend of Louisa's. Louisa visited Edith often in her Brookline, Massachusetts, home, moved in with her in 1914, and died there in 1917. HJFP, 758; "Lawrence L. Grinnell," New Jersey Deaths and Burials, Index, 1798–1971, film #589831; "Edith Grinnell," Massachusetts Death Index, 1901–1980, vol. 27, 291; Edith Willis (Grinnell) to Eugenie Webb, April 5, 1917, AWWP, in this edition.

23. President James A. Garfield died September 19, 1881.

24. The main contenders in the 1880 Republican National Convention in Chicago were Ulysses S. Grant (1822–1885), John Sherman (1823–1900), and James G. Blaine (1830–1893). James A. Garfield of Ohio had attended the convention for the sole purpose of nominating Sherman and was completely unprepared to be chosen as a dark horse candidate. After thirty-five ballots, Garfield was nominated as the Republican presidential candidate, and Chester Arthur (1829–1886) of New York was nominated as vice presidential candidate. Garfield's assassin—a disgruntled Grant supporter, Charles J. Guiteau (1841–1882)—had proclaimed after the shooting, "I am a Stalwart and Arthur

will be President," leading to unfounded rumors that Chester Arthur and his close associate, Roscoe Conkling, were behind the assassination.

25. The "mistaken step" may be Conkling's recent resignation from the state senate, or possibly the sex scandal surrounding him and Kate Chase (Sprague, 1840–1899), the wife of Governor William Sprague (1820–1915) of Rhode Island. In August 1879, Conkling's long-standing affair with Mrs. Sprague exploded with the well publicized story of Governor Sprague chasing his wife's lover off his Rhode Island cottage property, shotgun in hand. The Spragues were divorced in 1882. Peg A. Lamphier, *Kate Chase and William Sprague*, 288–96.

26. Owen Meredith (1831–1891) was the pen name of Robert Bulwer-Lytton, 1st Earl of Lytton—diplomat, statesman, and viceroy of India. Of his nine published books, the most popular was *Lucile*, published in 1860.

27. Julia Sanders (Venning).

28. Lafayette Square is across the street from the White House. HJFP, lxi.

29. In 1882 members of St. Luke's vestry petitioned the bishop for the removal of Alexander Crummell as rector. Dissatisfaction with Crummell's "secularity" and controversy about the church's music were part of the complaint. Wilson Jeremiah Moses, *Alexander Crummell*, 205.

30. Willowbrook was the country estate on Lake Owasco near Auburn, New York, of the large E. T. Throop Martin family. Martin's youngest son, Edward Sanford Martin (1856–1939)—poet, essayist, cofounder of Harvard's *Lampoon*, and the first literary editor of *Life* magazine—started work in 1879 as a clerk in the Department of State in Washington, DC, and may have been instrumental in getting Louisa the supervisory position in the family's booming canning and bakery business. In 1880 the Martin family employed eight live-in servants. William Cushing, *Initials and Pseudonyms: A Dictionary of Literary Disguises*, 495; Eveline Martin Alexander and Sandra Myres, *Cavalry Wife*, 136; "Cornelia Martin," 1880 U.S. Census, Owasco, Cayuga, New York, Roll 814, 242B; Paul K. Williams and Charles N. Williams, *Owasco Lake*, 106–7.

31. Miss Martin was one of the older unmarried Martin daughters, either Mary "Molly" Martin (1838–1884), who suffered from tuberculosis, or Cornelia "Nellie" Martin (1840–1927). Cornelia and Mary Martin managed the Willowbrook estate and supervised the canning business on the premises. Alexander and Myres, *Cavalry Wife*, 17.

32. Louisa provided for the Chew boys in her will.

33. Anna Brockett (Feeter, 1844–1913) was the daughter of Zenas Brockett.

34. This is the same address from which Louisa wrote in June 1880, and where Richard E. DeReef Venning also lived. Boyd's Washington City Directory, 1884, 1887.

35. Elizabeth Chase Akers (Allen, 1832–1911) first published "Rock Me to Sleep" in Philadelphia's *Saturday Evening Post* on June 9, 1860, under the pen name Florence Percy. Louisa quotes from the opening couplet, "Backward, turn backward, O Time, in your flight, / Make me a child again, just for to-night!" Edward T. James, ed., *Notable American Women 1607–1950: A Biographical Dictionary*, 1:36–37.

36. Louisa's and Genie's horror would have been compounded by the knowledge that their beloved Delie had been buried at Philadelphia's Lebanon Cemetery only

three years earlier. On December 4, 1882, a gang of grave robbers was caught carrying six cadavers from Lebanon Cemetery to the dissecting rooms of Jefferson Medical College. Dr. William Forbes (1831–1905), the chief anatomist at the college, along with other doctors and the cemetery's black superintendent, Robert Chew, were implicated in a nine-year "don't-ask-don't-tell" scheme of supplying the medical school with African American cadavers. When the news broke, distraught mourners rushed to the cemetery to retrieve their recently buried dead. An angry mob gathered the next day outside the magistrate's office and the courthouse. Two white men, Frank McNamee and Henry Pillet, and the Chew brothers, Robert and Levi, were convicted and sentenced to ten years in prison. The doctors were acquitted. The Chew brothers were not related to the Chew-Venning family. Emily Bazelon, "Grave Offence," *Legal Affairs: The Magazine at the Intersection of Law and Life* (July/August 2002), https://legalaffairs.org/issues/July-August-2002/story_bazelon_julaug2002.msp; Suzanne M. Schultz, *Body Snatching*, 81; "Robbing a Cemetery: A Body-Snatching Sensation in Philadelphia," *New York Times*, December 6, 1882.

One by One Bright Gifts from Heaven: 1883

1. Dr. Furman Jeremiah Shadd (1852–1908)—the brother of Louisa's school-teacher friend Marian "Mattie" Purnell Shadd (1856–1943)—married Alice Parke (b. 1854) on December 26, 1882, at the Fifteenth Street Presbyterian Church in Washington, DC. Reverend Francis Grimké conducted the service. Dr. Shadd was appointed assistant surgeon at Freedmen's Hospital, Howard Medical School, and became full professor in 1891. He was the third African American to be appointed to the faculty of Howard University, and he served as secretary and treasurer of the medical department from 1896 until his death. Henry S. Robinson, "Furman Jeremiah Shadd"; George Hendrick and Willene Hendrick, *Black Refugees in Canada*, 67.

2. Louisa and Harriet Jacobs and the Webb sisters were members of the Episcopal Church. Francis Grimké was a Presbyterian minister, but it seems that he performed an Episcopal marriage service.

3. Sallie Chew was William "Willie" H. Chew's sister, and the daughter of Charlotte Henson and John Chew of Philadelphia. She married Jefferson Coe, a waiter and caterer. "Sallie Chew," 1880 U.S. Census, Trenton, Mercer, New Jersey, Roll 788, 335D; "Sally Coe," 1900 U.S. Census, Cleveland, Cuyahoga, Ohio, Roll 1253, 1B; "Sally E. Coe," 1910 U.S. Census, Cleveland, Cuyahoga, Ohio, T624_1170, 4B; Sallie E. Coe, Lake View Cemetery, Cleveland, Ohio, http://www.findagrave.com/cgi-bin/fg.cgi?page=gr&GSln=COE&GSpartial=1&GSbyrel=all&GSst=37&GScntry=4&GSsr=881&GRid=78102249&.

4. "A Scandal in Colored Society," *Evening Star*, January 1, 1883, 3.

5. William E. Matthews (1843–1894), the son of a prominent mixed-race Baltimore family, was a wealthy financier and property owner in the District, and co-leader of the Lotus Club, criticized by many black Washingtonians for being a "blue vein" society (similar to the exclusive Brown Fellowship Society in Charleston) with a reputation for

color discrimination and exclusion. Its membership was largely made up of fair-skinned aristocrats from other cities who brought colorism with them. Many were associated with either Rev. Francis Grimké's Fifteenth Street Presbyterian Church or Rev. Alexander Crummell's St. Luke's congregation, which consisted of local white worshipers as well as distinguished mixed-race residents. Loren Schweninger, *Black Property Owners in the South*, 221; William J. Simmons and Henry McNeal Turner, *Men of Mark*, 246–51; Audrey Elisa Kerr, 46–48, 51–57, 105–9.

6. There was some truth to this scandal, and it particularly interested Louisa Jacobs and Genie Webb because the brother of Euretta Bozeman (Matthews, 1851–1915), William S. Boseman (b. ca. 1849), had married Annie Purvis's older sister, Sarah Purvis (1843–1890). Although her brothers in South Carolina and Kansas spelled the name "Boseman," Euretta used *z* in her spelling of the family name. She came from Troy, New York, to Washington, DC, to teach in 1876. In 1883 she married William E. Matthews (the same William E. Matthews who gave the Grimkés the large engraving of "Christ as the Good Shepherd" as a wedding gift in 1878). The Matthews' daughter, Aneuretta B. Matthews, was born in September 1883, nine months after the scandal broke. In 1890 Euretta Bozeman (Matthews) was working as a dressmaker in Philadelphia, and in 1892 she was back in Washington, where she remained—and was well regarded in elite colored society—until after the turn of the century. Her sisters were also teachers, and her eldest brother, Dr. Benjamin A. Boseman (1840–1881), served in the South Carolina state legislature from 1868 to 1873, and as postmaster of Charleston, South Carolina, from 1873 until his death in 1881. Julie Winch, *Gentleman of Color*, 365; "Euretta B. Matthews," Philadelphia, Pennsylvania, Marriage Records, 1885–1951, GSU # 4141877; "Mrs. Euretta Bozeman Matthews," *The Crisis* (New York: August 1915) www.marxists.org /history/usa/workers/civil-rights/crisis/0800-crisis-v10n04-w058.pdf; "Euretta B. Matthews," 1900 U.S. Census, Washington, Washington, District of Columbia, Roll T623, 129B; Gopsill's Philadelphia City Directory, 1890, 1274; "William E. Matthews," 2 May 1894, District of Columbia Deaths and Burials, 1840–1964; "Uretta Boseman," 1880 U.S. Census, Washington, Washington, District of Columbia, Roll 124, 76A; "Euretta Matthews," Boyd's Washington City Directory, 1892, 1895–1900; Gatewood, *Aristocrats of Color*, 72.

7. Isaac N. Carey (b. 1832) was a deputy marshal of the police court. 1880 U.S. Census, Washington, Washington, District of Columbia, Roll T9 0123, 81D.

8. Dr. Alexander Thomas Augusta (1825–1890) was a personal friend of Louisa Jacobs and Genie Webb. Dr. Augusta hosted the Jacobses in his home in Savannah, Georgia, in 1866 while Louisa taught in Dr. Augusta's Hospital for Freedmen and Refugees. He signed Genie Webb's autograph album in Atlantic City on August 25, 1884, with the note, "I hope you may ever retain the amiable disposition you seem to have inherited from your mother." His wife, Mary O. Augusta (1824–1904), also signed Genie Webb's autograph book with her Washington address, 1319 L Street. Dr. Augusta probably met Genie's mother, Annie E. Wood (Webb), in the late 1840s when he lived in Philadelphia and studied medicine privately with a faculty member of the University

of Pennsylvania. He may have met her again in the early 1850s in Toronto, where he studied medicine at Trinity College, University of Toronto. Dr. Augusta served as a surgeon in the Civil War, becoming the first African American doctor in the U.S. Army. He was the first black hospital administrator (Freedmen's Hospital in Washington) and professor of anatomy at Howard University. HJFP, 667; Genie Webb autograph book, AWWP; Jimmy B. Fennison, "Augusta, Alexander T.," The Black Past Remembered and Reclaimed: An Online Reference Guide to African American History, http://www.blackpast.org/?q=aah/augusta-alexander-t-1825-1890.

9. On January 3, Euretta Bozeman and William E. Matthews were married in her home by Reverend Alexander Crummell of St. Luke's Episcopal Church, assisted by Reverend Francis J. Grimké. The *Washington Bee* refrained from commenting on the scandal until January 6, when it stated in "Our Review" that "We shall show justice to those who were to be united in the holy bonds of wedlock." John H. Brooks's investigation found that the Matthews brothers were not in Washington on the evening he stated and that Matthews did indeed arrive in Baltimore early Sunday morning accompanied by a lady. On January 9, at an "interesting and somewhat exciting meeting of the School Board," teacher Euretta Bozeman was dismissed. Matthews responded with a defamation suit against school trustees John H. Brooks and Henry Johnson, and also against Isaac Carey and his housekeeper, Martha Alexander. On Thursday, January 18, Matthews resigned as trustee of the Fifteenth Street Presbyterian Church. On February 4, Mr. and Mrs. William E. Matthews attended the Fifteenth Street Presbyterian Church Sunday service and received congratulations. "Matthews-Bozeman," *Evening Star*, January 4, 1883, 3; "The Alleged Matthews Scandal," *The Critic*, January 8, 1883, 3; "Our Public Schools," *The Critic*, January 10, 1883, 2; "Mr. Matthews Sues for Damages," *The Critic*, January 13, 1883, 1; "Personals," *Washington Bee*, February 10, 1883, 3.

10. John G. Webb had celebrated his sixtieth birthday in January.

11. Harriet Jacobs would celebrate her sixty-eighth birthday. Cemetery inscription, interment record, Mount Auburn Cemetery, Cambridge, Massachusetts; Mary Maillard, "Dating Harriet Jacobs"; Harriet Jacobs, certificate of death, Vital Records Office, Washington, DC.

12. William E. Matthews.

13. Laura Iredell (Hawkesworth) was the sister of Sarah Iredell (Fleetwood) and a first cousin of Genie Webb. Laura's husband, James Malcolm Hawkesworth, was sued by his brother-in-law, Christian A. Fleetwood (1840–1914), but the nature of the lawsuit is not known. *Christian Fleetwood vs. J. Malcolm Hawkesworth surviving trustee, et al.*, filed January 9, 1883, with the Supreme Court of the District of Columbia, #8415, Eq. Doc. 22.

14. Genie probably sent Louisa a copy of the The *Bee*, edited by William Calvin Chase (1854–1921) in Washington, DC. In the March 10 edition, Genie and her sisters are mentioned as teachers at the Ferry Avenue Colored School in Camden, New Jersey, where they ran the night school. Louisa, in this letter, may be alluding to the *The Bee*'s recent attacks (in January and February) on Robert Purvis (1810–1898) as a "traitor" to his race, and Purvis's resulting libel suit against *The Bee*. Both Louisa and Genie were

friendly with the Robert Purvis family. "Camden and the Colored Schools," *The Bee*, Washington, DC, March 10, 1883, 2, 3; "Our Review," *The Bee*, February 17, 1883, 2; "A Warrant for Libel," "Mad About It Yet," "The Purvis-Chase Libel Case," *The Bee*, February 10, 1883, 2; "Our Exchanges," *The Bee*, February 4, 1883, 2; "Purvis Lame Defenders," *The Bee*, March 3, 1883, 2.

15. Genie's cousin Sarah Iredell (Fleetwood) was well known for her Thursday evening literary soirees, during which guests enjoyed music and discussed poetry and essays. Dorothy Sterling, ed., *We Are Your Sisters*, 430–32.

16. Sarah Iredell (Fleetwood) and Christian Fleetwood fostered two of the three children of Laura (Hawkesworth), and by 1900 Laura and all three children lived with the Fleetwoods. In 1886 Laura was listed in the Washington directory as a widow. Boyd's Washington City Directory, 1886, 442.

17. Richard Sanders Chew had been staying with his grandmother, Charlotte Henson (Chew), in Trenton, New Jersey.

18. Canadian-born Marian "Mattie" Purnell Shadd (1856–1940), daughter of Eliza (1829–1898) and Absolom Shadd (1815–1857), was a teacher at the John F. Cook School in Washington. Sallie Chew (Coe) was the sister of William "Willie" Chew and Annie E. Chew (Bishop, 1851–1909). HJFP, 769; "Marian P. Shadd," Massachusetts State Normal School at Framingham, 1875, American Antiquarian Society; "Marian P. Shadd," 1900 US Census, Washington, Washington, District of Columbia, Roll 160, 3A.

19. Zenas Brockett died May 28, 1883. *Beckwith's Almanac*, 409.

20. Lincoln University commencement exercises took place June 5, 1883. Minutes, United Presbyterian Church in the U.S.A., vol. 7, part 2 (1883), 742.

21. Annie E. Chew (Bishop) was Willie Chew's sister. In 1877 she had married Dr. William Bishop (1849–1904), a member of a prominent African American family of Baltimore. They lived in Annapolis, Maryland, and had four children, William, Charlotte, Martha, and James. "Annie E. Bishop," 1900 U.S. Census, Annapolis, Anne Arundel, Maryland, Roll 605, 4B; "Annie Elizabeth Bishop," Saint Anne's Cemetery, Annapolis, MD; Gatewood, *Aristocrats of Color*, 74.

22. Beef tea was a consommé made from lean beef given to invalids to stimulate the appetite.

23. Charlotte Henson (Chew) of Trenton, New Jersey.

24. The little sister is probably the third daughter of the Webb family, eighteen-year-old Miriam "Mame" Webb. By 1885 Miriam was established in Camden as a schoolteacher, where she worked five years before her marriage to William Waters Hegamin Jr. (1859–1942) in 1890. Undated obituary for Miriam Webb Hegamin [June 1942], marriage certificate, AWWP.

25. Charlotte Henson (Chew) had moved by this time from her home in Trenton, New Jersey, to live with her daughter, Annie Chew (Bishop), in Annapolis, Maryland. "Charlotte Louisa Chew," June 13, 1884, Philadelphia, Pennsylvania Death Certificates, film 2069689; "Annie Elizabeth Bishop," Saint Anne's Cemetery, Annapolis, Maryland.

One by One Thy Griefs Shall Meet Thee: 1884–1885

1. Louisa had recently been hired to teach sewing and cooking at Howard University. HJFP, 770.

2. Frederick Douglass served as recorder of deeds from 1881 to 1886. On January 24, 1884, Reverend Francis J. Grimké had performed the marriage ceremony for Douglass (ca. 1818–1895) and Helen Pitts (1838–1903) in his own home, witnessed by Lottie Forten (Grimké), Senator Blanche Bruce (1841–1898), and Josephine Willson (Bruce, 1853–1923). Francis J. Grimké, "Second Marriage of Frederick Douglass."

3. Annie alludes to the proverb "Man proposes, God disposes," translated from Thomas à Kempis's *Imitation of Christ.*

4. Sarah Louise Forten (Purvis) and Charlotte Vandine (Forten).

5. Annie alludes to the novel *Hope On, Hope Ever* (London: Thomas Tegg, 1840), written by British author Mary Botham Howitt (1799–1888).

6. Edith Louise Fleetwood (1884–1970) was born May 17 to Sarah Iredell (Fleetwood) and Christian A. Fleetwood. District of Columbia, Births and Christenings, 1830–1955; Social Security Death Index, #578-68-0024.

7. Glymont, Maryland, was a popular resort in the late nineteenth century, visited by citizens of Washington, Georgetown, and Alexandria, Virginia. Sara Poynor, "Long Past Days as Swanky Resort, Glymont Survives," Southern Maryland Newspapers Online, SoMdNews.com, September 9, 2009.

8. Alice Ann Purvis (1872–1934) was the daughter of Annie Purvis's double first cousin Dr. Charles Burleigh Purvis (1842–1929), the chief surgeon at Freedmen's Hospital, Howard University. Dr. Purvis's parents were abolitionists Harriet Forten (Purvis) and Robert Purvis. Bacon, *But One Race,* xiii.

9. Genie entrusted Louisa with the task of delivering the news of her aunt's death to her closest relatives in Washington. Ann A. Webb (1820–1884), Genie's paternal aunt, died August 30, 1884, and was buried at Olive Cemetery in Philadelphia on September 1, 1884. Elizabeth "Lizzie" Webb (Iredell, 1818–1888), Ann Webb's sister and Genie's paternal aunt, lived with the families of her daughters, Sarah Iredell (Fleetwood) and Laura Iredell (Hawkesworth). Genie's uncle in Texas, Frank J. Webb—author of *The Garies and Their Friends*—would also have been notified of his sister's death. "Ann A. Webb," New Jersey Deaths and Burials, 1720–1988, Camden, Camden, New Jersey, v16, 117; "Ann A Webb," State of New Jersey Burial Permit, Pennsylvania, Philadelphia City Death Certificates, 1803–1915, image 526; "Elizabeth Susan Iredell," District of Columbia Deaths and Burials, 1840–1964, District of Columbia, cn62414; Mary Maillard, "'Faithfully Drawn from Real Life.'"

10. "Tell Genie I don't think she will ~~the~~ teach in the public Schools in Camden long." John D. Webb to Edie Webb, August 3, 1884, AWWP.

11. Genie Webb's autograph book shows that she was in Atlantic City on August 25, 1884, five days before her aunt's death. On September 1, 1884, Lottie and Frank

Grimké signed Genie's autograph book with solemn messages, suggesting that they might have attended Ann Webb's funeral in Philadelphia. The *Christian Recorder* noted about the same time that Frank and Lottie Grimké attended an "entertainment" at the Philadelphia home of William Still (1821–1902). Autograph book, AWWP; Eric Gardner, *Unexpected Places*, 216n29.

12. Isaac Watts wrote the hymn "Am I a Soldier of the Cross" in 1709 to follow a sermon on 1 Corinthians 16:13. The referenced stanza reads, "Must I be carried to the skies / On flowery beds of ease, / While others fought to win the prize, / And sailed through bloody seas?" Amos R. Wells, *A Treasure of Hymns*, 84.

13. This was Louisa's second year as a home economics teacher (the only female instructor) at the newly founded Industrial Department at Howard University. HJFP, 770.

14. Thomas Willing Francis Forten lived with his brother William Deas Forten, his aunt Sarah Forten (Purvis), his cousin Annie Purvis, and her brother William B. Purvis (1841–1914) in the Lombard Street home of his mother Charlotte Vandine (Forten). A former U.S. marshal, Thomas Forten worked in the customs office until 1886. Winch, *Gentleman of Color*, 372.

15. Sarah L. Forten (Purvis) had died October 29, 1884, at the age of seventy-nine. Annie Purvis's grandmother, Charlotte Vandine (Forten), would live until December 30, just two days short of her one-hundredth birthday. "Sarah Louisa Purvis," "Charlotte Forten," Philadelphia, Pennsylvania, Death Certificate Index, 1803–1915, FHL #2069872, #2070088.

16. This address is confirmed in the name of Harriet J. Jacobs, "widow of Samuel." Boyd's Washington City Directory, 1885, 490. The "Samuel" that Harriet listed as her deceased husband was Louisa's father, Samuel Tredwell Sawyer.

17. Bailey Willis (1857–1949) was a geologist who eventually specialized in earthquakes and earthquake-resistant buildings. The son of Nathaniel Parker Willis and Cornelia Grinnell (Willis), Bailey Willis was raised in his early years by Harriet Jacobs. Bailey's cousin and first wife, Altona Grinnell (1848–1896), had recently lost a baby, born in September 1884. Bailey Willis had worked from 1881 to 1884 for the Northern Pacific Railroad under Raphael Pumpelly (1837–1923), a family friend and former lodger at Louisa and Harriet Jacobs's Cambridge boarding house. Inventory of the Bailey Willis Papers, 1856–1957, Huntington Library, Pasadena, California; HJFP, 779, 947; "Bailey Willis," 1870 U.S. Census, Cambridge, Middlesex, Massachusetts, Roll 593_623, 240B; Bailey Willis, "Biographical Memoir of Raphael Pumpelly."

18. Louisa and Harriet Jacobs were housekeepers at the Swedish minister Count Lewenhaupt's residence at 1021 Connecticut Avenue in the fall of 1884. In the summer they lived at the home of the Swedish secretary of legation, also on Connecticut Avenue. The minister's house was not occupied at the time, thus allowing for Bailey Willis's stay. HJFP, 778, 779.

19. Elizabeth "Lizzie" Landon (Cassey, 1833–1910) was the widow of Joseph W. Cassey, the eldest son of Joseph and Amy Matilda Cassey. Hairdresser Clara "Carrie"

Mitchell (Cassey, 1852–1912) was Lizzie's daughter-in-law and the widow of Joseph St. Leger Cassey (1854–1877), who, with his fifteen-month-old daughter, Amy M. Cassey (b. 1876), had died of diphtheria in 1877. Carrie Cassey remarried in 1895 to John William Jones (b. 1842) but continued to live with her mother-in-law until she died. Philadelphia City Directory, 1885, 322; "Elizabeth Cassey," "Amy M. Cassey," "Joseph Cassey," "Clara Aliniva Jones," Philadelphia, Pennsylvania, Death Certificates, 1803–1915, #1405375, #2028252, #2028144, 1421339; 1880 U.S. Census, Philadelphia, Philadelphia, Pennsylvania, Roll 1166, 269D; "Clara A Cassey," Philadelphia, Pennsylvania, Marriage Index, 1885–1951, GSU# 4140411; 1900 U.S. Census, Philadelphia, Philadelphia, Pennsylvania, Roll 1470, 6A; 1910 U.S. Census, Philadelphia Ward 28, Philadelphia, Pennsylvania, Roll T624_1402, 11A.

20. Activist, public speaker, and teacher, Caroline R. LeCount (1846–1923) was the Rosa Parks of her day. On March 25, 1867, she filed a complaint with the police after being ejected from a streetcar. Her act of civil disobedience, backed by new law, forced eighteen Philadelphia streetcar companies to end the practice of segregation. Judith Giesberg, "Caroline LeCount," Pennsylvania Civil War 150, http://pacivilwar150.com /ThroughPeople/AfricanAmericans/CarolineLeCount.html.

21. Matilda "Inez" Cassey (1851–1916) was the only child of Alfred Smith Cassey (1829–1903) and the granddaughter of abolitionists Amy Matilda and Joseph Cassey of Philadelphia. Inez Cassey was a pianist and talented musician. She graduated, with Laura Iredell (Hawkesworth), from the Institute for Colored Youth in 1869. "Inez Cassey," 1880 U.S. Federal Census, Philadelphia, Philadelphia, Pennsylvania, Roll 1169, 256C; Institute for Colored Youth, *Nineteenth Annual Report of the Board of Managers of the Institute of Colored Youth*, 17.

22. Grover Cleveland (1837–1908), the first Democratic president elected since before the Civil War, was not popular among African Americans.

23. Annie Purvis's unmarried uncles, Thomas and William D. Forten, lived at the Forten family home at 336 Lombard Street. William was a leader in Philadelphia's African American community, a champion for equal rights during the 1870s and 1880s, and an ardent Republican politician. After the illness and death of her mother in 1884, Annie Purvis assumed her mother's housekeeping duties. Winch, *Gentleman of Color*, 369–71.

24. William B. Purvis was an engineer and inventor. He invented numerous paper bag machines, a hand ink stamp, and an improved fountain pen, electrical railway switch, and magnetic car-balancing device. He lived with his sister Annie and never married. "Wm B Purvis," Philadelphia City Death Certificates 1803–1915, #14290148; "William Purvis," 1870 U.S. Census, Bensalem, Bucks, Pennsylvania, Roll M593_1313, 42B; "William B. Purvis," 1900 U.S. Census, Philadelphia, Philadelphia, Pennsylvania, Roll 1474, 2A; "William Purvis," About.com Inventors, http://inventors.about.com /library/inventors/blwilliampurvis.htm.

25. Linen was used as bandage for the dressing of wounds.

26. Mrs. Purnell was Julia A. Shadd (Purnell, Browne, 1844–1929), daughter of Absolom and Eliza Shadd, sister of Marian "Mattie" Purnell Shadd and Dr. Furman J.

Shadd, and widow of James Whipper Purnell (1834–1879). Julia Shadd (Purnell) was born in Washington, DC, and had returned there to teach school by 1890. She lived nearby the Webbs in Camden, New Jersey, in 1883 and 1884, while she taught at Mt. Vernon School, the same school at which the Webb sisters taught. In Philadelphia in the 1870s she lived near Genie Webb's Burr cousins. 1880 U.S. Census, Camden, Camden, New Jersey, Roll 774, 434A; "James W. Purnell," Camden City Directory, 1884, 415, and 1885, 421; 1870 U.S Census, Philadelphia Ward 7, Philadelphia, Pennsylvania, Roll M 593_1392, 274B; "Julia Ann Braune," District of Columbia Deaths and Burials, 1840–1964, gs# 2116044.

27. Three days later Cleveland delivered his inaugural address, in which he promised civil service reform. Grover Cleveland, "Inaugural Address," March 4, 1885, www.presidency.ucsb.edu/ws/index.php?pid=25824; "Grover Cleveland," www .whitehouse.gov/about/presidents/grovercleveland22.

28. Wiley Lane (1852–1885), born in Elizabeth City, North Carolina, graduated from Amherst in 1879 and earned a master of arts from Howard University in 1881. Professor of Greek language and literature at Howard University beginning in 1883, Lane died suddenly in February 1885. Among his eulogists were Frederick Douglass and Reverend Francis J. Grimké, who recalled in his tribute the heated debate over and white trustees' resistance to Lane's 1881 appointment. Lane's mother, like Louisa Jacobs and Genie Webb's mother, was a native of Chowan County, North Carolina. William Sanders Scarborough and Michele Valerie Ronnick, eds., *The Autobiography of William Sanders Scarborough*, 354; Eric Anderson and Alfred A. Moss, *Dangerous Donations*, 21; William W. Patton and George F. Hoar, *Obituary Addresses on the Occasion of the Funeral of Professor Wiley Lane*; "Wiley Lane," District of Columbia Deaths and Burials, 1840–1964, gs# 2135786.

29. Annie Purvis's mother, Sarah L. Forten (Purvis), died October 29, 1884.

30. Harriet Jacobs's illness was confirmed by Julia Wilbur in her April 10, 1885, diary entry. Julia Wilbur diaries, Haverford College, Quaker and Special Collections Transcriptions; HJFP, 779.

31. Genie's doctor, William H. Pancoast (1835–1897), wrote in her autograph book on January 12, 1886: "Rx Keep in the open air, and avoid nervous fatigue ~ William H. Pancoast A.M.M.D. &c, 1100 Walnut St." Dr. Pancoast was a leading surgeon and professor of general, descriptive, and surgical anatomy, and of clinical surgery at the Medico-Chirurgical College of Philadelphia. Born in Philadelphia, Dr. Pancoast graduated from Haverford in 1853 and from Jefferson Medical College in 1856. He was widely traveled, a member of various international learned societies, and the first president of the International Red Cross Society in Philadelphia. He gained some notoriety after performing an autopsy on the bodies of Chang and Eng Bunker (known as the Siamese twins) and concluding that they would have died if they had been surgically separated. Charles E. Sajou, ed., *Annual of the Universal Medical Sciences and Analytical Index*, vol. 4, 6; "Dr. William H. Pancoast," *The New York Times*, January 6, 1897.

32. Maud Cassey (b. 1875–1940) was the daughter of Joseph St. Leger Cassey Sr. (1854–1877) and Clara A. Mitchell (Cassey, Jones).

33. A four-wheeled horse-drawn carriage.

34. Annie Chew (Bishop).

35. Rev. Francis Grimké received a call to the Laura Street Presbyterian Church in Jacksonville, Florida, in 1885. He remained in Florida until 1889 when he was called back to the Fifteenth Street Presbyterian Church in Washington. Henry Louis Gates and Evelyn Brooks Higginbotham, eds., *African American Lives*, 363.

36. Martha "Mattie" S. Venning (1877–1885), a daughter of Julia Sanders (Venning) and Edward Y. Venning, died June 2, 1885. Philadelphia City Death Certificates 1803–1915, film 2070484.

37. Probably Richard Chew's aunt, Annie Chew (Bishop) in Annapolis.

38. The Webbs owned a farm property in Franklinville, Gloucester, New Jersey, purchased in 1855, and sold in 1971.

39. Emma Louise (Wardle, 1837–1907), widow of British-born doctor Thomas Wardle, patented medicines and was a close friend of the Purvis family. Her daughter, Harriet Newell Wardle (1875–1964), lived with Annie and William B. Purvis in 1910 while working as a museum bookkeeper. "Emma Louise Wardle," Philadelphia, Pennsylvania, death certificate #76103; "Wardle, Emma L.," 1893 Philadelphia City Directory, 2019; "Louisa Wardle," 1880 U.S. Census, Philadelphia, Philadelphia, Pennsylvania, Roll: 1172, 163D, FHL #1255172; "Harriet Wardle," 1910 U.S. Census, Darby, Delaware, Pennsylvania, Roll: T624_1339; 21A, FHL #1375352; "Harriet N. Wardle," Philadelphia, Pennsylvania, death certificate # 045613-64. Thanks to Sheila Jones, Eden Cemetery, Collingdale, Pennsylvania.

40. This may be the family of Annie L. Jones (b. 1853), a fellow teacher at Mt. Vernon School in Camden, New Jersey, who commuted from her family home at 1524 Lombard Street in Philadelphia. Annie L. Jones signed Genie Webb's autograph book January 9, 1885. Annie L. Jones was one of the eleven surviving children of Philadelphia barber Robert Jones (1817–1908), founding member of the Lombard Street Central Presbyterian Church, and his wife, Elizabeth Durham (Jones, b. 1825). "Anna L. Jones," Camden, New Jersey, City Directory, 1884, 298; Eugenie Webb autograph book, AWWP; "Robert Jones," U.S. Census 1880, Philadelphia, Philadelphia, Pennsylvania, Roll 1170, 147A; 1900 U.S. Census, Philadelphia, Philadelphia, Pennsylvania, Roll 1472, 7A; "Robert Jones," Philadelphia, Pennsylvania Death Index, #1402960; Fanny Jackson Coppin, *Reminiscences of School Life, and Hints on Teaching*, 171 (for information on Robert Jones's lineage); "Our Philadelphia Letter: Camden and the Colored Schools— Interesting Matter, &c," *The Bee*, Washington, DC, March 10, 1883, 3; William Carl Bolivar, "Dissertation on Robert Jones," ca. 1906, Slaughter Collection, Atlanta University Center–Woodruff Library, Atlanta, Georgia, in W. C. Bolivar file, Library Company of Philadelphia.

41. Julia E. Venning (1863–1891) was the daughter of Julia Sanders (Venning) and Edward Y. Venning of Philadelphia. Julia Venning married James E. Warwick (1860–1944). "Julia Elizabeth Warwick," Philadelphia, Pennsylvania Death Certificate Index, 1803–1915, #1888828; "James Edward Warwick," Pennsylvania, Death Certificates, 1906–1963, #70759.

42. The Novelties Exhibition of the Franklin Institute ran September 15 to October 31, 1885. In response to the numerous nonelectrical inventions submitted to the 1884 Electrical Exhibition, the board of managers hoped to attract applications for gas appliances. They offered "a chance for gas men to make a comparative showing against electricity," and awarded bronze, silver, and "Grand" medals in a competition for the invention that best contributed to the "welfare of mankind." *Bulletin of the Novelties Exhibition* 1, no. 5, Philadelphia, July 15, 1885.

43. Annie Purvis's uncle Thomas Willing Francis Forten and her brother William B. Purvis.

44. Probably Dr. William Pancoast of Philadelphia.

45. James "Joe" St. Leger Cassey (1877-1937) was the only son of Clara "Carrie" Mitchell (Cassey) and Joseph St. Leger Cassey, who died of diphtheria in September 1877 at the age of twenty-three. Either the 1880 census taker recorded the boy's name in error, or James was renamed Joseph—in honor of his father, grandfather, and great-grandfather—when he was young. His father was a student at Lincoln University in 1870 and the only child of Lizzie and Joseph W. Cassey of Philadelphia, and the grandson of Amy Matilda and Joseph Cassey. See also note with March 1, 1885, letter.

46. Joseph Hayne Rainey of South Carolina and William "Willie" H. Chew lived with the Jacobses at 2119 K NW in Washington. They managed a coal and wood yard at 1723 10th NW in Washington for one year after the failure of the banking and brokerage business Rainey had started in 1881. Rainey was the first black to be elected to Congress (1870-1879). Boyd's Washington City Directory, 1886, 11, and 1887, 71; "Joseph Hayne Rainey," Office of History and Preservation, Office of the Clerk, Black Americans in Congress, 1870-2007.

So Each Day Begin Again: 1886-1887

1. HJFP, 800.

2. Adelaide Proctor, "One by One," in Adelaide Proctor, *Poems of Adelaide A. Proctor*, 34.

3. Rev. Francis Grimké served as pastor at the Laura Street Presbyterian Church in Jacksonville, Florida.

4. Singleton T. Saunders (1848-1909) had been William H. Chew's partner in their barber business, Chew & Saunders. 1875 Philadelphia City Directory, 1312.

5. James Monroe Trotter served in the all-black 55th Massachusetts Regiment during the Civil War and afterward worked his way up through the U.S. Postal Service in Boston from 1866 to 1873. A respected music historian, Trotter published his comprehensive *Music and Some Highly Musical People* in 1878. A Democrat and supporter of Grover Cleveland, he was appointed recorder of deeds in 1887 in a tight vote: Republicans had objected to his political affiliation and Democrats to his color. Erina Duganne, "Black Civil War Portraiture in Context," http://mirrorofrace.org/blackcivilwar/, April 5, 2012.

6. James Campbell Matthews (1844-1930), a black Democrat from New York (the state's first African American law school graduate and first black judge), preceded James

M. Trotter as recorder of deeds and was one of the Jacobses' first boarders at 2119 K Street. After the Senate rejected President Cleveland's nomination of Matthews in July 1886, Cleveland went ahead and appointed him later in the summer after Congress had adjourned. In the fall, when the president nominated Matthews again, the nomination was rejected for a second time. James Monroe Trotter was Cleveland's next choice. HJFP, 793, 795; Mary Darcy and Greg Dahlmann, "James C. Matthews: New York State's first black judge, Albany Law graduate," All Over Albany, February 20, 2015, http://alloveralbany.com/archive/2015/02/20/albany-laws-james-c-matthews-new-york-state-first; "James C. Matthews," Menands, New York, Albany Rural Cemetery Burial Cards, 1891–2011.

7. The following morning, the headline "Recorder Trotter Very Ill" appeared in the *Washington Post*. The article reported that the "colored landlady" answered the door and informed the reporter, "No, it would be impossible for you to see Mr. Trotter this evening. He is better than he has been and is resting quietly. Pneumonia is a very dangerous disease, and as long as it remains he cannot be said to be out of danger, though unless there is a relapse I think he will improve rapidly." HJFP, 791.

Hours Are Golden Links: 1890–1911

1. Yellin, *Harriet Jacobs: A Life*, 252, 255, 363–64; HJFP, 263, 642, 711–16, 860; Butchko, *Edenton*, 89.

2. This was the address of Henry L. Dawes, Republican Senator from Massachusetts, who had boarded with the Jacobses ten years earlier. Louisa Jacobs had recently left the home of author and editor Charles Nordhoff, where she and her mother lived from 1888 to 1890. Nordhoff was the Washington correspondent for the *New York Herald* from 1874 until his retirement to California in 1890. Louisa Jacobs to Genie Webb, January 20, 1880, AWWP, in this collection; "Henry L. Dawes," Boyd's Congressional Directory, Washington, DC, 1891, 1057; HJFP, 799; "Louisa M. Jacobs," "Charles Nordhoff," Boyd's Washington City Directory, 1890, 517, 679; "Charles Nordhoff," *Encyclopedia Americana*, 1920, http://en.wikisource.org/wiki/The_Encyclopedia_Americana_(1920)/Nordhoff,_Charles.

3. Isaiah 48:10.

4. The poem "Chosen—In the Furnace of Affliction" by H. W. C., in Anson D. F. Randolph, comp., *Unto the Desired Haven and Other Religious Poems*, 85.

5. William Carl Bolivar (1849–1914), African American bibliophile, journalist, and cultural historian, wrote for the *Philadelphia Tribune*. William C. Welburn, "To 'Keep the Past in Lively Memory': William Carl Bolivar's Efforts to Preserve African American Cultural Heritage," *Libraries and the Cultural Record* 42, no. 2 (2007): 165–79.

6. Genie Webb's sister Charlotte Cordelia Webb was known as "Blink" by close family members. She had been named for her godmother and cousin, Charlotte Forten (Grimké).

7. Genie Webb's father, John Gloucester Webb, was the paternal uncle of Frank J. Webb Jr. (1865–1901).

8. Genie Webb's sister Miriam "Mame" Douglass Webb (Hegamin) had married William Waters Hegamin (1859–1942) in 1890 and moved to Reading, Pennsylvania. The babies were Cordelia "Pudge" Hegamin (1891–1980) and William "Webb" Hegamin (1893–1964).

9. Pinckney Benton Stewart Pinchback (1837–1921), a publisher, orator, and politician, had moved from Louisiana to Washington in 1892 and was well known for his gracious hospitality.

10. Mary Rosabelle Rodgers (Webb) was born in 1845 in Jamaica and emigrated with her children to Texas in late 1872. Her husband, Frank J. Webb, had returned to the United States in late 1869 to pursue a law degree from Howard University.

11. Genie Webb's youngest sister, Ada Webb (1872–1952).

12. Genie Webb's sister Miriam "Mame" Webb; her husband, William Waters Hegamin; and their children, Cordelia "Pudge" Hegamin and William "Webb" Hegamin.

13. Schoolteacher Ada Howell Hinton (1832–1903), daughter of Frederick Augustus Hinton (ca. 1804–1849) and Eliza Ann Howell (d. 1835), had grown up in Philadelphia with Genie Webb's mother, Annie Wood (Webb). She, along with Charlotte Forten Grimké, acted as godmother at the 1877 baptisms of Blink and Ada Webb. "Ada H. Hinton," Philadelphia City Directory, 1891, 863; Charlotte Cordelia Webb and Ada Virgil Webb baptism certificates, AWWP.

14. Frank's father, Frank J. Webb, wrote the second novel authored by an African American, *The Garies and Their Friends* (1857), and he published poems, articles, and two novellas in the *New Era* in 1870. After moving to Texas, he worked as a newspaper editor and, by the time of this letter, had worked for thirteen years as the principal of the Barnes Institute, an African American school in Galveston, Texas. He would die four months after this letter was written. Werner Sollors, "Frank J. Webb (1828–1894)," 27.

15. Frank J. Webb Jr., known earlier in life as Frank R. Webb, lived in Washington in the home occupied in 1893 by his (and Genie's) first cousin Sarah Iredell (Fleetwood). He was a member of the "Middle Class" of Howard University Medical School and graduated in 1895. He also worked for the Treasury Department in Washington, DC. In 1896–1897 he continued his medical studies at Howard University as a postgraduate student. "Christian Fleetwood," Boyd's Washington City Directory, 1892, 419; "Frank J. Webb," Boyd's Washington City Directory, 1893, 954; "Frank J. Webb," Howard University Catalogue 1893, 15, 1894, 13, and 1895, 54 (American Antiquarian Society at ancestry.com); "Frank J. Webb," July 1, 1895, Register of Civil, Military, and Naval Service, 1863–1959, ancestry.com; "Frank J. Webb," Directory of Deceased American Physicians, 1804–1929, ancestry.com.

16. In public records Louisa Jacobs first appeared at this address in 1894; she had probably moved there by late 1893. Boyd's, Washington City Directory, 1894, 572.

17. This was the home of Philadelphia barber Robert Jones (1817–1908), founding member of the Lombard Street Central Presbyterian Church, and his wife, Elizabeth Durham (Jones, b. 1825).

18. Address confirmed by the census listing, "Annie Purvis," 1900 U.S. Census, Philadelphia, Philadelphia, Pennsylvania, Roll 1474, 2A, and by William B. Purvis's listing in the Philadelphia city directory, 1894. Annie and William B. Purvis moved from the old Forten home at 336 Lombard Street in 1893.

19. Elizabeth "Lizzie" Cassey.

20. Genie's cousin, Laura Iredell (Hawkesworth).

21. Like Louisa Jacobs, Genie Webb went into the business of selling preserves. On June 30, 1897, wealthy Philadelphia businessperson George Harrison Fisher (1849–1925) responded to her offer to sell homemade preserves with a loan of fifteen dollars "to assist you in your work." The Fisher family had employed Genie's grandmother, Louisa Burr (Webb, Darius, ca. 1785/88–1878), as a nursemaid and housekeeper and supported her in her later years. George Harrison Fisher to Eugenia Webb, June 30, 1897, AWWP; Maillard, "'Faithfully Drawn from Real Life,'" 273–77.

22. From David Garrick, *Prologue on Quitting the Stage in 1776*: "Their cause I plead,— plead it in heart and mind; / A fellow-feeling makes one wondrous kind." John Bartlett, *Familiar Quotations*, 10th edition (Boston: Little, Brown, 1919), 387.

23. Louisa's mother had broken her hip in March 1896 and never walked again. The strain of caring for her mother—especially the heavy lifting—took its toll on Louisa's health, and she was unable to earn a living. Ednah Dow Cheney (1824–1904) had proposed a public appeal to raise money to help the Jacobses but reconsidered and solicited aid from William Garrison Jr. (1838–1909), who sent a check in July 1896. Louisa was grateful, but "grieved and hurt at the necessity of calling on friends for aid." Harriet Jacobs died six months after this letter was written, on March 7, 1897. HJFP, 822, 827.

24. The Great Hurricane of 1896 was a Category Three storm that hit Florida, Georgia, the Carolinas, Virginia and Washington, DC, on September 29 with maximum sustained winds of 130 mph. It caused a hundred deaths and $1.5 million (1896 dollars) in damages. Kevin Ambrose, "Washington's Worst Five Hurricanes and Tropical Storms," *Washington Post*, August 25, 2011; National Oceanic and Atmospheric Administration, U.S. Department of Commerce, http://www.srh.noaa.gov/images/tbw/paig/PresAmHurricane1896.pdf.

25. Possibly the same Jones family mentioned in Annie Purvis's letter of September 6, 1885.

26. Louisa worked as matron of the National Home for the Relief of Destitute Colored Women and Children in Washington, DC. 1900 U.S. Census, Washington, Washington, District of Columbia, Roll 158, 12A.

27. Republican president William McKinley (1843–1901) was elected for a second term with Theodore Roosevelt as his vice-president. McKinley would be assassinated in September 1901.

28. "Blink" was the family nickname for Genie Webb's sister Cordelia. AWWP.

29. Dr. Rebecca J. Cole (1846–1922) was the second African American woman to earn an M.D. She was hired as the superintendent of the National Home for the Relief of Destitute Women and Children in Washington, DC, in 1899, the same year that

Louisa Jacobs was hired as assistant matron. Born in Philadelphia and educated at the Institute for Colored Youth and the Woman's Medical College of Pennsylvania, Cole practiced medicine in South Carolina and in Philadelphia, where, in 1873, she established the Women's Directory Center to assist poor women and children. "Dr. Rebecca J. Cole," Changing the Face of Medicine, U.S. National Library of Medicine, www.nlm .nih.gov/changingthefaceofmedicine/physicians/biography_66.html; HJFP, 846.

30. Ada Virgil Webb had married Reverend John H. Simons (1866–1925), a native of Bermuda, in 1900. "John Henry Simons," Illinois, Deaths and Stillbirths, 1916–1947, 5 Feb 1925, FHL microfilm 1877618; "Ada Simons," 1910 U.S. Census, Plainfield, Union, New Jersey, Roll T624_910, 6A.

31. National Association for Destitute Colored Women and Children, Washington, DC, U.S. Registry of Civil, Naval, and Military Service, 1863–1959, volume 1, 1901, 1269; 1903, 1270.

32. John G. Webb was now seventy-nine years old, senile, and living in Philadelphia with his three unmarried daughters, Edith, Genie, and Cordelia. He died two years after the writing of this letter. "John Webb," 1900 U.S. Census, Philadelphia, Philadelphia, Pennsylvania, Roll 1472, 3B; "John Webb," Pennsylvania, Philadelphia City Death Certificates, 1803–1915, Philadelphia, Philadelphia, Pennsylvania, film #1003721.

33. Louisa Jacobs lived at this address until 1914. District of Columbia directory, 1914, 699.

34. Genie and her sisters, Edith and Cordelia, lived together in Philadelphia and were out of work for the entire year of 1909. "Edith L. Webb," 1910 U.S. Census, Philadelphia, Philadelphia, Pennsylvania, 624_1402, 3A.

35. Probably Louise Sanders Venning at the Fitzwater house in Philadelphia.

36. Edith Willis (Grinnell), daughter of Cornelia Grinnell (Willis) and Nathaniel Parker Willis. "Edith W. Grinnell," 1920 U.S. Census, Brookline, Norfolk, Massachusetts, Roll 625_721, 6B; "Deaths," *New York Times*, March 24, 1938.

Epilogue: The Pilgrimage Be Done

1. HJFP, 863–70; "Loretta C. Simms," 1910, 1930, U.S. Census, Washington, Washington, District of Columbia; Washington City Directory, 1914, 699; letter from Janet Heywood at Mount Auburn Cemetery to Jean Fagan Yellin, September 11, 1992, Harriet Jacobs Family Papers, Wilson Library, University of North Carolina, Chapel Hill.

2. Reginald Heber Howe (1846–1924) had served as the rector of the Church of Our Savior in Longwood, Brookline, Massachusetts, since 1877. HJFP, 870–71.

3. Genie Webb's unmarried niece, Miss Cordelia Webb Hegamin.

Select Bibliography

Manuscript Collections

Haverford College, Quaker and Special Collections Transcriptions
    Julia Wilbur diaries
Historical Society of Pennsylvania, Philadelphia
    Dr. and Mrs. Henry Drinker Collection (Collection 3125)
Library Company of Philadelphia
    African American Friendship Albums
    Stevens-Cogdell-Sanders-Venning Collection (SCSVC)
    W. C. Bolivar file
Library of Congress, Washington, DC
    Christian A. Fleetwood Papers
Missouri History Museum
    Thomas Butler Gunn diaries
Moorland-Spingarn Learning Center, Howard University
    Francis J. Grimké Papers
Private Collections
    Annie Wood Webb Papers (AWWP), Philadelphia
    Blair/Iredell Bible records, Silver Spring, Maryland
St. Paul's Episcopal Church records, Edenton, North Carolina
St. Thomas African Episcopal Church records, Philadelphia
Southern Historical Collection, University of North Carolina, Chapel Hill
    Harriet Jacobs Family Papers
    Hayes Collection

Primary Sources

Alexander, Eveline Martin, and Sandra Myres. *Cavalry Wife: The Diary of Eveline M. Alexander, 1866–1867.* College Station: Texas A&M University Press, 1977.

Beers, Henry Augustin. *Nathaniel Parker Willis*. Boston: Houghton, 1885.

Brockett, Edward J. *The Descendants of John Brockett*. East Orange, NJ: The Orange Chronicle Company, 1905. https://archive.org/details/descendantsofjohooinbroc.

Brooklyn School Board. *Annual Report of the City Superintendent of Schools of the Consolidated City of Brooklyn*. Brooklyn, NY: George C. Bennett, 1863, 1865, 1868–1872.

Coppin, Fanny Jackson. *Reminiscences of School Life, and Hints on Teaching*. Philadelphia: A.M.E. Book Concern, 1913. http://docsouth.unc.edu/neh/jacksonc/jackson.html.

Cushing, William. *Initials and Pseudonyms: A Dictionary of Literary Disguises*. New York: Thomas Y. Crowell, 1888.

Dorr, Mrs. Julia C. R. "The Spirit Teachings." *The Columbian Magazine* 9 (1948).

Forten, Charlotte. "The Angel's Visit." November 1858, reprinted in William Wells Brown's *The Black Man: His Antecedents, His Genius, and His Achievements* (Boston: James Redpath, 1863), 196–99.

Greene, Homer. "Mizpah." *Lippincott's Monthly Magazine* 43 (1889): 222.

Griffin, Farah Jasmine, ed. *Beloved Sisters and Loving Friends: Letters from Rebecca Primus of Royal Oak, Maryland, and Addie Brown of Hartford, Connecticut, 1854–1868*. New York: Knopf, 1999.

Grimké, Francis J. "The Second Marriage of Frederick Douglass." *Journal of Negro History* 19 (July 1934): 325.

Harrison, R. S. *Nome and Seward Peninsula*. Seattle: Metropolitan, 1905.

Herron, Carolivia, ed. *Selected Works of Angelina Weld Grimké*. New York: Oxford University Press, 1991.

Institute for Colored Youth. *Nineteenth Annual Report of the Board of Managers of the Institute for Colored Youth*. Ithaca, NY: Cornell University Library, 2012.

Jacobs, Harriet. *Incidents in the Life of a Slave Girl: Written by Herself*, ed. Jean Fagan Yellin. Cambridge, MA: Harvard University Press, 2000.

———. "Life Among the Contrabands." *The Liberator*, September 5, 1862. http://docsouth.unc.edu/fpn/jacobs/support5.html.

Jacobs, John S. *A True Tale of Slavery*. London: Stevens and Co., 1861. http://docsouth.unc.edu/neh/jjacobs/menu.html.

Jones, J. McHenry. *Hearts of Gold*, ed. John Ernest and Eric Gardner. Morgantown: West Virginia University Press, 2010.

Loomis, Lafayette Charles. *Mizpah, Prayer, and Friendship*. Philadelphia: Lippincott, 1858.

Patton, William W., and George F. Hoar. *Obituary Addresses on the Occasion of the Funeral of Professor Wiley Lane: Delivered in the University Chapel, February 18, 1885*. Washington, DC: Judd & Detweiler, 1885.

Payne, Daniel Alexander. "The Triumphant End of Mrs. Mary Virginia Forten." *The Colored American*, August 29, 1840.

Pike, John Gregory. *The Works of the Rev. J. G. Pike of Derby: With a Biographical Sketch*. London: Simpkin, Marshall & Co., 1862.

Proctor, Adelaide. *The Poems of Adelaide A. Proctor.* New York: Thomas Y. Crowell & Co, 1853.

Randolph, Anson D. F., comp. *Unto the Desired Haven and Other Religious Poems.* New York: Anson D. F. Randolph & Co, 1881.

Sajou, Charles E. ed. *Annual of the Universal Medical Sciences and Analytical Index: A Yearly Report of the Progress of the General Sanitary Sciences throughout the World,* Volume 4. Philadelphia: F. A. Davis Company, 1890.

Scarborough, William Sanders, and Michele Valerie Ronnick, eds. *The Autobiography of William Sanders Scarborough: An American Journey from Slavery to Scholarship.* Detroit, MI: Wayne State University Press, 2005.

Simmons, William J., and Henry McNeal Turner. *Men of Mark: Eminent, Progressive, and Rising.* Cleveland, OH: W. W. Williams, 1887. http://docsouth.unc.edu/neh/simmons/simmons.html.

Stevenson, Brenda, ed. *The Journals of Charlotte Forten Grimké.* New York: Oxford University Press, 1988.

Trotter, James M. *Music and Some Highly Musical People.* Boston: Lee and Shepard, 1880.

Webb, Frank J. *The Garies and Their Friends.* 1857; reprint, Baltimore: Johns Hopkins University Press, 1997.

Wesley, Dorothy Porter, and Constance Porter Uzelac, eds. *William Cooper Nell: Nineteenth-Century African American Abolitionist, Historian, Integrationist; Selected Writings, 1832–1874.* Baltimore: Black Classic Press, 2002.

Whittier, John Greenleaf. *The Letters of John Greenleaf Whittier,* Volume 3. Boston: Harvard University Press, 1975.

Willis, Bailey. "Biographical Memoir of Raphael Pumpelly, 1837–1923." *National Academy of Sciences* 16 (1931).

Yellin, Jean Fagan, Kate Culkin, and Scott Korb, eds. *The Harriet Jacobs Family Papers.* Chapel Hill: University of North Carolina Press, 2008.

Secondary Sources

Alexander, Leslie. "Alexander Crummell." In *Encyclopedia of African American History,* ed. Leslie Alexander. New York: ABC-CLIO, 2010.

Alonso, Harriet Hyman. *Growing Up Abolitionist: The Story of the Garrison Children.* Amherst: University of Massachusetts Press, 2002.

Anderson, Eric, and Alfred A. Moss. *Dangerous Donations: Northern Philanthropy and Southern Black Education, 1902–1930.* Columbia: University of Missouri Press, 1999.

Andrews, William L., Frances Smith Foster, and Trudier Harris, eds. *The Concise Oxford Companion to African American Literature.* New York: Oxford, 2001.

Bacon, Margaret Hope. *But One Race: The Life of Robert Purvis.* Albany: State University of New York, 2007.

Biddle, Daniel R., and Murray Dubin. *Tasting Freedom: Octavius Catto and the Battle for Equality in Civil War America.* Philadelphia: Temple University Press, 2010.

Butchko, Thomas R. *Edenton: An Architectural Portrait.* Edenton, NC: Edenton Women's Club and Chowan County Government, 1992.

Campbell, Ballard C. *Disasters, Accidents, and Crises in American History: A Reference Guide to the Nation's Most Catastrophic Events.* New York: InfoBase, 2008.

Dunbar, Erica Armstrong. *A Fragile Freedom: African American Women and Emancipation in the Antebellum City.* New Haven, CT: Yale University Press, 2008.

Gardner, Eric. "Charlotte Forten." In *Encyclopedia of African American History*, ed. Leslie Alexander. New York: ABC-CLIO, 2010.

———. *Unexpected Places: Relocating Nineteenth-Century African American Literature.* Jackson: University Press of Mississippi, 2009.

Gates, Henry Louis, and Evelyn Brooks Higginbotham, eds. *African American Lives.* New York: Oxford University Press, 2004.

Gatewood, Willard B., Jr. *Aristocrats of Color: The Black Elite, 1880–1920.* Fayetteville: University of Arkansas Press, 2000.

Hatfield, Gabrielle. *Encyclopedia of Folk Medicine: Old World and New World Traditions.* Santa Barbara, CA: ABC-CLIO, 2004.

Hendrick, George, and Willene Hendrick. *Black Refugees in Canada: Accounts of Escape during the Era of Slavery.* Jefferson, NC: MacFarland, 2010.

Hine, Darlene Clark, ed. *Black Women in America: Science, Health, and Medicine.* New York: Facts On File, 1997.

———. "Rape and the Inner Lives of Black Women in the Middle West." *Signs* 14, no. 4 (Summer 1989): 912–20.

Howe, M. A. DeWolfe. *The Life and Labors of Bishop Hare: Apostle to the Sioux.* New York: Sturgis & Walton, 1911.

James, Edward T., ed. *Notable American Women 1607–1950: A Biographical Dictionary.* Boston: Harvard University Press, 1971.

Jefferson, Margo. *Negroland: A Memoir.* New York: Knopf, 2015.

Katz, William Loren, ed. *History of Schools for the Colored Population.* New York: Arno, 1969.

Kerr, Audrey Elisa. *The Paper Bag Principle: Class, Colorism, and Rumor and the Case of Black Washington, D.C.* Knoxville: University of Tennessee Press, 2006.

Lamphier, Peg A. *Kate Chase and William Sprague: Politics and Gender in a Civil War Marriage.* Lincoln: University of Nebraska Press, 2003.

Lane, Roger, and Benjamin R. Collins. *William Dorsey's Philadelphia and Ours: On the Past and Future of the Black City in America.* New York: Oxford University Press, 1991.

Lapsansky, Phillip S. "Afro-Americana: Family Values, in Black and White." In *The Annual Report of the Library Company of Philadelphia, 1991*, 26–40. Philadelphia: Library Company of Philadelphia, 1991.

Maillard, Mary. "Dating Harriet Jacobs: Why Birthdates Matter to Historians." *Perspectives Magazine* (July 2013). http://www.blackpast.org/perspectives/dating-harriet-jacobs-why-birthdates-matter-historians.

———. "'Faithfully Drawn from Real Life': Autobiographical Elements in Frank J. Webb's *The Garies and Their Friends*." *Pennsylvania Magazine of Biography and History* (July 2013): 261–300.

McKivigan, John R. *The War against Proslavery Religion: Abolitionism and the Northern Churches, 1830–1865*. Ithaca, NY: Cornell University Press, 1984.

Millard, Candice. *Destiny of the Republic: A Tale of Madness, Medicine and the Murder of a President*. New York: Anchor, 2012.

Moses, Wilson Jeremiah. *Alexander Crummell: A Study of Civilization and Discontent*. New York: Oxford, 1989.

Perry, Mark. *Lift Up Thy Voice: The Grimké Family's Journey from Slaveholders to Civil Rights Leaders*. New York: Penguin, 2002.

Peterson, Carla L. *"Doers of the Word": African American Women Speakers and Writers in the North (1830–1880)*. New York: Oxford University Press, 1995.

Robinson, Henry S. "Furman Jeremiah Shadd." *Journal of the National Medical Association* 72, no. 2 (1980): 151–53.

Schecter, Patricia Ann. *Ida B. Wells-Barnett and American Reform, 1880–1930*. Chapel Hill: University of North Carolina Press, 2001.

Schultz, Suzanne M. *Body Snatching: The Robbing of Graves for the Education of Physicians in Early Nineteenth Century America*. Jefferson, NC: McFarland, 1992.

Schweninger, Loren. *Black Property Owners in the South, 1790–1915*. Urbana: University of Illinois Press, 1997.

Scudder, Jennie W. *A Century of Unitarianism in the National Capital*. Boston: Beacon, 1922.

Smith, Jesse Carney, ed. *Notable Black American Women*, Volume 2. Detroit: VNR AG, 1996.

Smith, Mark M. "'All Is Not Quiet in Our Hellish County': Facts, Fiction, Politics, and Race—The Ellenton Riot of 1876." *South Carolina Historical Magazine* 95, no. 2 (April 1994): 142–55.

Smithsonian Anacostia Museum and Center for African American History and Culture. *The Black Washingtonians: 300 Years of African American History*. Hoboken, NJ: John Wiley & Sons, 2005.

Sollors, Werner. "Frank J. Webb (1828–1894)." In *African American Literature beyond Race: An Alternative Reader*, ed. Gene Andrew Jarrett. New York: New York University Press, 2006.

Sterling, Dorothy, ed. *We Are Your Sisters: Black Women in the Nineteenth Century*. New York: W. W. Norton, 1997.

Stewart, Anne M. "Desegregation of Pennsylvania Schools." *Pennsylvania Heritage* 36, no. 2 (2010).

Warren, Joyce W. *Fanny Fern: An Independent Woman*. New Brunswick, NJ: Rutgers University Press, 1992.

Wells, Amos R. *A Treasure of Hymns: Brief Biographies of One Hundred and Twenty Leading Hymn-Writers with Their Best Hymns*. Boston: United Society of Christian Endeavor, 1914.

Williams, Andrea N. *Dividing Lines: Class Anxiety and Postbellum Black Fiction*. Ann Arbor: University of Michigan Press, 2013.

Williams, Max. R. "The Johnston Will Case: A Clash of the Titans, Part I." *North Carolina Historical Review* 67, no. 2 (1990).

Williams, Paul K., and Charles N. Williams. *Owasco Lake*. Charleston, SC: Arcadia
    Publishing, 2002.
Winch, Julie. *The Clamorgans: One Family's History of Race in America*. New York: Hill &
    Wang, 2011.
———. *The Elite of Our People: Joseph Willson's Sketches of Black Upper-Class Life in Antebellum
    Philadelphia*. University Park: Pennsylvania State University Press, 2000.
———. *A Gentleman of Color: The Life of James Forten*. New York: Oxford University Press,
    2002.
Yellin, Jean Fagan. *Harriet Jacobs: A Life*. New York: Basic Civitas, 2004.
Zboray, Ronald J., and Mary Saracino Zboray. *Literary Dollars and Social Sense: A People's
    History of the Mass Market Book*. New York: Routledge, 2013.

Index

Page numbers for illustrations are in italics.

207

Wisconsin Studies in Autobiography

WILLIAM L. ANDREWS
Series Editor

Mark Twain's Own Autobiography: The Chapters from the "North American Review,"
second edition
Mark Twain
Edited by Michael J. Kiskis

Graphic Subjects: Critical Essays on Autobiography and Graphic Novels
Edited by Michael A. Chaney

A Muslim American Slave: The Life of Omar Ibn Said
Omar Ibn Said
Translated from the Arabic, edited, and with an introduction by Ala Alryyes

Sister: An African American Life in Search of Justice
Sylvia Bell White and Jody LePage

Identity Technologies: Constructing the Self Online
Edited by Anna Poletti and Julie Rak

Masked: The Life of Anna Leonowens, Schoolmistress at the Court of Siam
Alfred Habegger

We Shall Bear Witness: Life Narratives and Human Rights
Edited by Meg Jensen and Margaretta Jolly

Dear World: Contemporary Uses of the Diary
Kylie Cardell

Words of Witness: Black Women's Autobiography in the Post-"Brown" Era
Angela A. Ards

A Mysterious Life and Calling: From Slavery to Ministry in South Carolina
Reverend Mrs. Charlotte S. Riley
Edited with an introduction by Crystal J. Lucky

American Autobiography after 9/11
Megan Brown

Reading African American Autobiography: Twenty-First-Century Contexts and
Criticism
Edited by Eric D. Lamore

Whispers of Cruel Wrongs: The Correspondence of Louisa Jacobs and Her Circle, 1879–1911
Edited by Mary Maillard